By the Same Author:

Skyways and Landmarks Revisited
    (with Jimmy Goddard and Paul Baines) (1985)
Earth Mysteries: An Exploratory Introduction
    (with Brian Larkman) (1985)
Tony Wedd: New Age Pioneer (1986)
The Elements of Earth Mysteries (1991)
Secret Places of the Goddess (1995)
Earth Mysteries (1995)
Mirrors of Magic (1997)
Magical Guardians: Exploring the Spirit and Nature of Trees
(1998)
Leylines: A Beginner's Guide (1999)
Wiccan Roots: Gerald Gardner and the Modern Witchcraft
    Revival (2000)
Gerald Gardner and the Cauldron of Inspiration (2003)
Newland Avenue School 1896-2006 (2006)

Witchfather

A Life of Gerald Gardner

Volume 1

Into the Witch Cult

Witchfather

A Life of Gerald Gardner

Volume 1

Into the Witch Cult

by

Philip Heselton

THOTH PUBLICATIONS

Loughborough, Leicestershire

Published by Thoth Publications
64 Leopold Street, Loughborough, LE11 5DN

EAN: 9781913660161

web address: www.thoth.co.uk
email: enquiries@thoth.co.uk

For Hilary, Owen and Aidan

CONTENTS

ACKNOWLEDGEMENTS

A book of this sort is far from being the work of only one person. Indeed, I have had help from a very large number of people. Some have given me great assistance over many years; others may have provided a small but useful snippet of information. To all who have helped me I give my thanks: there is no doubt whatever that this book would never have been written without you.

I give thanks to Mike Allen, Jo Anderson, Bridget Archer, M.Y. Ashcroft, Paul Atkin, Pat Badham, Suzi Balls, Hilary Bartle, Lesley Barton, Helen Bassett, John and Julie Belham-Payne, Ian Bell, Simon Bennett, Bali Beskin, Geraldine Beskin, Gavin Bone, Adrian Bott, Desmond Bourke, Lois Bourne, Roger Bristow, Jane Brodley, Ray Buckland, Fran Burgon, Cora Burke, Hilary Byers, Francis Cameron, Kenn Capps, Philip Carr-Gomm, Keith Chisholm, Else Churchill, Marilyn and Trevor Clark, Ann Cook, Rory Cook, Jerry Cornelius, Zach Cox, Phyllis Croft, Barbara Croom, Angela Crow-Woods, Patricia Crowther, Nick Culpeper, Mags Currie, Anne Dacre, Karen and Evan Dales, Morgan Davis, Dayonis, Roger Dearnaley, Kim and Tracey Dent-Brown, Peter Dickens, Elizabeth Doria, Lalita du Peron, Beverley Emery, Peter English, Janet Farrar, Michael Farrar, Jani Farrell-Roberts, John Ferguson, Ben Fernee, Alan Franklin, Ken and Marita Freeman, Don Frew, Adrian Gardner, Gay Gardner, Robert A.Gilbert, Kate Gladstone, Lynne Sydelle Gordon, Clare Goulder, Kenneth Grant, Simon Green, Paul Greenslade, Clive Harper, Christina Oakley Harrington, Melissa and Rufus Harrington, Lizzie Harris, Ralph Harvey, Jeanne Heaslewood, Nigel and Susan Heselton, Trevor Hildrey, Martin Hinchcliffe, Gillian Hodges, Michael Hodges, John Hopkins, Beryl Housley, Michael Howard, Nick Howson, Ronald Hutton, Nigel Jackson, Deric James, Richard and Tamarra James, Larry Jones, Prudence Jones, Steve Jones, Suzanne Josefowicz, Aidan Kelly, J Elwyn Kimber, Graham King, Richard Knight, Anna Korn, Fred Lamond, Andrew Lee-Hart, Ian Lilleyman, Ray and Lynda Lindfield, Grevel Lindop, Carey Littlefield, Catherine Lloyd, Nagia Lombardo, Chris Lycett, Beverly Lyon Clark, John and Kitty Macintyre, Jonathan MacQueen, Mary Kay

Mahoney, Laurence Main, Maria Malo, Carolyn Maunder, Gareth Medway, Hugh and Beryl Midgley, George Monger, Alan Moorhouse, Levannah Morgan, Marian Mozley, William Mullan, Tony Naylor, Paul Newman, Sue Newman, Jeremy Newson, Andy Norfolk, Caroline Oates, Dáithí Ó Geanainn, Jo Pearson, Julia Phillips, Doug Pickford, Joy Piper, Carol Price, Richard Price, Shelley Rabinovich, Jon Randall, Ken Rees, Andrew Robertson, Caroline Robertson, Jean Rose, Penny Rudkin, Jane Rutter, W.F. Ryan, Olive Samuel, Edward Saunders, George Schrager, Melissa Seims, Eleanor Sergeneson, Elizabeth Silverthorne, Geoffrey Basil Smith, Tony Steele, Ian Stevenson, Tim Stimson, Jean Stirk, Derek Stokes, Andrew Stoodley, John Tait, Jonathan Tapsell, Keith Thompson, Anthony Thorley, Helen Thorne, Kevin Tingay, Jane Estelle Trombley, Jean Tsusima, Julie Venner, Miranda Vickers, Bill Wakefield, Chris Wallis, Gareth Watkins, Sibyl Webster, Martin Westlake, Iseult Weston, Nicky Westwood, Roy and Grace Wheadon, Cerys Williams, Jean Williams, Steve Wilson, Caroline Wise, Allyn Wolfe, C.M. Woolgar, Jim Wright, John Yeowell and Kalisha Zahr.

I would also like to give my thanks to all those who wish to remain anonymous.

It is inevitable, with such a large number who have contributed their assistance, that I will have missed someone. This is no reflection on the value of their contribution: it is merely due to my failing memory!

My thanks to you all, and to those who will read this book.

PICTURE AND TEXT CREDITS

Bridget Archer 41; Boscastle Museum of Witchcraft 30, 38; British Federation of the International Order of Co-Freemasonry, Le Droit Humain 21; Patricia Crowther 40, 44, 45; Adrian Gardner 1-7, 11, 12; Rufus and Melissa Harrington 34, 46; Gillian Hodges 10; Richard and Tamarra James 9, 14, 15, 16, 29, 39; Larry Jones 48; Jonathan MacQueen 13; Sefton Libraries and Information Services 8; Ian Stevenson 22,23; Keith Thompson 17-20, 42, 43; Miranda Vickers 31, 32; Westminster Libraries 25. All other illustrations by or in the collection of the author. The author has made every effort to identify copyright holders and to obtain their permission but would be glad to hear of any inadvertent errors or omissions.

I must thank Ian Bell for his skills with Photoshop in improving many of the photographs included in this book. I must also thank Grevel Lindop and Gareth Medway for valuable detailed comments on the text.

My thanks go to John Belham-Payne for permission to quote from Doreen Valiente's published works. He has asked me to mention his websites www.doreenvaliente.com and www.paganismstudies.org which are both very good and informative.

I would also like to thank Graham King for permission to quote from letters and other documents held in the Boscastle Museum of Witchcraft archives; and to Richard and Tamarra James for permission to quote from various documents in the Toronto collection.

I would like to thank Pat Badham, Barbara Croom and other members of Five Acres Club for permission to quote from letters in their archives; and to Adrian Gardner for permission to quote from documents in the Gardner family archive.

Many others mentioned in the Acknowledgements section have given me permission to quote from documents in their possession, or which they have written, and I am most grateful to all of them.

ILLUSTRATIONS

Between pages 174 and 175:

Fudge, Rosetta Mason and Edna Fudge. The child is Judith
Ann Fudge. Beechwood Hall, Osborne Road, Southampton -
January 1935
22 Dorothy St. Quintin Fordham (née Clutterbuck)
23 Katherine Oldmeadow (in centre with wide-brimmed hat)

DIAGRAMS

MAPS

A NOTE ON USAGE

I have used the names and spellings of countries and towns as they were when Gerald Gardner was living in or visiting them, so I refer to Ceylon, Borneo, Malaya, Johore and Gold Coast, for example, rather than the current Sri Lanka, Sabah, Malaysia, Johor and Ghana. This also applies to the boundaries of English counties and to organisations such as the Folk-Lore Society, which changed its name to the Folklore Society in 1960. Lois Bourne is referred to by that name when I am quoting from her book *Dancing with Witches*, but by the name Lois Pearson, when referring to the time when she knew Gerald Gardner. The building which was known as the Witch's Cottage while at the Abbey Folk Park, I refer to as the Witches' Cottage after rituals started to take place there in the mid-1950s. The naturist club of which Gerald was a member was known as both Fiveacres and Five Acres. I have preferred the latter form, partly in order to distinguish it from the former Fouracres Club. I have used the terms 'the Wica', 'the witch cult' and 'the Craft' as interchangeable. I have generally referred to Gerald Gardner by his first name because, as explained elsewhere, whilst I never knew him in this life, I feel I have got to know him very well in the process of writing this biography. I have also often referred to others, such as Edith Woodford-Grimes, Cecil Williamson and Frederic Lamond by their first names. Where I quote directly from Gerald's letters or other writings, I have preserved his somewhat idiosyncratic spelling, as I feel that in some way it enables us to get closer to him. For year dates, the suffixes 'CE' and 'BCE' are used in preference to the specifically Christian 'AD' and 'BC'.

FOREWORD

In 1960 I borrowed a book entitled *Witchcraft Today* from our local library. It was by one Gerald B. Gardner, who claimed to be a "member of one of the ancient covens of the Witch Cult which still survive in England".

That phrase echoed around my innermost being: I found an excitement in those words that has never left me. Whilst the historical scholarship in that book has been rightly questioned, the hints scattered through its pages that the 'witch cult' still survived were enough to propel me on to further investigation.

In time, after much reading and even speaking to real live people, I put down my findings in two books of my own, *Wiccan Roots* and *Gerald Gardner and the Cauldron of Inspiration*. And in between the publication of the two books, I was finally, over forty years after that initial encounter, initiated into 'the witch cult', more usually known today simply as Wicca.

Gerald Brosseau Gardner lived from 1884 to 1964, had five books published, and revived, virtually single-handedly, a tradition of witchcraft which has, since his death, expanded vigorously, not just in England but in America, the rest of Europe and many other parts of the world. He was well into his retirement from an active employment 'out East' as tea and rubber planter and customs officer, when the one key event in his life took place: his initiation into 'the witch cult' in September 1939.

He devoted the remaining quarter century of his life to ensuring the survival of this joyous and exciting thing into which he had been welcomed. And so he researched and wrote, he lectured and ran a museum. And he initiated people who had read his books. And so the witch cult did not die out. After a few false starts, it not only survived but grew, until today it is strong beyond his wildest dreams.

Of recent years I have become convinced that the position of Gerald Gardner as the publicist for what Professor Ronald Hutton, in a memorable phrase, has called "the only religion that England has ever given to the world", was a worthy subject and sufficiently important to deserve a full-scale biography. I also began to realise that I would have to do it myself! Some have held it against me that I have written about Gerald Gardner without knowing him. Yet, if that is to be the criterion, should no-one ever again write about Shakespeare or Dickens or Jane Austen or Queen Victoria? In any case, in the course of my researches over many years I feel that, even though I never met him, I have got to know Gerald sufficiently well to be on first name terms with him, so that is how I refer to him in the current volume.

This is, however, not the first biography of Gerald Gardner. In 1960, *Gerald Gardner Witch* was published.[1] It is a very good book, based largely on Gerald's own reminiscences, and in no way has this current work made it redundant. It really is virtually the only source of information for much of Gerald's life and the broad narrative is largely accurate. There are details which are wrong, but I put this down in most cases to his failing memory for names and dates and sometimes to a misconception as to the true state of affairs. I have certainly found *Gerald Gardner Witch* invaluable in writing the current work and ideally they should be read together. Yet, despite its strengths, there is a lot about Gerald's life that it didn't cover, even superficially. Most obviously, it was published four years before his death, so those years are unrecorded. There are also many aspects of Gerald's life that are hardly touched upon, such as any examination of the context and content of his various books, the organisations of which he was a member, his homes, the circumstances surrounding the establishment of the museum (Cecil Williamson, for example, is never even mentioned) and, perhaps deliberately, the group into which he was initiated, the subsequent individuals he initiated and covens with which he was associated. Now, fifty years later, I can be more informative about these matters, though even here I have had to be circumspect about certain names.

Some have criticised me for destroying the mystery concerning the origin of the Craft. I have tried to present the basic facts in Gerald Gardner's life as clearly and straightforwardly as I can. But there is still much mystery left. We will never know everything, but I firmly believe that it is as well to try and sort out the

---

1. J. L. Bracelin, *Gerald Gardner Witch*, (Octagon Press 1960); republished I-H-O Books, 1999.

truth while we can. Another few generations and we will be presented with a 'creation myth' as potent as any other religion. I happen to believe that the real story is every bit as interesting and inspiring as any made up myth.

Gerald Gardner Witch has been described as a 'hagiography'. I take this to mean that it was intended to be entirely favourable to him. If so, then the current volume is certainly not a hagiography. Gerald had many faults (as well as many virtues) and I have tried to chronicle them in a fair and unbiased way. However, I could not, and would not, have written this book unless I was basically sympathetic to Gerald Gardner as a person.

When I started to write, I felt I was putting pressure on myself to come up with a conclusion as to how it all started. But this book is not intended to delve deeper into the truth and origins of the group into which Gerald was initiated: much work remains to be done, and that is for a future book. The present volume is more limited in scope. As it is intended to be a biography of Gerald Gardner, I write it as far as possible from his perspective and what he is likely to have known about the background to the whole thing. I am comforted by the fact that almost certainly he did not know the answers either, and since this is a book about his life, my failure for the present to find a definitive origin is perhaps not as damning of my narrative as it might otherwise be. In many cases, he was probably even more in the dark than we are, and I do take the liberty of including brief biographical material on the various individuals involved.

It is in the nature of a biography that it can never be complete. As I carried out my investigations I found that when one answer revealed itself, it brought along three new questions with it! I was clearly fighting a losing battle. And yet, I have found out a lot about Gerald Gardner that has never before been published, including some remarkable photographs.

I do not claim that this is an academic text in any way. I hope it is readable and that I don't use too many big words! Also, I hope that I make clear the distinction between fact and speculation. I try to be honest and admit when I don't know something and when I have failed to find out some crucial feature in Gerald's life. I do engage in what I call "intelligent speculation", trying to think logically about what is likely to have happened.

In writing this book I have not only made extensive use of *Gerald Gardner Witch*, I have also borrowed extensively from my own books on the subject. Some of the material in those books has been used as a basis for chapters in the current work, in some cases substantially amended and in other cases largely unchanged.

A book of this nature is far from being the work of one person. A glance at the acknowledgements section will give some idea of the very large number of people who have helped me. Almost without exception they have been enthusiastic and supportive. I hope that I have repaid their trust.

In conclusion, I would just say that I have enjoyed writing this book enormously. If those who read it enjoy it as well, then I am content.

Philip Heselton
Hull
December 2009

❊ PART I ❊

Fertile Ground

CHAPTER ONE

The Gardner Inheritance: Myth And Reality

We are all a mixture of the environment into which we are born and what we make of ourselves. Gerald Gardner was a self-made man, teaching himself to read and, through his own efforts, becoming expert in many fields. Yet this was achieved with the benefit of a privileged background and an unconventional upbringing. We can often get insights into a person's character, as to why they are how they are, by looking at their ancestors. Yet this is an area where "creative genealogy" is notoriously present: not all claims are true and people are not always who they say they are.

This is certainly true of Gerald Gardner's attempted reconstruction of his ancestry. Sometimes this was deliberate fabrication, such as in an interview in 1954 when he stated[1] that he was born in Scotland. In another interview with a Scots paper he was more specific, claiming to have been born in North Berwick, haunt of witches in the 17th Century. By 1960 he had reverted to the truth of the matter, that he was born in Blundellsands, a few miles north of Liverpool, a major seaport in the county of Lancashire in north-west England. And another story which he told,

---

1. "I Am A Witch", *Daily Dispatch,* 5 August 1954.

at least as far back as the 1930s, was that there was a family connection with Grissell Gairdner of Newburgh in Scotland who in 1610 was executed for consulting with the Devil.[2]

Gerald definitely wanted to give the impression that he was Scots; he put himself down as such on the passenger list on his trip to America in 1947 and, in an interview in the early 1960s he referred to his fellow countrymen drinking whisky, a clear reference to Scotsmen.[3] Whether it had any validity, Gerald was very proud of his Scottish ancestry as can be seen in the splendid photograph of him in Highland dress. In his will, he bequeaths to his sister-in-law:

> My Grandfather's dirk
> My Grandfather's Skign-Dhoo (stocking knife)
> My kilt with all its belongings
> My Plaid with its brooch
> My Grandfather's sword with its Cross belt (known as
>   the Rhyming Sword)

He also expresses the wish that such articles be treated as heirlooms and remain in the Gardner family. A rhyming sword is, apparently, one of a matching pair of ceremonial or ornamental weapons that had the halves of a rhyming couplet etched onto each blade.

It is not clear how this "regalia" ended up with Gerald. I suspect that these were the possessions of his mother's father, John Jay Ennis (1829-1880), whose name may have a Scottish origin, which 'Gardner' most certainly does not. Indeed, it is rumoured that the Barony of Ennis was started in 1116CE near Inverness and that the Ennises were one of the most powerful clans in the Moray area until the mid 17th Century.

The tartan in the photograph appears to be a Hunting Maclean, but the wording of Gerald's will suggests that he had acquired rather than inherited it, perhaps just because it was visually attractive.

---

2. Margaret Murray, *The Witch Cult in Western Europe* (Oxford, 1921) quoting Robert Pitcairn - *Criminal Trials in Scotland* (Edinburgh: 1833, iii, 96)
3. CD accompanying Gardner Witchcraft Series (Restivo Enterprises, 1999).

Gerald often talked about two Gardners who made a name for themselves.[4] Alan Gardner (1742-1809), who was later to become Baron Gardner of Uttoxeter, was a naval officer who rose to the rank of Admiral by 1795. In 1797, in the Spithead Mutiny, he lost his temper with the mutineers and threatened to 'hang every fifth man in the fleet'. The Dictionary of National Biography says: "This led to a violent outburst, from which Gardner with difficulty escaped." Bracelin gives more, and subtly different, details, reporting that Gardner was captured by the mutineers and was about to be hanged by them. In response, he said "Pull away and be damned to you" whereupon the mutineers' anger changed to admiration and he was released while being cheered by the mutineers.[5] This is not given in any other account, including a book on the mutiny,[6] and I suspect some romanticisation of the incident by Gerald or one of his family. Alan Gardner later became Member of Parliament for Plymouth and was created Baron Gardner of Uttoxeter, his birth-place, in 1800.

Following the death of Alan Gardner there were two claimants to the title of Baron Gardner. It all centred around how long the gestation period of a woman could reasonably be and a report chronicles the seemingly endless evidence and arguments presented.[7]

William Linnaeus Gardner (1770-1835) was the nephew of Alan Gardner. He spent most of his life in India and became a skilled rider and swordsman. Initially he was a "soldier of fortune" in the service of Jaswant Rao Holkar and the Raja of Jaipur. In 1809 he raised the cavalry corps which was named in his honour – 'Gardner's Horse'. In about 1796 he married a Royal Princess of the Mughal Dynasty, a descendent of Genghis Khan. He died in 1835 at his estate at Khasgunge at the age of 65.

These are the sort of ancestors who appealed to Gerald: one, the successful Admiral of the Fleet, the other the self-made adventurer. However, I have found no family connections

---

4. J.L. Bracelin, *Gerald Gardner Witch*, (Octagon, 1960) 11-12.
5. Ibid., 12.
6. G.E. Manwaring and Bonamy Dobrée, *Mutiny: The Floating Republic* (Geoffrey Bles, 1935).
7. Denis Le Marchant, *Report on the Proceedings of the House of Lords on the Claims to the Barony of Gardner*, (Henry Butterworth, 1828).

between Gerald Gardner and either Grissell Gairdner, Baron Gardner of Uttoxeter or Gardner of Gardner's Horse. If there is a family connection it is a remote one, dating back to at least the 16th Century. I don't think that Gerald intended to make such precise claims. It was rather that he saw all those with the name Gardner as having something in common, part of the larger Gardner family or clan, which is a valid, if unorthodox, way of looking at things.

꧄

In 1948, a booklet[8] was published to celebrate the bi-centenary of the family firm of Joseph Gardner and Sons, which was described as "the oldest private company in the timber trade within the British Empire". Gerald clearly had access to that booklet and most of the historical information which he gives comes from that source.

An appendix to that volume gives an account of the celebrations held on 30th June 1948 to mark the anniversary. Part of those celebrations involved a talk by J.L. Kirkbride, who refers to the Gardner family dating back to 1379 and to one Simon le Gardinor. With all the genealogical resources now available, I can find no trace of Simon le Gardinor, but Gerald must have taken Kirkbride's statement at face value and proudly added it to the pedigree which appears in *Gerald Gardner Witch*.[9]

The surname Gardner, also spelt Gardiner, Gardener, Garner and, occasionally, Gard'ner, probably arose in different places independently and all individuals of that surname are not necessarily related to each other. The most obvious origin of the name is also the most likely: that they were gardeners, what is known as an 'occupative patronymic': the family was named because of their work. Gerald tells the story of some individual who was boasting about the longevity of his family tree, to which he quietly replied: "Well, you know, I can beat that, because Adam was a gardener!"

---

8. *History of Joseph Gardner & Sons Limited*, (Liverpool and London: 1748-1948)
9. Bracelin, 222.

Thomas
b. 1559
m. **Ellen** 1585
d. 1604

Nathaniel
b. 1585
m. **Elizabeth Pendleton**
d. 1610

Hugo
b.
m. **Maud**
d. 1659

Thomas

Thomas
b. 1617

William
b. 1617
d. 1674

John
Margaret
Sara
Ann
[all died young]

Thomas
[from whom is
descended **Richard
Cardwell Gardner** -
Mayor of Liverpool 1862]

Richard [I]
b. 1645
m. **Elizabeth Waring**
1682
d. 1700

Darcus
Elizabeth
Katheren
Henry
[all died young]

Richard [II]
b. 1689

John
William
Nicholas
Ann
[all died young]

Henry
b. 1725
d. 1790

Edmund
b. 1721
m. **Ann Charnock** 1747
d. 1795

Richard
Elizabeth
Ann
[all died young]

Thomas
b. 1749
d.1818

Richard
b. 1785
m. **Martha Jones** 1815
d. 1845

Thomas
b. 1787
d. 1840

Joseph
["Grandfather Joseph"]
b. 1791
m. **Maria Jackson** 1830
d. 1865

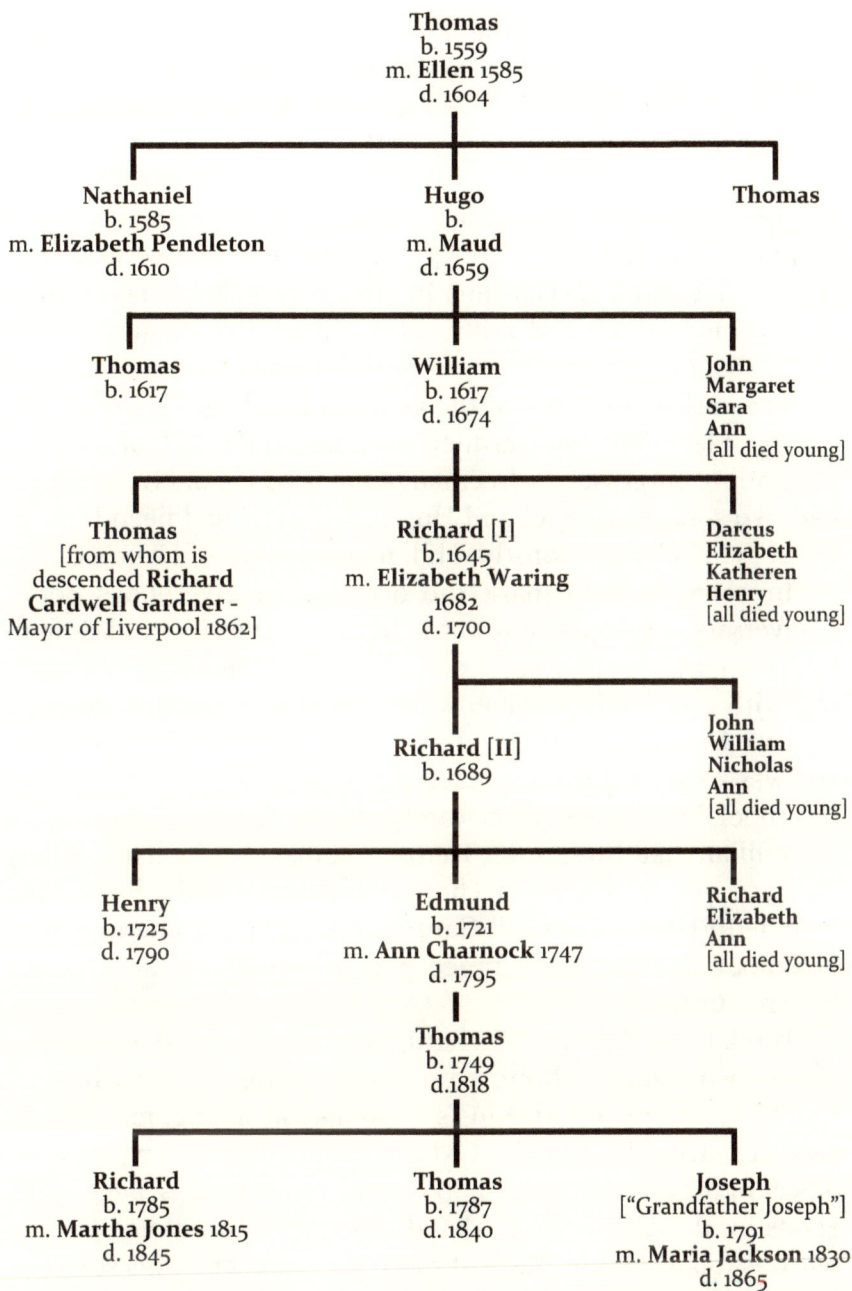

Gardner Family Tree up to 1850

The earliest record of the Gardner/Gardiner surname appears to be Sir Osbern Gardiner, born about 1089, who lived in Orrell, near Wigan in Lancashire. This suggests a very long association of the Gardners with that county. Osbern had a son of the same name who is said to have earned the crest on his Coat of Arms by chopping through the shoulder of a Saracen who was about to kill Richard Coeur de Lion. In the 13th Century there are recorded references to Geoffrey le Gardiner in Oxfordshire, Ralph le Gardiner in Huntingdonshire and William le Gardiner in Lincolnshire and Hertfordshire.

The earliest member of the Gardner family given in the history booklet is Thomas Gardner, who died in 1604. He was one of the leading burgesses, or freemen of the borough of Liverpool. He had two sons, Nathaniel and Hugo. Nathaniel had been born in about 1585 in Walton-on-the-Hill, now a suburb of Liverpool.

In 2007, to help mark the occasion of Liverpool's 800th anniversary, a competition was held to find the city's oldest family. The Gardners came second, with documentary evidence starting with the birth of Hugo's son, William Gardner, in 1617. William became a member of the Common Council of Liverpool and was a Bailiff. It was expected that he would become Mayor of Liverpool, but he died prematurely in 1674.

William had three sons, Henry, Thomas and Richard. Henry died at a young age. From Thomas was descended a line which included Richard Cardwell Gardner, who did become Mayor of Liverpool, in 1862. We will meet this branch of the family again later in our story!

William's oldest son, Richard, born 1645, started a tradition which lasted several hundred years by taking a job with H.M. Customs, ending up as King's Searcher, a prestigious post. A searcher, according to the Oxford English Dictionary, was "an officer of the custom-house appointed to search ships, baggage or goods for dutiable or contraband articles". Richard died in 1700 but was followed into the post of King's Searcher by his son, also Richard, born in 1689, presumably not immediately, since he would have been only 11 years old on his father's death.

It was Richard's son, Edmund, born in 1721, who founded the company that became Joseph Gardner and Sons. In 1748 he set up business as a block and pump maker. This provided a service to the maritime trade: blocks were the pulleys used in ships' rigging and pumps were used to extract water from ships' bilges. The particular skills of the blockmakers were recognised by the authorities, who in 1749 had bought a fire engine and had decided that blockmakers were best able to look after it. Edmund subsequently became a Freeman of Liverpool.

In the 1750s, the expansion of the slave trade resulted in full employment for the local shipyards and associated businesses such as Edmund's. Indeed, it cannot be denied that the Gardners and the family firm prospered greatly as a result of that trade. Slave trading merchants made a lot of money, much of which was being spent on building, fitting out and furnishing mansions in Liverpool and the surrounding area, the result being that the carpentry and cabinet-making trades expanded rapidly. As a consequence, the timber trade grew until it quickly became the largest employer in Liverpool. Exotic hardwoods, such as mahogany, started to be imported by the slavers on their return journey from the West Indies. Not only did the wealth of the slave owners result in increasing demand for tropical hardwoods, but the felling and moving of the trees was very likely done by slave labour. Moreover, the fitting-out of the slave ships would have provided work for the branch of the family who were involved in block, pump and mast making.

Later in the 18th Century the prosperity of Liverpool's seven shipbuilding yards was augmented by the award of Government contracts for ships to take part in wars with France, Holland and America. Edmund did well out of these trends. On his death in 1796, the firm was taken over by his son, Thomas, and nephew, William. Following William's death in 1799, Thomas ran the firm alone until he took his second son, also Thomas, into partnership and changed the name of the firm to Thomas Gardner and Son.

Following a slump during the Napoleonic War, the opening up of trade to the East Indies and the introduction of steam power resulted in another rapid expansion of the port of Liverpool.

Thomas had three sons, Richard, Thomas and Joseph, all of whom were involved in the business. In 1817 Thomas and Richard took over the firm, by which time it had enlarged its scope to cover mast making. This attempt to diversify was perhaps an indication that block and pump-making on its own was not a viable trade. By 1820, Thomas had obviously recognised this fact, for he set up in business on his own as a timber merchant. He was joined by his brother Joseph (Gerald Gardner's grandfather), by which time the firm was being described as Timber Merchants.

In the 17th Century, timber merchants generally did not have their own yards but left their timber where it was landed: on the beach until it was needed. After the docks were built (Salthouse Dock in 1739 and King's and Queen's Docks in the 1780s) timber was stored on adjacent land.

It was a good moment to become involved in the timber industry. The 1820s saw an unprecedented construction of churches and other public buildings, all of which required large quantities of imported hardwood timber, not to mention large numbers of private dwelling-houses. By the end of the 1820s, there were no less than 87 timber merchants in Liverpool. As the "History" says: "...it is probable that the Gardners entered the trade just in time to secure their share of the business".[10]

Between the years 1829 and 1848 the storage space needed for the business continued to increase. The Brunswick Dock had opened in 1832 specifically for the timber trade, and Gardners moved in 1839 and, in 1848, to still larger premises and storage yard at 113 Park Lane.

The following year, Joseph's eldest son, Joseph (Gerald's 'Uncle Joe') entered the firm as an apprentice at the age of 15. He remained associated with the firm for the rest of his life.

By the early 1850s, wooden shipbuilding had ceased, but this was more than compensated for by the expansion of house building and the furniture trade.

We have already noted that Thomas and Richard Gardner had split in about 1820, leaving Richard to run his block-making business from his property in Hurst Street, taking on his eldest son,

---

10. Op. cit., 11.

William, when he was old enough. He continued in the block making business when the rest of the family had turned to the timber trade, though he continued to have a hand in the family firm for several years.

In 1848, William was taken into partnership in the family firm, which became Richard, Joseph and William Gardner. This partnership lasted for 14 years until 1862, when it was dissolved and Richard and William withdrew from the business, leaving Joseph in sole control. The reason for this dissolution is not known, but it has been suggested that it was due to the somewhat forceful personality of Joseph junior ("Uncle Joe"). However, following the split, Joseph junior was brought in as a partner together with his elder brother, Thomas Richard, but Joseph senior died soon after in 1865.

Particularly during the 1850s, the firm had expanded its trade in African and American hardwoods as well as importing Caucasian boxwood and walnut from such ports as Smyrna in the eastern Mediterranean. They also dealt in native British hardwoods.

Canada Dock, to the north of the town, opened in 1859 and timber operations became centred there and in Brocklebank Dock, where a special timber basin with wide quay storage opened in 1862. The firm, which was now Joseph Gardner and Sons, moved to new offices at 123 Regent Road, Bootle as a result in 1868 to be nearer these operations, also opening a sawmill in Clyde Street, Kirkdale, later moving to Derby Road, Bootle.

The "History" notes an interesting point:

> *The new offices were equipped with a telephone and it is believed that Gardners were the first Merseyside firm to adopt what has now for so long been an indispensable aid to the conduct of business. For some seventy years the telephone number of the firm was Bootle 1.*[11]

Grandfather Joseph and his wife, Maria, had five sons and three daughters, Mary Ann (b. 1831), Maria (b. 1832), Joseph (b. 1834), Thomas Richard (b. 1836), Edmund Harold (b. 1837, died in

---

11. Ibid., 15.

infancy), Elizabeth (b. 1839), James Edward (b. 1841) and William Robert (b. 1844).

Gerald told[12] of a family tradition that the Gardners were involved in piracy and smuggling. He refers to a tunnel discovered when their old house was being demolished which was lined with barrels and which led directly to the harbour. He also refers to the tradition of one member of the family always being in the Customs Service, for what would seem to be obvious reasons. I was inclined to dismiss this as just a story until I came across a report of a talk given in 1863 by Thomas Berry Horsfall, Member of Parliament for Liverpool, to the Liverpool Chamber of Commerce.[13]

A committee of the House of Commons (the Select Committee on Inland Revenue and Customs Establishments) had been looking into a proposal to combine the Customs and Inland Revenue services under one body, and generally to reform them. In his talk, Horsfall mentioned that *The Economist* was against the proposal, but revealed that the article in that journal had been written by a Commissioner of Customs, who had a vested interest in opposing any reform of the departments and simplification of taxation. Horsfall accused the Customs service of nepotism:

> *There is considerable anxiety manifested among the officers of the Customs in reference to the promotions that take place. We hear a great deal of the competitive examinations: and I am not prepared to say that one family may not be more talented than others; but I will take a specimen of the promotions which do take place. There is Mr. Francis Gardner, secretary to the Customs, with a salary of £1,400 a year; a worthy relative of his, Mr. Wm. Pugh Gardner, collector of Customs, Dublin, has a salary of £1,000 a year, and £500 as collector of ballast dues, making £1,500; Mr. F.W. Gardner, the secretary's son, clerk in the solicitor's office, £200; Mr. H.J. Gardner, secretary's son, clerk in the Comptroller-General's office, £250; Mr. Gardner, son of the collector at Dublin, landing waiter in Dublin, £250; Mr. H.W.*

---

12. Bracelin, 11.
13. "Consolidation of the Revenue Departments", *The Bankers' Magazine*, 1863 Vol. XXIII.

Gardner, son of the collector at Dublin, clerk in the bill of entry office, £160; ... I am not prepared to say that these are not the most talented men who are to be found; but their having by the influence of this gentleman, the secretary, been brought forward bears very materially on the question at issue. ... Here we have a parcel of lads receiving larger salaries than many excellent clerks and valuable public servants who entered the Customs before they were born, but who have the misfortune, in a pecuniary point of view, not to be connected with a Gardner.[14]

Whether the Gardners in this account were relatives of Gerald, or whether he had read about it and assumed they were, I do not know. However, I suspect that in this particular case, Gerald was not exaggerating and that it was indeed the practice to have at least one member of the family in the Customs service (and, it would appear, often many more than one!). The local directories indicate that this was the case up until at least the end of the 19th Century.

⚜

William Robert Gardner (1844-1935), Gerald's father, was the youngest son of Joseph senior. In 1867, at the age of 23, he was sent to New York to represent the company's interests in the United States. There, he arranged for the erection of seven timber mills for the manufacture of ash oars, boat-hook poles, cornel and persimmon shuttle blocks and sawn hickory.

While in New York, William met Louise Burguelew Ennis, daughter of a wholesale stationer, John Jay Ennis (1820-1896), and his wife, Emma Louise Burguelew, who were living at 128 West 29th Street, Manhattan. This was a typical brownstone house, now demolished, which was subsequently, from about 1907 to 1911, the first New York residence of the composer Scott Joplin, where he began to write his opera, *Treemonisha*. John and Emma had earlier (1850) lived in Poughkeepsie, Dutchess County, New York State.

---

14. Ibid., 935-936.

There was a lot of flexibility in the matter of surnames among immigrants to America. There appears to have been no formal registration of births with the issuing of a Birth Certificate, as there had been in England and Wales since 1837. Not only were many of the individuals illiterate but those recording names in, for example, Census documents were sometimes less than diligent in their endeavours. Indeed, the individuals themselves would often not know how to spell their names, since spelling was an alien concept to those who could neither read nor write.

The earliest definitive record is from 1839/40 which refers to one Elizabeth Burguelew, widow of Daniel, living at 64 Henry Street, Manhattan. No earlier records of the surname 'Burguelew' appear to exist, though if the 1880 Census is to be relied on, both Elizabeth and her parents were born in the state of New Jersey.

'Burguelew' is a unique name, unheard of elsewhere. As mentioned, the Census returns can be unreliable with regard to spelling, and Emma's mother's surname is given variously as Burgalews and Burgelow in the 1870 and 1880 Censuses respectively.

Burguelew sounds French and, in fact, Gerald did claim in an interview he gave for a French newspaper that he had French ancestry. Unfortunately, the cutting I have does not give either the name of the newspaper or the date. The article is, however, entitled "Le dernier des sorciers crée le "musée de la magie" (The last witch opens a "museum of magic"), so it probably dates from 1951 when the museum opened in the Isle of Man, or from 1954, when Gerald took over. In it he is quoted as saying:

> *Et savez-vous, ajoute-t-il sans liaison apparente, que je suis d'origine française? Mes ancêtres vivaient dans un petit village, non loin de Paris.* (And did you know, he said, changing the subject, that I have French roots? My ancestors lived in a little village not far from Paris.)

How much reliance we can put on this statement is open to question, bearing in mind the fact, mentioned earlier, that he claimed that he was born in Scotland when being interviewed for a Scottish newspaper!

Joseph
["Grandfather Joseph"]
b.1791
m. Maria Jackson 6 Jan 1830
d. Huyton 2 Feb 1865

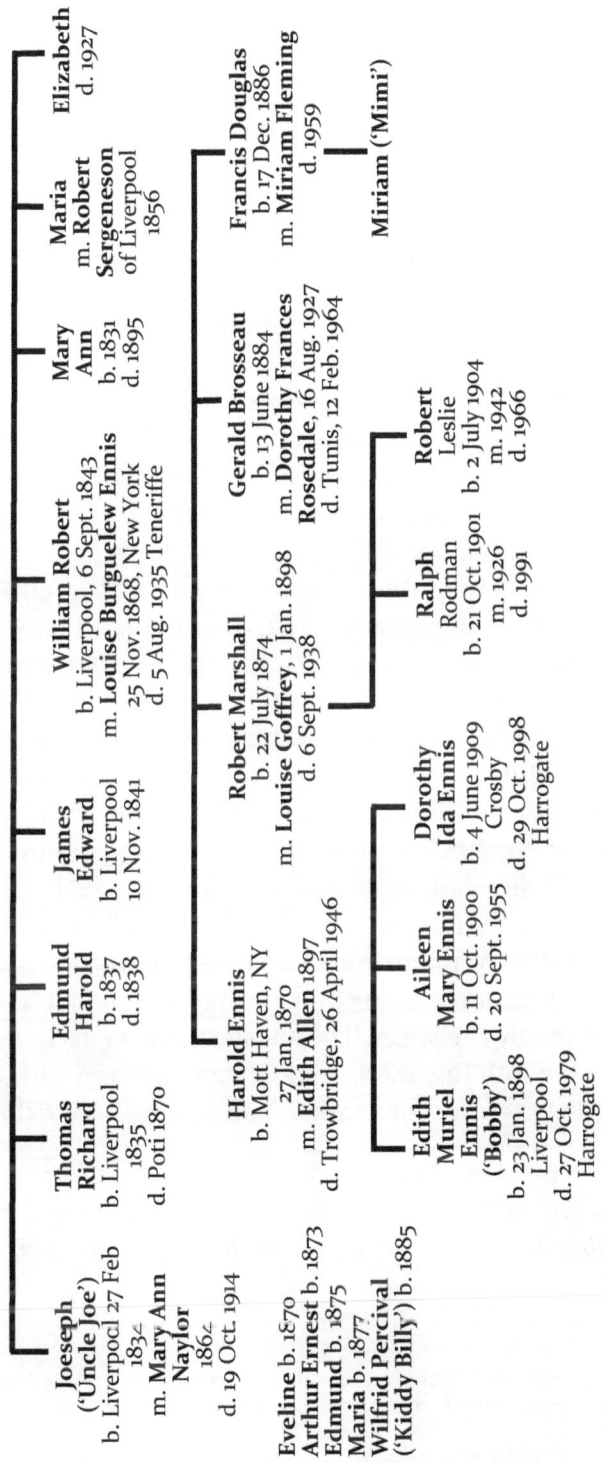

Joeseph ('Uncle Joe') b. Liverpool 27 Feb 1834 m. **Mary Ann Naylor** 1864 d. 19 Oct 1914

Thomas Richard b. Liverpool 1835 d. Poti 1870

Edmund Harold b. 1837 d. 1838

James Edward b. Liverpool 10 Nov. 1841

William Robert b. Liverpool, 6 Sept. 1843 m. **Louise Burguelew Ennis** 25 Nov. 1868, New York d. 5 Aug. 1935 Teneriffe

Mary Ann b. 1831 d. 1895

Maria m. **Robert Sergeneson** of Liverpool 1856

Elizabeth d. 1927

Eveline b. 1870
Arthur Ernest b. 1873
Edmund b. 1875
Maria b. 1877
Wilfrid Percival ('Kiddy Billy') b. 1885

Harold Ennis b. Mott Haven, NY 27 Jan. 1870 m. **Edith Allen** 1897 d. Trowbridge, 26 April 1946

Robert Marshall b. 22 July 1874 m. **Louise Goffrey**, 1 Jan. 1898 d. 6 Sept. 1938

Gerald Brosseau b. 13 June 1884 m. **Dorothy Frances Rosedale**, 16 Aug. 1927 d. Tunis, 12 Feb. 1964

Francis Douglas b. 17 Dec. 1886 m. **Miriam Fleming** d. 1959

Edith Muriel Ennis ('Bobby') b. 23 Jan. 1898 Liverpool d. 27 Oct. 1979 Harrogate

Aileen Mary Ennis b. 11 Oct. 1900 d. 20 Sept. 1955

Dorothy Ida Ennis b. 4 June 1909 Crosby d. 29 Oct. 1998 Harrogate

Ralph Rodman b. 21 Oct. 1901 m. 1926 d. 1991

Robert Leslie b. 2 July 1904 m. 1942 d. 1966

Miriam ('Mimi')

Gardner Family Tree after 1850

Nevertheless, the name 'Burguelew' may be a corruption of a French name, perhaps associated with the town of Bourgueil in the Loire valley, which is not, however, particularly near Paris. Further research is clearly needed. The village of Burguilla in the Tajo valley in Spain has also been suggested, but the origins of the name Burguelew for the moment remain shrouded in mystery.

A possible origin was provided by Miriam (Mimi), Gerald's niece, Douglas' daughter,[15] who believes that her grandmother, Gerald's mother, was of Dutch descent. I had already noted the research which had been carried out into the variations of surname, mostly in the states of New York and New Jersey, of the descendants of the Van Borculo or Barkelo brothers, who originated in the village of Geesteren near the town of Borculo in the Province of Gelderland, Netherlands, near the border with Germany. They emigrated to America in the 17th Century, settling in the New York and New Jersey area. There are many variants of the surname, including Barkalow, Barricklow, Barkuloo, Burklow and Bartlow. The extensive research carried out by David Bartlow[16] into the history of these various branches of the family does not reveal a 'Burguelew' spelling and I have not been able to demonstrate that the Burguelews were Van Borculo descendants, but Mimi's comment means that it is a strong possibility. I am hopeful that American readers of this book may feel inclined to follow up this line of inquiry.

Whether William and Louise met on his first journey, starting in July 1867, or on his second journey, in June 1868, I do not know, but probably the latter. The engagement seems to have been fairly rapid. On 16th July 1868, on notepaper printed with the heading of a single letter "E", for "Ennis", Louise writes to William:

> *Mr. Gardner, In response to an invitation from Miss Miller, Gettie and I have gone to take tea at 357 W. 19th St. If agreeable to yourself, we will be happy to see you there this*

15. Telephone conversation between Mimi Gardner and Morgan Davis, 12 July 2001.
16. http://burklowfamily.com/bartlow/IndexVanB.html, email David Bartlow to the author, 25 July 2007.

Ada Winants
b. 1776 New Jersey
d. 19 Apr 1858

Elizabeth Winants
b. 1795

=

Daniel Burguelew
d. before 1839

Emma Burguelew
b. c1820
d. after 1880

=

John Jay Ennis
b. c1820
d. New York City 6 Jan 18976

Hester
b. 1859

Ada
b. 1857

Geraldine
b. 1854

Emma
b. 1847

Elizabeth
b. 1845

Louise Burguelew Ennis
b. 1843
m. 25 Nov 1868
d. 1920

=

William Robert Gardner
b. Liverpool 6 Sept 1843
m. New York 25 Nov 1868
d. Teneriffe 5 Aug 1935

Ennis Family Tree

evening. But do not disarrange any plans which you have made, on my account, for Gettie has promised to see that I get home safely. Yours truly Louise B.E.[17]

Just over a month later, on 25th August 1868, the relationship had advanced to the extent that in a letter written on that date she addressed William as "My Dear Willie" and finished the letter "Yours Very Affectionately, Louise". It is still, however, very formal in tone, the first part of it reading:

I was sorry not to see you yesterday morning. The fact is, I had so thoroughly tired myself out the day before, that I was in a perfectly unconscious state long after the sun had set me his praiseworthy example. If you are here next Monday morning, I shall try to rival him. I suppose you will like to suggest that it may be a fortunate thing for me if it should prove a stormy day, for then I would most likely succeed. No, be the weather fair or foul, I promise to do better than I did this week ...[18]

In other words, "I overslept: it won't happen again!"

The marriage of William Robert Gardner and Louise Burguelew Ennis took place just three months later, on 25th November 1868 in Manhattan.

William brought Louise back to England in December 1868. They divided their time between staying at the family home, The Rooley, at Huyton, and visiting various friends in Cheshire and elsewhere.

In about June 1869, they returned to the United States, by which time Louise was pregnant. They settled in Mott Haven, Morrisania, West Chester County, New York State (in present-day Bronx) and, on 27th January 1870, their first child, Harold Ennis Gardner (Gerald's eldest brother), was born.

---

17. Letter from Louise Ennis to William Gardner 16 July 1868 in the Gardner Family Archive.
18. Letter from Louise Ennis to William Gardner 25 August 1868 in the Gardner Family Archive.

For some reason, perhaps William's desire to make a permanent home back in England or the firm's wish to have him back in Head Office, the couple moved back from New York some time in late 1871 or 1872. Anyway, William and Louise and their young son, Harold, came to England to settle. They lived in Waterloo Cottage, Crosby but by 1873 they were in 'The Glen', a very different residence, in time for the birth of their second child, Robert Marshall Gardner, on 22nd July 1874.

At this juncture, to take our story further, we have to follow the life of William's eldest brother, Joseph, the redoubtable "Uncle Joe".

Liverpool was expanding in population in the mid 19th Century and those who could afford it were moving out to more attractive villages and planned suburbs on the outskirts of the city. One of the most exclusive, which became home to most of the Gardner family, was Blundellsands. The environment was an attractive one for the development of what were known at the time as "villas".

Along this part of the Lancashire coast was a substantial belt of sand dunes, the largest in England, extending from the northern suburbs of Liverpool right up to Southport, some twenty miles to the north. The existing towns and villages were along a line on the landward side of the dunes. There was agricultural land to the east, but the dunes themselves were unproductive: the nearest thing in England to a desert.

Adjacent to the small town of Great Crosby, the Lord of the Manor, William Blundell, owned the sandhills. I think he saw the potential for development because when the idea for a railway from Liverpool to Southport was first suggested in the 1840s, he became Chairman of the Liverpool, Crosby and Southport Railway Company and managed to convince the other members that the line should be built through the sandhills rather than the alternative, which was closer to Crosby itself. A Parliamentary bill for the construction of a Liverpool, Crosby and Southport Railway got royal assent in 1847 and work on it started the following year. The through route from Liverpool to Southport was completed in 1850.

The opportunity now opened up for Blundell to develop the whole of his land on the sand-dunes - a substantial area. It had great potential for, not only was it within convenient commuting distance of Liverpool, but the environment was of the finest. To quote one future resident, Sir William Bower Forwood (1840-1928), shipowner and merchant, Mayor of Liverpool in 1881:

Probably no place in the United Kingdom possesses a finer marine prospect. Its wide expanse of sea, with its back-ground of the Welsh mountains, Snowdon standing in the far distance, and in the near foreground the constant parade of great merchant ships and steamers which pass and re-pass the day long, make a picture which for beauty and varying interest it is difficult to surpass.[19]

Blundell employed Liverpool architect, Thomas Mellard Reade, and surveyor and engineer, George William Goodison, to come up with a design for the estate which, perhaps inevitably, became known as Blundellsands. Reade (1832-1909) was also a civil engineer and later became architect for the Liverpool School Board. He wrote extensively on Lancashire geology and became a Fellow of the Geological Society in 1872. Goodison, who is now best known as the name of Everton Football Club's ground, was the Surveyor and Engineer to the Walton and Much Woolton Local Boards, and they went into partnership as "Reade and Goodison, Civil Engineers, Architects and Surveyors".

William Blundell died in 1854, but his son, Nicholas, took over the project. We will come across Nicholas again later in our story.

Reade and Goodison drew up a formal plan in 1865. The main feature was a sinuous road known as The Serpentine which ran in three long reverse curves from the railway station at Crosby almost to the coast and then back to the railway at Hall Road. I think this is probably one of the earliest roads of this deliberately curved nature in any housing development in England. Superim-

---

19. Roger C Hull, "Social Differentiation in a North Liverpool Suburb: The Case of Great Crosby and Waterloo 1841-1901", a thesis presented to the University of Liverpool for a Master of Arts Degree (in Local History) September 1989.

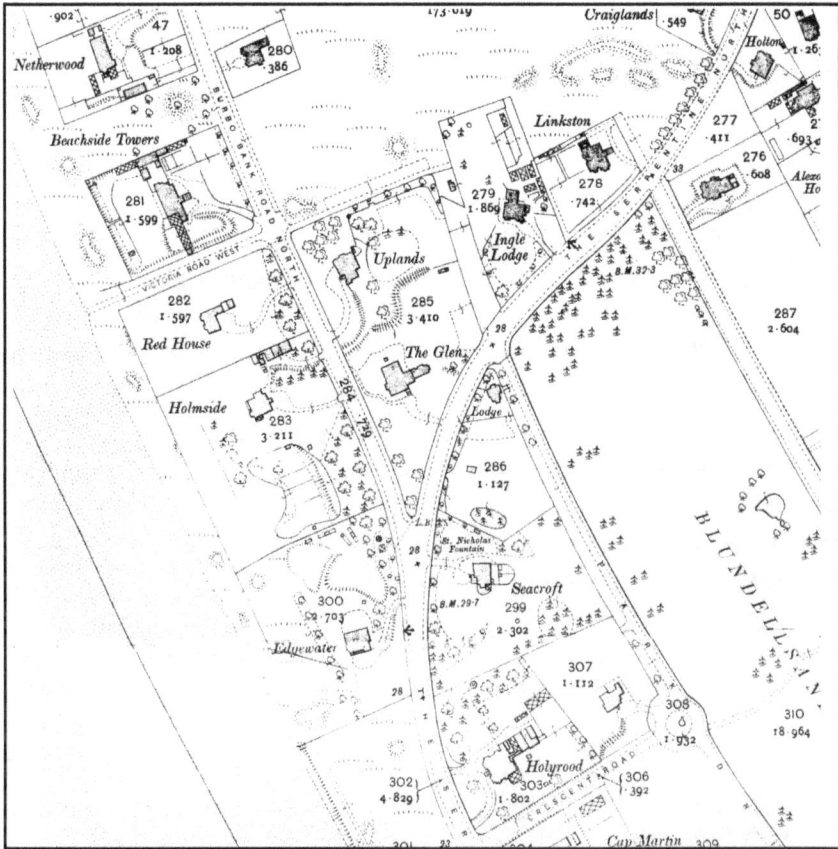

*Gerald Gardner's birthplace – Ingle Lodge, Blundellsands –
and other houses built for Gerald's uncle, Joseph Gardner
(Extract from the 1891 25-inch Ordnance Survey map)*

posed on this is a more orthodox pattern of roads running
roughly parallel to the coast but not rigidly straight.

The land was then subdivided into individual plots each of
roughly an acre or more in extent. The area was clearly intended
to be developed with houses of superior quality and this was
ensured by clauses in contracts for the sale of the land, such
that each house must have cost at least £1000 to £1200 to build,
or £1800 per pair of semi-detached. This was successful, since a
contemporary commentator noted that "Blundellsands ... now

consists of little else but large and palatial residences for Liver-pool's commercial and professional men". Greatbatch confirms this when he writes that: "... Blundellsands was home to more shipowners, brokers and merchants than any other part of north Liverpool".[20]

At the centre of the estate was a large park. This was (and is) retained for the benefit of the residents and is commonly known as Key Park. Apart from tennis courts and a pavilion at the south-ern end, it is not the well-manicured municipal enterprise that its name might suggest. Whereas the housing development has resulted in the levelling of the sand dunes and the building up over the years of layers of topsoil to create in most cases some very elegant and luxurious gardens, the Park has retained the sand dunes in their natural state and, apart from an area of woodland which has either been protected or has grown up in the last 150 years, the only sign of human activity is a network of paths which are maintained where necessary by the Blundellsands Park Trust.

Joseph Gardner, Gerald's "Uncle Joe", probably the most enterprising of the family, was the one who first established the family connection with Blundellsands. Gerald described him as "a pompous man with a forked beard"![21] He married in 1864 and went to live in Great Crosby, at Stanley Villas.

He obviously quickly became aware of the potential for devel-opment at Blundellsands. Indeed, this may have been the reason for his moving to Crosby in the first place. I have not studied the original deeds of the properties, but I imagine what probably happened is that Uncle Joe, at a fairly early stage, bought a sub-stantial tract of land as a speculative venture. In any case, he was soon the owner of a large block of land towards the north end, adjacent to what is now Burbo Bank Road North.

When the plan for the estate was drawn up, presumably in consultation with Uncle Joe, as a key landowner, he agreed to develop part of his land for housing and would donate the remaining land for a park. He obviously donated this land as an

---

20. Mike Greatbatch,Notes accompanying Old Ordnance Survey Maps, Blundellsands 1907, (The Godfrey Edition).
21. Bracelin, 13.

altruistic act or perhaps it was required as part of the contract for the purchase of the land. This was almost certainly not the whole of the Park, as Bracelin implies, but a substantial proportion nonetheless. In fact, his motives were probably not entirely altruistic, as the use of the land as a park would prevent development overlooking one of his houses, 'Seacroft', to the north.

The remainder of the land was subdivided into large building plots, some of three acres, and Joseph himself was the first to have built and occupy a house. This was 'Uplands', off Burbo Bank Road North in 1871, which was reputedly the first house to be built in the northern part of Blundellsands. It was in red brick, with blue and white banding, something which critics of the time somewhat contemptuously described as 'streaky bacon style'. 'Uplands' had a turret with a viewing platform from which to see the many ocean liners and other ships leaving the port of Liverpool. There were also many other extravagant and decorative features, as can be seen from the photograph.

Two years later, Gerald's father, William Robert Gardner, had built and moved into 'The Glen', a large house built on a site immediately to the south of 'Uplands'. Indeed, judging from the maps of the time, there was no dividing line between the properties: they just shared a garden of almost 3½ acres.

At about this time, Joseph seems to have had built three other large houses on land which he owned in the vicinity. These were 'Ingle Lodge' to the east, 'Seacroft' to the south, on the opposite side of The Serpentine, and 'Holmside', between Burbo Bank Road and the coast. Of these five houses it is sad that none still survives. Today they would undoubtedly have been Listed as being of Architectural and Historic Interest.

One of the reasons for building the houses was that Joseph lived close to the railway line but had a fifteen minute walk to the nearest station, Blundellsands and Crosby. So, he asked the railway company to build a new station, but, understandably, they refused to build one for just one customer. They told him, however, that if a further five houses were built, they might consider his request more favourably. So, this is what he did and, as a result, Hall Road station opened in 1874.

The families seem to have played 'musical chairs' with these houses. In 1876, Gerald's father had moved into 'Ingle Lodge',[22] whereas Joseph's family had moved into 'Seacroft'. By 1891, Joseph's family were occupying 'Holmside', but this was increasingly being affected by the encroachment of the sea, and by 1901 they were back in 'Seacroft'. Joseph continued to live in 'Uplands' until his death in 1912.

Joseph Gardner was a very public figure in Blundellsands. In about 1901-6 he became a J.P. (Justice of the Peace) and he was a well-respected character locally. In 1881 he had a fountain erected at the junction of The Serpentine North and Burbo Bank Road North. This was intended for the 'Cockle Mollies' (cockle pickers) who had previously called at the door of 'Uplands' begging for water. It was named 'St. Nicholas Fountain' after the local St. Nicholas Church.

Joseph seems to have been a somewhat eccentric philanthropist. He donated land for part of the park, planting esparto grass to help stabilise the dunes. He quarrelled with the Church of England curate, accusing him of 'Popish tendencies', going over to the Methodists and giving them the funds to build a chapel. When, in turn, he quarrelled with them, he returned to the Church of England by providing money for a new church.[23]

The first church in the Blundellsands area was St. Nicholas, at the junction of Agnes Road and Warren Road. Initially, in 1864, the year Joseph Gardner moved to the area, a 'tin tabernacle' known as the 'iron church' was built, to be replaced by a more permanent stone building ten years later. This would probably have been the church that Joseph attended and of which he accused the curate of "Popish tendencies". The Wesleyan Methodist Church in Mersey Road would have been the one that Joseph then financed and which was built between 1889 and 1891.

22. Letter from Harold Ennis Gardner to Ralph Rodman Gardner 31 October 1943 in the Gardner Family Archive.
23. Bracelin, 13.

Following his break with the Methodists, Joseph financed the building of another 'tin tabernacle', this time on Crescent Road closer to his house. This was St. Michael's Church, and it was occasioned by the increase in population in the Blundellsands and Crosby area. It was dedicated by the Bishop of Liverpool on 1st August 1907 (and I find by coincidence that I am writing these words exactly 100 years later, on 1st August 2007!)

So the Gardner family ended up living, not just in the same suburb of Liverpool but in the same part of that suburb: they were all neighbours! But enough of this historical and geographical background! It is time to meet the subject of our book—Gerald Gardner.

CHAPTER TWO

Venturing Abroad

William and Louise had come to England in late 1870 or early 1871, to move into their new house, 'The Glen'. It was large for the young couple with their two year old son, Harold, even allowing for the obligatory servants. The house was similar to 'Uplands', being in red brick with yellow brick banding and decorative detail. It had steeply sloping tiled roofs with large chimney stacks and a tower with a conical tiled roof. The first impression of the building (from a photograph: the building itself was demolished in 1963) is of a primary school: its style seems strongly influenced by that of William Butterfield. Gerald remembered it as "a huge Victorian monstrosity of a house, its brickwork, stained glass and dull gables surmounted by an ornamental tower".[1]

Two years later, in 1874, William and Louise's second son, Robert Marshall Gardner, was born. In 1876 the family moved into 'Ingle Lodge', the neighbouring house to the east. This was perhaps slightly smaller than 'The Glen' but still a substantial property. The reason for the move is not clear. I suspect that behind it lay Joseph Gardner's juggling with his various properties

---

1. Bracelin, 13.

27

like chess pieces and the families had to play 'musical chairs' whether they liked it or not. It is strange, though, that Gerald is clearly describing 'The Glen' as the place he lived when young, so perhaps, whilst Ingle Lodge is indicated in the directories as being William's residence from 1880 to 1885, they may have moved back into 'The Glen' when Gerald was very young.

Anyway, William Robert Gardner and Louise Burguelew Gardner's third son, Gerald Brosseau Gardner was born on Friday 13th June 1884 at Ingle Lodge, The Serpentine North, Blundell-sands, Great Crosby, Lancashire.

Many have spelled his middle name "Brousseau", including Bracelin,[2] but it is quite clearly "Brosseau" on his birth certificate, which is the definitive statement in the matter. His marriage and death certificates also spell it that way. Perhaps the determining blow must come from Gerald himself. Whilst he was notoriously bad at spelling, I think we can take it that he could spell his own name! I have a copy of an inscription in Gerald's handwriting in a book that he was presenting to his sister-in-law: it says, unequivocally, "from Gerald Brosseau Gardner". I think that settles the matter.

I have failed to find any reason why Gerald was given the middle name "Brosseau". It sounds French and there may have been some family connection with his mother via the French-speaking part of Canada. However, I have so far failed to find such a connection. I suspect that there was no particular reason: probably Louise just liked the name. However, I am still looking!

Gerald's early years at Blundellsands can at present only be seen through his eyes. His father is described as "a sturdy man, kind and gentle, with nothing of the heavy Victorian paterfamilias about him". By the time Gerald was around, William had been made a J.P. (Justice of the Peace - a magistrate), an award in those days only made to those who had achieved a certain status and reputation in society. He was also nearing the end of his working life and was apparently finding the travelling less enjoyable than previously and his return home to Blundellsands a welcome event.

---

2. Bracelin, 222.

Gerald's mother seems to have had a strong character:

... despite a certain comfortable placidity, [she] dominated the house, not merely as manager and mistress, but also with her wide, mainly literary interests. She belonged to the Browning Society, and was of the number who are convinced that Bacon wrote Shakespeare's plays. The house would buzz with bazaars and meetings which Mrs. Gardner would arrange to further her causes.[3]

When Gerald was born, in 1884, his eldest brother, Harold Ennis Gardner, was 14 and his other brother, Robert Marshall Gardner, whom he knew as 'Bob', was ten. By the time Gerald was old enough to be aware of his environment, Harold, was away studying for a Law degree at Oxford University. Bob, however, used to entertain Gerald by drawing pictures for him. A younger brother, Francis Douglas Gardner, was born in 1886, two years after Gerald. He shared the nursery with him, but he was really too young to be much of a companion.

Ruling over the nursery was Elizabeth, whom Gerald describes as a "forceful nursemaid", but she was soon replaced by a woman who was to have a major influence on Gerald's life, arguably greater than his mother or wife, and who went by the nickname of 'Com'. Her full name was Georgiana Harriet Wakefield McCombie, shortened almost universally to 'Com'. Bracelin refers to her as 'Josephine', which I had imagined was a mistaken memory on Gerald's part. After all, if she was always known as 'Com' he may only rarely have heard her proper name. However, her great niece tells me[4] that she was known in the family as "Aunt Jo", so Gerald may well have heard her being referred to as "Jo" and come to the mistaken conclusion that her full name was Josephine.

Bracelin describes her as Irish, as does the 1881 Census, although in the passenger lists of voyages made with Gerald she is put down as 'Scotch'! I can find no trace of her birth in the Scottish records, so perhaps the answer is that she came from the north of Ireland, where many people, particularly Protestants, might use

3. Bracelin, 13.
4. Letter from Gillian Hodges to the author, 5 May 2008.

that description. Irish birth records are notoriously incomplete and I have so far been unable to track down any birth record for her.

The other problem is her age, which seems to have fluctuated wildly over the years! In 1881 she was 22. Ten years later, she had attained the advanced age of 24, and eight years after that she was still only 26! The same year, she told Gerald she was in her early thirties. Even her death certificate, in 1945, gives her age as 80, which sounds very much like an approximation by someone who was unfamiliar with her actual age. I think the truth of the matter is probably that she was over-stating her age in 1881, possibly to get employment, and that she may only have been 16 rather than the 22 that she claimed. This would have made her 33 in 1898 when she told Gerald that she was in her early 30s and would imply a birth year of 1865, which would make the age on her death certificate nicely correct.

What then do we know about Georgiana McCombie? The earliest record is from the 1881 Census, where her first name is given as Georgina and where she appears as a Private Governess to the family of George F. Wilson, a Captain in the Royal Artillery, living in St. James House, Maple Road, a superior part of the town of Surbiton in Surrey. He had been serving in Bengal but had returned to England in 1870, being stationed in Southampton, Woolwich and Southsea before moving to Surbiton the previous year. Georgiana is indicated as having been born in Ireland, as was George Wilson, so there may have been some connection there. There were four children. Mary, the eldest, was ten; Violet was nine; Richard was seven and the youngest, Grace, was two.

Some time in 1887, 'Com' started to work for the Gardners as a nursemaid. We don't know how she came to be in their employment. Her post with the Wilsons may have come to an end, probably as the children grew older, and she may have come to Liverpool as somewhere she may have known someone, as quite a few Irish people had settled there. It may then have been a simple matter of answering an advertisement placed in a local newspaper.

Gerald remembers her as 'erupting' onto the scene and as being "a flamboyant, deep-bosomed, blarneying Irish girl". Bracelin calls her the dominant personality of Gerald's childhood.

Gerald saw far more of her than he did of his parents and she was the background against which his personality was formed and his interests developed. She certainly seems to have been able to wind Gerald's parents around her little finger.

Gerald was allowed out of her sight on occasions, however. His cousin, Uncle Joe's youngest son, Wilfred Percival Gardner, known as 'Kiddy Billy', was only a year younger than Gerald and as they lived next door to each other they used to play together frequently in the park, with its sand dunes, secret paths and undergrowth and, of course, on the beach, which was only a minute's run away from their houses. Gerald remembers Kiddy Billy's long golden hair flying in the sea breezes.

Such was the carefree life led by Gerald during the long summers at Blundellsands. But the winters were different: he suffered with his breathing and it was at about the age of three that asthma was diagnosed. This is a condition which causes the tubes that carry air into and out of the lungs to become swollen, making breathing difficult and causing wheezing and coughing, particularly at night. It has long been known in certain circles as 'the occultists' disease', as so many involved in the occult, such as Aleister Crowley, seemed to suffer from it.

One of the crucial decisions came when Gerald reached the age of four and school was being considered. Gerald's father had gone to Liverpool High School and The Royal Institution School, a boys' grammar school, in Liverpool.[5] It was a matter of some pride in the family that in the 1858 Oxford Local Examinations, William was "second in order of merit in all England". But more recently, the family had something of a tradition of attending the local prestigious Merchant Taylors' School at Crosby as day pupils. It had been founded in 1620 and moved to its present site in 1878. Gerald's Uncle Joe had attended, as had his two elder brothers. His younger brother, Douglas, would, in due course, go there as well.

Gerald was the only one of the family not to go there. Indeed, he never attended school at all, anywhere. The fact that he is the only one of the family to have made it into the Dictionary of

5. Letter from Harold Ennis Gardner to Ralph Rodman Gardner, 31 October 1943, in the Gardner Family Archive.

National Biography and is the subject of this book may well be because of the difficulties that he had to overcome in order to become the avid reader and writer which he later became.

The reason he was not sent to school was, of course, his asthma. In the late 19th Century there were very few things like inhalers to alleviate the symptoms of asthma. It was certainly considered that cold, damp conditions and atmospheric pollution made the condition worse, so, since the family was reasonably well off, it was suggested that Gerald should winter abroad. Whether it was Com who saw such a trip as being potentially more exciting than winter days in a Liverpool suburb or the recommendation of Gerald's doctor, we don't know. Perhaps it was just generally accepted that a warmer, cleaner climate would be better for him.

Anyway, it was agreed that Gerald would go to the south of France for a few months, accompanied by Com. It set a pattern which Gerald continued whenever he could when he was living in England, for the whole of his childhood and after his retirement. Indeed, he died on one of these winter trips in 1964.

So, in autumn 1888, when Gerald was just four, he and Com set off from Liverpool Lime Street station after waving his mother goodbye. It was after the train had set off for London, away from the eyes of Gerald's parents for the first time, that another side of Com's personality became evident. Gerald asked her to read to him from Sir Walter Scott's *Ivanhoe*, but she refused. It was clear that she was now in charge, acting 'in loco parentis' and Gerald would just have to get used to it.

In fact, the sights of the journey were exciting enough for Gerald to put this to the back of his mind. They stayed overnight at the Grosvenor Hotel, adjacent to Victoria Station in London, strangely enough right opposite where Gerald would be living after he retired in 1936. The hotel was advanced for its time, having not only electric light and telephones (Gerald was familiar with these since they already had one at home!) but also one of the first lifts in London, or, as Gerald describes it, a "...surprisingly small room - which without warning began to move!"[6]

6. Bracelin, 15.

They caught the Boat Train the following day and then there was the first of many sea voyages for Gerald who, on this first experience, was sea-sick. He recovered quickly, however, as they boarded the overnight sleeper train to Nice. He was excited by the whole experience: eating a meal while on the move, with everyone speaking French.

Nice had become, by the late 19th Century, the epitome of elegance and sophistication, which was reflected in the architecture, the costume and the whole ambience of the place.

It was probably not an atmosphere which held much interest for a four-year-old, though he remembered the warm sun and the blue waters of the Mediterranean. One event which did strike him, though, was the Battle of the Flowers. Over the years the custom built up of throwing flowers at parades as they passed, but it was really only in the 1870s that the Bataille des Fleurs was instigated as a way of opening the Mardi Gras festivities. There were numerous floats, almost completely covered with mountains of all kinds of flowers, but particularly honey-scented mimosa blossoms and branches in profusion. They went along the Promenade des Anglais as flowers were tossed to the onlookers until the floats were bare. Gerald remembered "...horse-drays piled high with colourful set-pieces, and people everywhere pelting friends and strangers with the blossoms, coming by in carriages and landaus and firing multi coloured broadsides".[7] He had never experienced anything like it and his immediate reaction was that it seemed a terrible waste of flowers!

It seems as if for several years there were similar winter trips to 'the Continent'. Gerald's memory of events which happened over 60 years previously when he was a young boy are, perhaps unsurprisingly, not always as accurate as they might be. The more definite dates given in shipping passenger lists can be relied on a lot more, although the names and ages noted down on them are often incorrect.

Bracelin says[8] that in 1891 there came a change and they went to the Canary Islands. However, we now have access to passenger

---

7. Bracelin, 15.
8. Bracelin, 15.

lists for all ships leaving England from 1890 onwards[9] and there is no mention of journeys by Gerald and Com in 1891. The journeys for 1892 onwards more or less tie in (with one exception) with what Gerald says about them, so this first trip beyond the Mediterranean is a bit of a mystery. Perhaps Com had been given enough freedom and money by the Gardners to make such a trip a real possibility. Perhaps she had become a little tired of the pleasures which the south of France had to offer and, on impulse, during the winter of 1891/92, had taken Gerald on the first passenger ship to dock in Nice or Marseille, which just happened to be going to the Canary Islands.

These were only 50 miles off the coast of Morocco and Spanish Sahara. It was here that one of Gerald's lifelong obsessions first became apparent: his interest in weapons. He had noticed that all the men seemed to wear knives, and, when Com gave him his pocket money, he bought one. His pride in owning such an item was short-lived, however, for it was confiscated by Com, who considered him to be too young at seven to own such a potentially lethal weapon.

According to Gerald's memories, we have a vivid picture of Com on these trips abroad as being in pursuit of pleasure in its traditional form - in her case, whisky, music and men! She attracted eligible young men with her singing and flirtation. Gerald recalls being very much a spectator in these enterprises, sitting, as he described it, "unnoticed in a corner of her room". There were times when he was called upon to take a more active part: as bait! Com would point out a young man who seemed impervious to her charms, and Gerald would go up and engage him in conversation, eventually "dragging him into her clutches"!

Exactly what Com's relationship was with these various young men, I do not know. Although Gerald does not mention it, there was clearly a sexual element. It was not purely looking for a husband and yet it was also not purely a matter of selling sexual favours since Gerald seemed to have been present throughout the proceedings. Com was a very strong woman, probably unusually so, and would have been attractive to a wide variety of men. As

---

9. See, for example, www.findmypast.com.

far as she was concerned, she was on holiday and Gerald was a bit of a nuisance to be put in the corner or hidden away unless he could be pressed into specific use.

They had only been in the Canary Islands for a few weeks when the proximity of the African coast became only too evident. Every so often an east wind picks up sand from the Sahara Desert, takes it out over the sea and deposits it many miles away, sometimes as far as the Caribbean. This wind goes by many names, such as the sirocco, leveche, the calima and the Tiempo del Sur. The wind, which can be quite strong, brings fine white sand, causing visibility to drop considerably and a dramatic temperature rise. In this situation it is most unwise to go out with any part of the body exposed. With his asthmatic condition, Gerald's breathing was particularly affected by the fine sand getting into his lungs, and Com decided that they needed to get away - and fast! They took the first ship available, not worrying where it was going.

In fact, it happened to be going to Accra, in the Gold Coast, a British colony on the west coast of Africa, not far from the Equator.

The ocean-going ships could not dock in Accra because of the shallow water, so passengers were transferred in surf boats, paddled by the native people. Gerald found this fascinating, though Com seemed rather apprehensive about it and screamed in fear!

Arriving in the town, it was the first time that Gerald had made contact with a culture significantly different from his own. He became vividly aware of the stiffness and, as he described it, 'stuffiness' of his clothes as contrasted with the natives, who were almost naked. Perhaps in this experience we can detect the first stirrings of an approach to life which would lead him, many years later, to naturism.

It was, however, not a peaceful period to visit Accra. Indeed, it had something of the Wild West frontier town about it. There were, for example, the 'Palm Oil Ruffians', European traders who had endured the triple perils of malaria, dysentery and blackwater fever to trade beads and gin for palm oil and ivory. Most did not survive, but those that did often made a fortune, which they were determined to spend in Accra. Although they were rough,

Mary Kingsley[10] admired them more than the missionaries and settlers that were generally favoured by European governments.

For Com, these 'Palm Oil Ruffians' offered fruitful possibilities. She acquired a piano and seemed to Gerald to have wild parties every night, with much singing and drinking.[11] There are hints, however, that it was something more. Notice of Com's activities began to reach the local missionaries, who took objection to them. This strongly suggests some sort of sexual content. Indeed, one could scarcely imagine the 'Palm Oil Ruffians', newly into town with money to burn, being content with merely a sing-song!

We will, perhaps, never know, as Gerald is not specific on this point. It, nevertheless, seems to be true that after only three weeks, he and Com took, if not the first then certainly an early sailing away from Accra. Their destination was Funchal, in the Portuguese colony of Madeira, an island in the North Atlantic further out from the coast than the Canary Islands. This was to be a successful choice on Com's part, since she and Gerald continued to visit the island every winter for the next nine years and it was here that she would meet her future husband. The tourist industry was just starting in Madeira in the 1890s and was attracting English visitors and residents because of its equable climate.

The passenger lists show that in most years it was far more for Gerald and Com than just "wintering abroad". The general pattern was to embark on a ship from England to Madeira from about mid to late October, not returning until June or July the following year. Therefore, most of Gerald's year was spent with Com in foreign climes with only three or four months spent in the summer back in England.

As usual, Com established herself, but this time in a much more fashionable environment. She again acquired a piano, which was as indispensable to creating a party atmosphere as electronic means of playing music are today. She also placed screens around the bed. Whether this was in pursuit of a more elegant environment, to provide a degree of privacy for sexual activity, or to prevent the sleeping Gerald from being seen by

---

10. Mary H Kingsley, *Travels in West Africa*, (Macmillan: 1897).
11. Bracelin, 17-18.

anyone, it would be difficult to determine. The environment was certainly enhanced or, one might at least say, made more distinctive, by Gerald's collection of weapons, which were displayed on the wall. This suggests a degree of permanence in the arrangement: they were obviously in the same hotel for several months. One gets the impression of a lively round of parties, whisky and wine flowing freely, music of course and a succession of men partaking in the delights that were on offer.

Some special friends seemed to emerge from this process. An early one whom Com may have met on this first visit to Madeira was Clifford England. Bracelin describes him as "a short, sturdy man who liked his whisky, chain-smoked incessantly, and regretted the youthful days when he had been at sea". This is likely to have been the same Clifford England who had been born in Liverpool in 1855 and who, by the 1890s, was a surgical dressing manufacturer, living in a superior part of Birkenhead, just over the River Mersey from Liverpool, probably working for the firm of Stephenson and Travis in Liverpool, manufacturers of Stypium, an absorbent anti-septic surgical dressing which had won several international prizes.

Gerald liked Clifford England because, unlike most of Com's suitors, he would find time to talk to him. In fact, England was married with two children of his own and in subsequent years the family came out to Madeira with him. Clifford remained good friends with Com and Gerald for several years.

The most significant liaison that Com made during her years abroad with Gerald - significant both for her and for Gerald - was with David Elkington. Exactly when they met is not clear. Gerald and Com wintered in Madeira every year from 1892 to 1896, but I suspect it was in 1893 that they first met David.

He had been born in 1874 in the King's Norton suburb of Birmingham, Warwickshire, to Jane and Hyla Elkington. He had at least three brothers and two sisters. The firm of Elkington and Co. is well known to antique collectors. It was founded in 1824 by George Richards Elkington (1801-1865), David's grandfather, and George's cousin, Henry Elkington (1810-1852). During the 1830s, they experimented with electroplating: the coating of a metal object with another layer of metal using an electric current. In 1840, they patented the world's first commercial electroplating process. As a result they quickly expanded from their works in Birmingham's Jewellery Quarter until by 1880 the firm employed over 1000 people in six factories, including London and Liverpool. They created a market for plated imitation gold and silver jewellery, which they dominated for many years. They also made everyday household objects like dishes, trays and cutlery and larger sculptural works such as those on Holborn Viaduct in London. They have examples of their work in the Victoria and Albert Museum in London, including two life-size copies of 17th Century silver lions from Rosenborg Castle, Copenhagen.

David was sent to St. Peter's College, Radley, just south of Oxford, one of the most prestigious private schools in the country.

Bracelin says that David was "not much more than fifteen" when he stopped at Madeira on his way to South Africa and fell under Com's "magic spell". This is likely to be an exaggeration. The first record we have from the passenger lists was at the beginning of April 1893, when David would have been 18, which is a more likely age anyway to have left school and about to take a job in South Africa. The ships on route to South Africa would only stay in Madeira a few days at the most, so we can perhaps imagine that David fell for Com and re-arranged his passage to South Africa on a later ship.

Gerald's niece, Mimi, believed that Com met David when he was put off a British freighter because he was ill and she, being a nurse, nursed him back to health.[12]

David certainly had time to go for several long walks on the beach with Gerald, impressing him by shooting seagulls with his walking-stick gun.

Com was less impressed with David. In fact, she found him boring. She even moved with Gerald to a different hotel to be away from him. But, of course, he followed them.

Eventually, David had to go on to the promised job in South Africa and then, in 1895, his father sent him, at the age of twenty, to Ceylon to learn the skills of a tea planter. From Ceylon, he

12. Telephone conversation between Mimi Gardner and Morgan Davis, 12 July 2001.

began to write long letters to Com. These she referred to as "the epistles of David" and threw them away unread.

One gets the impression that Gerald was left to do more or less as he wished, going out exploring, meeting people and observing life in general. Whether with Com's blessing or not, he probably persuaded someone to take him on a trip up to Monte above the town, to be propelled down again on one of the wicker-work toboggans on wooden runners that were guided by locals down the narrow winding streets at speeds of up to 30 mph. Exciting but apparently quite safe!

He certainly observed the variety of characters who frequented Funchal, either as residents or "wintering abroad" like himself. Gerald recalled a visitor whom Bracelin describes as "his local squire". He had a red face and seemed to drink a lot. He used to buy lots of caged canaries and release them, saying "I'm happy. Let them be happy as well." The squire's father is supposed to have taken off all his clothes and sat on them if it started to rain.[13]

A squire is an English country gentleman, the chief landowner in a parish. Gerald's "local squire" would be the squire of Blundellsands. The Lords of the Manor were the Blundell family, well-known Catholic landowners, of Crosby Hall. The anecdote about the father, Nicholas Blundell, sounds very much like a story told by someone (presumably Com) who knew the family in question rather than through direct experience. Nicholas Blundell, who had been squire since his father, William, died in 1854, had himself just died, in July 1894, and the title had fallen on his oldest surviving son, Osbert, who was a 37-year-old Lieutenant in the Submarine Mining Service of the Royal Engineers, a small elite unit which mined estuaries against the possibility of foreign attack. Osbert visited Madeira in January and August 1895 and then again in December 1896, so he could have come to Gerald's attention at either the first or last of these visits.

Com seems to have changed her mind about Gerald possessing knives as he got older and he enthusiastically went around acquiring more of them whenever his allowance from Com would

13. Bracelin, 18.

permit. It was only 80 years since the Napoleonic Wars and there were apparently quite a few cutlasses and bayonets still in the ownership of those whose grandfathers had fought in that conflict. Some of these at least were amenable to Gerald's earnest requests to let him have those weapons. Perhaps it was in such negotiations that Gerald's persuasive powers that he used to great effect in later life were first forged.

It is not clear the extent to which Com acted as a governess and gave Gerald lessons. My impression is very little indeed. But Gerald was an inquisitive boy and he needed to exercise his mind. One obvious way was to talk to people. He recalled Billy Dewey, an old man with a long white beard who may well have been an Ulster Protestant, with whom he had long discussions and arguments about religion and philosophy. This was something new for Gerald: he hadn't previously had anyone with whom he could talk in this manner. He clearly enjoyed this very much and it was something which stayed with him for the rest of his life.

An indication that Com did not take much interest in Gerald's education is that he taught himself to read. He did this by looking at magazines, particularly *The Strand*, which was very popular in the 1890s, having serialised the Sherlock Holmes stories of Sir Arthur Conan Doyle. Gerald used to look at the pictures and then pester people to read the captions to him. Gradually he learned the letters and the sounds that they made and, as he gained confidence, he used to practise by trying to decipher the fairy tale at the back of each issue. Gerald recalls a 'Eureka!' moment when he ran to Com shouting "I can read! I can read!". Her reaction to this news is not recorded! However, it had profound implications for Gerald: he now had potential access to all the written knowledge in the world, and he probably valued it the more from having achieved it entirely by his own doing.

Gerald immediately began to use his newly-acquired ability on any books and newspapers that he happened to come across. In particular, he found that departing hotel guests often used to leave books behind, which he deftly appropriated. Some were more interesting than others. One which made a lasting impact was *There Is No Death* by Florence Marryat (1838-1899). She was the youngest of the eleven children of Captain Frederick Marryat, author of *The Children of the New Forest*. After her husband's death in 1890, Florence became interested in spiritualism and wrote at least three books on the subject. *There Is No Death*, which appeared in 1891,[14] is an account of the various spiritualist mediums whom she had met and séances which she had attended.

This book affected Gerald deeply. Bracelin calls it "the first real step in his life's destined journey". His reaction to it was to become convinced of survival beyond death. The other effect of this book on Gerald is that he found no mention of Hell, somewhere that Com was always telling him he would end up, and concluded that such a place did not actually exist.[15]

A change of some significance occurred, probably in 1896, with the arrival in Madeira of Robert Lawrence Thornton, DL, JP, a barrister-at-law, together with what Bracelin describes as his "general factotum", one A. Rowley. Thornton was extremely rich, not merely because he was a barrister of the Inner Temple but because seven years previously he had succeeded his father as owner of the High Cross estate at Framfield in Sussex. He was Sheriff of East Sussex and provincial grand master of the Sussex freemasons. An indication of his wealth is that by 1901 he had nine servants. He is described as being "big and fat and sandy-haired"[16] and as being easily amused.

It was, however, Thornton's assistant, Rowley, who attracted Com's interest. He was tall and dark-haired and very soon Com was deeply in love with him, a feeling that appeared to be mutual.

Things were wonderful for a while and Gerald was being treated better as a result, but Rowley's devotion to Com started to affect his work, which Thornton obviously did not appreciate, so he arranged to move to another hotel and took Rowley with him, using the same ploy that Com had used against David a few years previously. Com was not easily discouraged, however, and very shortly she and Gerald had moved into the same hotel!

14. Florence Marryat, *There is no Death*, (Kegan Paul 1891)
15. Bracelin, 19.
16. Bracelin, 21.

Even when back in England, Gerald was taken on summer holidays and other trips by Com. London was an obvious destination, looking at all the famous sights. The main interest as far as Gerald was concerned, however, was the collections of weapons in the Tower of London and the Wallace Collection.

The Isle of Wight was the destination on at least one occasion in 1896, but what Gerald most remembered was not the scenery or the beaches but the library in Ryde where he located more of Florence Marryat's books. They had a profound effect on Gerald, even though he was only 12 years old. Bracelin says that Gerald "... dates his firm belief in the survival of the spirit from this time".

1897 was the occasion of the Diamond Jubilee: Queen Victoria had been on the throne for 60 years. The celebrations culminated on 22nd June with a grand procession ending with a service of thanksgiving outside St. Paul's Cathedral. Com probably used this as an excuse to come down to London to see Rowley. It seems as if her relationship with Thornton had improved by that time, for she and Gerald were invited to visit them at Thornton's 'town house' at Trevor Lodge in Oakhill Road, Surbiton Hill. Com was familiar with Surbiton, since it was there that she had been governess to the Wilson family some 15 years previously. Bracelin refers to the house as being in Richmond, which is probably Gerald's uncertain memory of the geography of south-west London suburbs and towns. In fact, Surbiton Hill is only a few miles from Richmond.

Gerald would never forget the Jubilee festivities, with the presence of soldiers from all corners of the empire, in their bright colours, flags, the parades with bands and banners, horses with plumes, breast-plates and the "glint of steel". He was less impressed by Queen Victoria, whom he describes as a "tiny, dumpy elderly woman in black" who seemed to nod like an automaton.[17]

Later on that year, something unusual happened. In mid-October 1897, Com and Gerald travelled to London and, as usual, took the ship which would take them to Madeira, as they had done for the previous five years. And, indeed, they did go to Madeira but, when the ship called at the port of Funchal, they did

17. Bracelin, 21-22.

not disembark as usual but stayed on board. In fact, Com had booked them straight through to Cape Town: they were going to visit David! He was either working in South Africa or, more likely, had come over from Ceylon to his old haunts to meet them. I think this was all intended to be secret. I don't think Gerald's parents knew about it. For all they knew, Gerald and Com were going to Madeira as usual, and there were, of course, no international telephone lines to enable them to check up on the travellers. David had obviously paid for the extra cost of the tickets.

Whilst it is in the passenger lists, this trip is not mentioned in *Gerald Gardner Witch* and I think the explanation is clear: Gerald had given his word to Com that he would keep it a secret. It is perhaps a matter worthy of attention to those who accuse Gerald of betraying the secrets of the Craft that the word of a 13-year-old boy was so important that it was kept over 60 years later when all the other participants had been dead for many years.

Gerald often remarked that if you are telling an untruth, it is easier if it is in fact partially true, so I suspect that he and Com spent at least part of the 1897/1898 winter in Madeira. They probably arrived from South Africa by January 1898, to coincide with the visit by Thornton and Rowley. I suspect that Com learned about that visit and curtailed her stay in South Africa as a result.

On their return to England in June 1898, Com had to make a decision. David had asked her to marry him. She wanted to get married, for she was in her early thirties, and David came from a wealthy family and owned a tea plantation. Yet she was in love with Rowley, who did not seem to be able to provide her with the standard of living that David could and that she had aspired to since working for the Gardners. This was something that was clearly important to her.

All that summer, Com was trying to choose between Rowley, whom she loved, and David, who would provide security. Bracelin describes the "long tearful sessions with Rowley, during which the whisky flowed as freely as her tears."[18] In the end she decided to choose David and to go out to Ceylon and marry him.

---

18. Bracelin, 22.

It was also decided that Gerald would go with her and get a job on David's plantation. Who decided this is uncertain, but it is likely to have been, at least in part, Com's idea. She put it to Gerald's parents that he would be 16 in 1900. His health required a warm climate and he would be learning a trade. Also, whilst it may not have been reciprocated, I think that Com had grown quite fond of Gerald and would miss him if he were not there with her.

Gerald's father agreed. Probably it would be a good thing financially if Gerald did not enter the family firm. He agreed to pay for his upkeep while he was learning the trade of a tea planter.

After this was settled, things went on much as before. For another three winters, Gerald and Com made the usual trip to Madeira, in 1898, 1899 and 1900.

David returned to England in the summer of 1900 to see Com and, presumably, his family, and, a year later, Gerald and Com joined him in Ceylon. Clifford England accompanied them to Marseille and, at the beginning of November 1901 they embarked on the *Shropshire*, bound for Colombo. As Bracelin put it, Gerald was "sailing toward manhood".[19]

---

19. Bracelin, 23.

CHAPTER THREE

The Enchanted Isle

After boarding the ship at Marseille, Gerald and Com stopped off briefly at Port Said, with all its bustling activity. And then, through the Suez Canal, and many days at sea: the next port would be Colombo.

As the ship steamed across the Indian Ocean, Gerald had time to ponder on his future. He was bound for Ceylon, but what did he know of the place? David had undoubtedly kept him informed, probably through the medium of his long 'epistles', as to what he could expect. He knew that Ceylon (now known as Sri Lanka) was an island off the southern tip of India, just north of the Equator and about half the size of England and Wales (or, for those on the western side of the Atlantic, about the size, and incidentally the shape, of West Virginia).

Whilst so near the Equator, the highlands in the central part of the island have a climate more amenable to the Europeans who settled there. Indeed, the area around Nuwara Eliya, one of the highest of the hill towns, was popularly supposed to have a climate similar to that of the Highlands of Scotland.

Until the 1870s, coffee had been Ceylon's main export crop. It had been introduced by the Arabs and was first systematically cultivated by the Dutch in 1740. Production increased markedly in the 1830s, reaching a peak in the late 1860s. However, in 1869, the coffee-rot fungus, *Hemileia vastatrix*, (known to the planters as 'Devastating Emily'), first appeared and spread rapidly, so that by the early 1880s only a quarter of the coffee was being exported that there had been but 13 years previously. Estate owners were thus forced to diversify into other crops. Tea was one obvious candidate, which seemed to have some advantages, as Ferguson makes clear:

> *Untimely showers, which so often wreck the blossoms and the hopes of the coffee planter, do no harm to the leaf crop of the tea planter; and the tea shrub is found to be hardier and more suitable to the comparatively poor soil of Ceylon than coffee.*[1]

From an initial yield of just 23 pounds in 1873, tea production expanded rapidly throughout the 1870s and 1880s, reaching 81,595 pounds in 1878, 623,292 pounds by 1881 and to over 22,000 tons by 1890. Today, Sri Lanka is the largest tea exporter in the world.

So, by the time Gerald arrived on the island in 1901, tea was well established as the major export crop and a worthy investment, as David's purchase of the Ladbroke Estate indicated. Most tea plantations in Ceylon were in the highland areas in the centre of the island at a height of between 3,000 and 8,000 feet. The climate at this altitude was more equable, not just for the planters, who mostly originated from Britain, but also for the tea crop.

Ladbroke Estate was in the Maskeliya district, some 250 acres in extent at a height of 4,500 to 5,000 feet on the northern slopes of the ridge which runs between Adam's Peak and the World's End. Obtaining ownership of the estate had not been straightforward. David had completed the purchase of the estate on 1st June 1900, but the widow of the former owner had complained to the courts that he had been in unlawful possession of one fourth of the estate which she claimed was hers. Her husband, James Cantlay, had died intestate with certain debts

---

1. John Ferguson, *Ceylon in 1883: The Leading Crown Colony of the British Empire* (Sampson Low: 1883), 67.

which required that the estate be sold. His widow claimed that she owned part of the estate and that therefore her share should not have been sold to pay off James' debts. In the end, her claim was not upheld by the courts and so David's ownership of the whole estate was confirmed.[2]

As they approached Colombo harbour in the dusk, Gerald thought the town looked European, rather like an English seaside resort, an impression that was reinforced when the large "G.O.H." illuminated sign on the Grand Oriental Hotel suddenly lit up.

After a reunion with David on the quayside they may well have stayed at that very hotel overnight (Gerald certainly did so in future years). David had already arranged the marriage ceremony, which took place in Colombo a few days later.

There was no time for a honeymoon, however, for the following day they all took the train, with their luggage, to the hill town of Kandy, where David had rented a bungalow pending completion of the new dwelling which he was having built on his tea estate.

Kandy had plenty to interest Gerald. It was an old centre of Buddhism, often considered the religious capital of the island, and had the two largest Buddhist monasteries in the country. It was also the location of the Dalada Maligawa, the Temple of the Sacred Tooth, supposedly containing a great treasure - one of the teeth of the Buddha, which was publicly paraded every July in the great parahera ceremony. In fact, the original was probably stolen and a fake substituted several hundred years ago, but this did not seem to affect the religious fervour which the relic generated.

Bracelin states that at "...about the same time, a neighbouring bungalow was occupied by Arnold Bennet and Aleister Crowley the magician".[3] Crowley does feature in our story and it has been suggested by some that he and Gerald first met in Ceylon. This is actually highly unlikely, not only because neither man mentions it in his writings, nor claimed it when they met almost 50 years later, but because the timing is wrong. Gerald was sharing the bungalow in Kandy with David and Com from about December 1901 to perhaps March 1902 at the latest. Crowley and Allan Bennett (not

2. www.lawnet.lk/docs/case_law/nlr/common/html/NLR9V168.htm, Cantlay v Elkington D.C. Kandy 15,378.
3. Bracelin, 26.

Arnold Bennet!) did indeed rent a bungalow called 'Marlborough' overlooking the lake and temple at Kandy, but it is clear that this was only from August to November 1901, so they had gone before Gerald arrived.4

Gerald had time to explore the city and found its sights and back streets fascinating. Kandy is considered to be one of the most beautiful cities in the world, something which has recently been confirmed by its being designated as a World Heritage Site by UNESCO. It was the country's capital in the 17th and 18th Centuries.

But Kandy was sufficiently small that Nature was never far away. The city was full of trees, and Gerald was able to get close to a tropical natural environment for the first time. He seemed strangely attracted to the jungle and took long walks, giving him what Bracelin calls "a nearness to reality".5 He didn't mind coming home covered with leeches, for he felt alive and happy.

At last, the bungalow on the Ladbroke Estate was ready and they moved in. The bungalows in the hill country were well-built because they needed to withstand the low temperatures which could occur. They were timber framed, with mud infill. The ceilings were of cloth, above which snakes seemed to pursue rats on a regular basis.6 The building was a substantial one. Gerald would probably have had a separate apartment around the back.

Having settled in to the bungalow, Gerald, for the first time in his life, at the age of seventeen, had to work. Trainee planters, or 'creepers' as they were popularly known, were really apprentices but, rather than being paid, they had to pay a certain amount for the privilege of learning the trade, and for their board and lodging. For some reason, Gerald's father had agreed to pay £300 a year for this rather than the usual rate of £50. Why Gerald's training should cost six times as much as anyone else's, I do not know. Perhaps it was because he was almost considered a relative of Com and David and that William Gardner did not want his son to

---

4. Lawrence Sutin, *Do What Thou Wilt: A Life of Aleister Crowley*, (St. Martin's Press: 2000).
5. Bracelin, 26.
6. Bracelin, 28.

be a burden on them financially, particularly in their first years of marriage. Perhaps it was in the nature of a wedding present, or perhaps he just wanted to give them the impression that he was well off and could afford to give away a few hundred pounds here and there without concern. Or perhaps he was aware that he had paid school fees for his other sons and that he owed Gerald something to make up for it.

It must be remembered that Gerald had never been to school. Indeed, it seems highly likely that he had never experienced any formal teaching of any sort from Com. The discipline of work would therefore perhaps be even more of a contrast with his former life than for someone who had previously experienced the discipline of school. Bracelin quotes Gerald as disliking the "dreary endlessness" of the work, and gives an outline of the daily routine, which started at six in the morning with a roll-call and assignation of work to particular groups. Breakfast followed and then the morning spent checking on the workers. After an hour's lunch, work continued until four in the afternoon, when Gerald was responsible for supervising the weighing of the crop. At least he was working largely in the fresh air, and he greatly appreciated the natural scenery and beauty which surrounded him.

Even though Gerald was working full time, Com was still in the habit of trying to order him around. There was, for example, the incident where she asked Gerald to make a special drinks tray for her, to try to hide the extent of her drinking from David. The idea was that the recess in the tray that her glass went into was deeper than the others and therefore her glass could be filled higher without David noticing.[7] This sounds highly unlikely to have been carried out in practice. Why would the tray need recesses anyway? One could understand it on board ship but not in the highlands of Ceylon. Com's glass would also have to be specially made to be taller than the others, and the depth of the recesses would be clearly seen to vary once the glasses had been removed. Even Bracelin says that this did not remain undetected for long and I suspect strongly that this, like many of Gerald's other stories, was just an idea that never saw the light of day.

---

7. Bracelin, 27.

After two years, probably at the beginning of 1904, Gerald began to feel that it was time to move on. His spirit had expanded with the landscape and the ideas with which he was surrounded, and he felt claustrophobic living so close to David and Com. It is natural for a young person to want to leave home and branch out on their own, and Com was still very much the parent figure. Gerald, now almost twenty, wanted to get out of her shadow, so he started to look for a job that would pay money rather than one which was being subsidised by his father.

He very quickly found one. This was on the Non Pareil estate, on the south-western slopes of the highlands, below Horton Plains. It had been a coffee estate in the 1880s, but like so many had converted to tea. It stretched from 3,000 feet above sea level at its lower end to 5,800 feet at its upper limit. It had over 400 acres in tea cultivation. The estate still exists today and has the reputation of producing some of the finest teas (Uva high grown) in the whole of Sri Lanka.

For the first time in his life, Gerald was on his own, earning his own keep and not relying on his father. His manager, A. Atkinson, lived three miles away, but Gerald was responsible for day-to-day decisions. He was also able to spend more time getting to know the local people and his environment.

Gerald was in the habit of hunting deer. One day, he went further than usual and got lost. This didn't worry him and he just settled down for the night. Meanwhile, Atkinson had sent out native workers to look for him. In fact, they knew he would be all right and didn't actually do much looking. The following morning he found his way back, was surprised at the concern that his absence had caused and was in fact "exhilarated by the experience".[8] This gives an indication that, unlike many of his compatriots who found themselves working 'out East', Gerald did not cut himself off from the locality and the native people and pretend that he was still in England.

The landscape in the vicinity of Non Pareil is some of the most dramatic in the whole of Sri Lanka. Gerald undoubtedly went for long walks on his own, when he could, exploring the

8. Bracelin, 28.

area. His own bungalow was directly below the famous viewpoint of World's End, where the land suddenly drops away in a cliff face 2000 feet in height. Undoubtedly Gerald would have made the long and arduous climb up to the World's End for the spectacular view over the estate and far beyond, for Bracelin comments: "Looking from the top, Gardner felt as if he could have dropped a biscuit straight down to where his bungalow lay. In reality, however, the house was some distance from the cliff."[9]

Haeckel gives a vivid description of the World's End:

> ... *a famous, but rarely visited ravine, where the southern edge of the great tableland is cut off in a perpendicular wall five thousand feet high. The stupendous effect of this sudden fall is all the more startling, because the wanderer comes upon it after walking for a couple of hours through the forest, emerging immediately at the top of the yawning gulf at his feet. The rivers far below wind like silver threads through the velvet verdure of the plain, and here and there, by the aid of a telescope, a bungalow can be discovered in its plantation. Waterfalls tumble from the top of the ravine, which is overgrown with fine tree-ferns, and, like the Staubbach at Lauterbrunnen, vanish in mist before they reach the bottom.* [10]

Gerald would also probably have climbed Sri Pada, also known as Adam's Peak (7380 feet; 2243 metres), which was sacred to three religions and which drew pilgrims from all faiths. It was once, improbably, thought to be the highest mountain in the world. And he would undoubtedly also have been familiar with the nearby Dafther Jailany, which is a natural cave where a Muslim saint is said to have meditated.

For the first time in his life, Gerald was living somewhere where Christianity was not the dominant religion. Most of the native people were Buddhist and there was a substantial Muslim presence as well. To what extent he actually discussed religion and philosophy with the native people I do not know. He certainly did later in Borneo and Malaya, but I suspect that it may

---

9. Bracelin, 27.
10. Ernst Haeckel, *A Visit to Ceylon*, (Peter Eckler: 1883).

have taken quite a while for the young 'creeper' to pluck up enough courage to do what most Europeans did not do - talk to the native people as equals. I am sure that he made what contact he could with the Singhalese natives, though this was difficult outside the narrowly prescribed work relationship.

Certainly the job gave Gerald time to think. He learned what he could about the local religion, which was a mixture of Buddhism and older more local beliefs. He came to realise that Buddhism had survived longer and in more of its original form in Ceylon than anywhere else. He was attracted by what he learned about Buddhism, such as the firm belief in reincarnation. There was also the ready acceptance of local gods and goddesses, a belief that in no way came into conflict with Buddhism. The Buddhist scholar, Richard Gombrich, confirms this when he writes:

> *Sinhalese villagers have been judged corrupt Buddhists because they say and do things which the judges think are incompatible with what is said in the Pali Canon. In particular, most Sinhalese believe gods and demons to exist and make offerings to them under various circumstances. ... The judgement that this is corrupt Buddhism is based on a misunderstanding which has arisen because the original people to make it were westerners, raised in a Christian culture, whose background made them think of religion as god-centred. ... An ordinary Buddhist layman is no more concerned to accept or deny the existence of some new supernatural being than a western layman is concerned to accept or deny the existence of some newly discovered type of nuclear particle or natural force. Both are just facts of life.*[11]

In December 1904, Gerald received a visit from his parents, his youngest brother Douglas and an American cousin, Jenny Tompkins. She seemed to have been a remarkable woman. She had brought Gerald the present of a bible and told him to study it. This was not the usual pious sentiment, however, for on giving it to him, she commented: "I read it from cover to cover when I

---

11. Richard F. Gombrich, *Buddhist Precept and Practice: Traditional Buddhism in the Highlands of Ceylon*, (Kegan Paul: 1971), 54–55.

was your age ... and I have never believed a word of it since!"[12] She was clearly a free-thinker, which was somewhat rare at the time, and one can imagine that she had long discussions with Gerald ranging far and wide. Her attitudes certainly helped to encourage in him the wide-ranging approach to religion and philosophy which characterised his later years.

The visit was only in part to see how Gerald was getting on: it was also because William Gardner wanted to investigate the commercial potential of growing rubber. He had previously invested heavily in South African mining stock, on which he had incurred large losses, and he was looking to invest in other, more fruitful, directions.

The cultivation of rubber (*Hevea braziliensis*) outside its native Brazil was still in its infancy in 1904. It had been introduced into Ceylon in the wake of the coffee blight in 1877. By 1900, there were 1000 acres of rubber plantation in Ceylon and by 1905 this had increased to 66,000 acres, so William Gardner was looking at a crop for which there was a lot of enthusiasm.

He decided to take the plunge and invest. Atkinson had some land to spare near the village of Belihul Oya and he sold it to William. It was at an altitude of over 3000 feet, which was quite high for a rubber plantation, the consequence being that the rubber trees would grow relatively slowly.

The estate was to be known as Atlanta Estate and Gerald was to be in charge of the enterprise. This involved quite a lot of work to start with in planting out and keeping the various diseases at bay, but after the initial activity, it was not really a full-time job for him. Whether he retained his job with Atkinson on a part-time basis or got a different job at one of the other tea plantations in the Kelani Valley is unclear.

Haeckel's description of the hamlet of Belihul Oya is very much how Gerald would have experienced it 20 years later:

The little village of Billahooloya, literally the Sacrificial Torch-brook, derives its name from the mountain torrent which here falls in rushing cataracts through a fine gorge in

---

12. Bracelin, 28.

the southern rampart of the plateau, and which is fed by a small rivulet which rises at the World's End, besides several tributary streams. The narrow channels of these tumbling brooks are shrouded in luxuriant verdure, and enclosed between steep rocky walls, all opening westwards, and these ravines give the scenery a very grand and imposing aspect. As we came down from Nonpareil, the beauty of the country charmed us so much that we decided on spending a few days at the village. The rest-house is delightfully situated, under the shade of a mighty tamarind tree, close to a stone bridge which spans the torrent; the background is formed by the vast amphitheatre of the cliffs of the World's End.[13]

Social life seemed to be centred on the small town of Balangoda, which had a 'rest house'. These were founded in the colonial era along the main roads to provide fairly basic and cheap accommodation and meals for travellers. They were also often centres for social gatherings and entertainment, as at Balangoda. Whilst Gerald was probably happier exploring the local landscape and talking with the local Sinhalese people, he was able to mix with other planters and take part in sports and social activities with growing confidence. Whilst he did not drink alcohol, he took an active part in what sounds as if they were quite lively music evenings which sometimes got out of hand.

Two of the participants made a particular impact on him. One was Walter Dermott Holland (1865-1912), universally referred to as "Old Man Holland". He was the manager of the 200 acre Dik Mukalana tea estate, not far from Balangoda. On his land were caves where remains of some of the most ancient inhabitants of the island were found. He also discovered a rare mineral, thorianite (ThO_2). But his main quality as far as Gerald was concerned was his ability to come up with satirical songs about those in power, such as the Visiting Agents, who inspected estates on behalf of their owners and who were greatly feared, as their word could get a man dismissed. Holland was: "... very old and thin, hollow-chested and rather consumptive-looking: but he was really

---

13. Haeckel, 314.

tough. He could drink more than anyone else, shout louder, take the initiative - the archetype of a leader in those parts."[14]

The other character which Gerald mentions is C.J. Smale, manager of Massena, a much larger estate than most, over 1000 acres, though less than 300 acres were in cultivation. Like Non Pareil, it was originally an old coffee plantation which had, at least in part, been turned over to tea. Gerald liked Smale. He was half German, and drank beer rather than whisky. He had a large laugh and knew how to enjoy himself, but he also had the very useful skill of being able to stop fights, often before they had really started.

In time, Gerald felt that he wanted to spend some of his time in public service, and his continuing interest in weapons led him towards the military. The Ceylon Volunteers, a reserve military force, had been established in 1881 to help the regular army if there were threats to internal security or a possible invasion and also to provide supplementary manpower for overseas military campaigns such as the Boer War. They were not a regular force and only received occasional training. Gerald joined one of the divisions, the Ceylon Planters Rifle Corps, the members of which, as its name suggests, were drawn from the largely British planters, and supposedly served from 1906 to 1910. In fact, I have not found Gerald's name in the directories for 1904, 1905-6 and 1909-10, which list all the members, so I can only suggest that he was either romanticising about being a member of the Corps, or else that he joined in 1907 following his return from England but, in typical fashion, he had ceased to be a member by 1909.

Certainly Bracelin's account is detailed enough to confirm Gerald's membership of the Corps. He refers to camps being held at Diyatawala, which was the site of a prisoner-of-war camp where Boers were kept during the Boer War, along with other isolated locations such as St. Helena and Bermuda. It was certainly the biggest of all the prisoner-of-war camps. Gerald remembers visiting in the early days with Com when the Boers were still being held there. He describes the Boers as being "enormous" and requiring specially large handcuffs when they

---

14. Bracelin, 29.

were restrained following a break-out.[15] There is one anecdote that suggests strongly that Gerald had been a member of the Corps, possibly introduced by Walter Holland, as it presupposes "inside knowledge". To quote Bracelin:

> *The Rifle Corps used to march past to a tune which the authorities fondly imagined to be "A Life on the Ocean Wave"; but the volunteers knew that it was really one of the immortal songs by Old Man Holland:*
>> *"A life on a tea estate,*
>> *Is a life that is dull and drear;*
>> *The same monotonous round,*
>> *The whole of the live-long year ..."*
> *The rest is unprintable, but it describes how the planter did in fact have some pleasures.*[16]

In January 1906, Gerald's father made another visit to Ceylon. William Gardner was 61 at the time and was really retired from his work in the family timber firm. So he was obviously both willing and able to spend what amounted to a whole year on the Atlanta Estate. He may also have done some business on behalf of the family firm, which imported satinwood from Ceylon.

In the November of that year, Gerald's mother joined them, to see her husband and Gerald again and probably to join them in a holiday to various parts of the island.

When Gerald and his father were sure that the rubber plantations were coming on satisfactorily, they left the estate in the hands of a caretaker manager, possibly Atkinson, and Gerald returned to England with his parents for a well-earned break, in April 1907. The story of his return to England is told in the next chapter.

As an indication of the extent to which they had grown apart from Gerald and his family over the years, it is interesting to note that David and Com had been on a visit to England during 1906 and they took a ship back to Colombo in January 1907.

---

15. Bracelin, 34.
16. Bracelin, 35.

CHAPTER FOUR

An Edwardian Interlude

Gerald returned with his parents on the *Warwickshire* from Colombo, arriving in London on 25th May 1907. It had been six years since he had last seen England. Bracelin refers to Gerald's visit home as being 1905, but it is quite clear from the passenger lists that the year was 1907.

He had arranged to stay with his brother, Harold, his wife Edie (Edith Amelia, née Allen) and their three daughters, Edith Muriel (known as 'Bobby'), born 1898, Aileen Mary (known as 'Betty'), born 1900, and Dorothy Ida, born 1903. Gerald's father had retired from the family firm and was living with Harold and Edie at 'Treleaven', a large house at the junction of Warren Road and Blundellsands Road West, quite close to Blundellsands and Crosby railway station.

Gerald had seen very little of Harold and tended to feel that he was rather 'putting on airs'. Gerald "... had always taken the social prominence of the Gardner family somewhat for granted ..."[1] and thought that Harold's posturings rather unnecessary. However, he was a barrister, which probably explained it, although in Gerald's opinion he seemed to lack what he called

1. Bracelin, 118.

'the gift of the gab", which seemed to Gerald to be a prerequisite for the job.

Gerald's brother, Bob (Robert Marshall Gardner) was very much part of the family firm. He lived with his wife, Louise (née Goffey), whom Gerald describes as "a very sporting kind of girl", and their two sons, Ralph Rodman, born 1901, and Robert Leslie, born 1904. They lived at 'Leighton', Merrilocks Road, Blundellsands, and Gerald visited them regularly while he was home.

The atmosphere in England in 1907 seemed to Gerald to focus on military matters. There had been concern about the lack of preparedness which had come to light during the Boer War and there were also fears about a possible German invasion, of which Erskine Childers' *The Riddle of the Sands*[2] and Ernest Oldmeadow's *The North Sea Bubble*[3] were only two of many fictional representations. The Altcar rifle range, just north of Blundellsands, was frequented by trainloads of reservists and territorials from Liverpool. This was clearly something that excited Gerald and with which he wanted to get involved. His interest in weapons meant that he sought out some group that would fulfill that desire.

The Legion of Frontiersmen seemed exactly the right sort of thing and, enthusiastically, Gerald applied to join. The Legion had been founded by adventurer and author, Roger Pocock. A letter from him appeared in ten major newspapers on Boxing Day 1904. It read, in part:

> ... it is time to enlist the Legion, for good fellowship, mutual help, and possible service to the State in time of war. A few thousand men would form a sufficient army of observation, a unit for field intelligence in peace and war, its duties being those of scouting – to see run and tell – in case of any menace to the British peace.[4]

The Legion of Frontiersmen was inaugurated in April 1905 and was intended to have branches throughout the British Empire, recruiting volunteers, primarily ex-servicemen. It had

---

2. Erskine Childers, *The Riddle of the Sands*, (Smith Elder: 1903).
3. Ernest Oldmeadow, *The North Sea Bubble*, (Grant Richards: 1906).
4. Geoffrey A. Pocock, *One Hundred Years of the Legion of Frontiersmen*, (Phillimore: 2004), 28.

romantic aims, being described as "an organisation of roguish patriots who did all they could to ensure that Britain was prepared to defend itself". Pocock was a great expert on horses and saw the Legion in terms of "mounted scouts for the British Army, riding the frontiers of the British Empire and reporting back directly to the War Office".

The organisation grew rapidly and by 1907 there was almost certainly a branch in Liverpool. Gerald gave his impressions: "The members were mostly Colonials, seasoned men, wily in bush or desert and always carried guns. This precursor of the Commandos was formed to give instruction in fighting in rough country."[5]

Whilst in practice it was all probably rather quixotic and the precursor of the Home Guard rather than the Commandos, Gerald was able to study fighting methods with them, which he was able to use back in Ceylon when he enlisted with the Planters' Rifle Corps.

❧

One day, a letter arrived on the doormat at 'Treleaven' addressed to Gerald. It was an invitation to visit the Sergenesons, a family that so far he hadn't heard of. They lived in Formby, a village about five miles north of Blundellsands.

So, the following Saturday, Gerald set out by train. Just as the construction of the Liverpool-Southport railway had made possible the creation of Blundellsands, so it was transforming the small village of Formby into a thriving dormitory for workers from Liverpool. Judging from its name, Formby was of Viking origin, growing up on the small strip of land between the Altcar and Formby Mosses, which were marshlands to the east, and one of the largest areas of sand-dunes in England known as Formby Hills, between the village and the sea.

Gerald would have used the railway to get there and it had recently been electrified, in 1904, at a cost of £340,000, one of the first lines in England to be so treated. He alighted at Formby

---

5. Bracelin, 120.

station and walked along Freshfield Road looking for 'Red-holme'. It was, as might be expected from its name, a red brick house standing in a garden rather larger than the other houses in the road: someone seemed to be a keen gardener!

Nellie Sergeneson immediately introduced herself. Bracelin says that she was "kind and motherly, pleasant and friendly to everyone" and that she was the "placid centre of the activities of the house".

The gardener was Nellie's husband, Ted (Edmund) (1857-1925). He seems to have had a natural affinity with the land. He had been a boxer in his earlier days and had retained an enthusiasm for life which was centred on his gardening and bee-keeping. He was very much aware of, and could sometimes see, nature spirits (or "the Little People", as he called them) and kept part of the garden wild just for them.[6]

It seems as if the Sergeneson household was rather different from the typical Edwardian household. It was far more informal and had a constant stream of local visitors, as Gerald remarked: "Just how many people lived there was uncertain"! He says that he "had a feeling that he really belonged there". And so, it seemed, did half the village!

Gerald was 23 when he first came into contact with the Sergenesons and it is clear that this had a profound effect on him after the Victorian, though somewhat unusual, upbringing which he had experienced. For the first time in his life, he came across a group of people whose attitudes and approach he felt in harmony with. This happened to him again in 1936 when he fell in with the naturists and, more strongly still, in 1939 when he met the witches. Gerald's interest in unusual things, spiritualism and psychic phenomena was accepted as normal by the family.

In the midst of all this activity, Nellie took Gerald aside and explained to him that she was his godmother and explained what was puzzling Gerald: the connection between the Sergenesons and the Gardner family. She explained that there were two separate connections. First of all, Ted's father, Robert Sergeneson, a master cooper, had, in 1856, married Maria Gardner, who was one

---

6. Bracelin, 121.

of Gerald's father's sisters – Gerald's aunt, in fact, though he had never met her. The second link was through Nellie's side of the family. Her maiden name was Williams and she was one of ten children, four girls and six boys. Her father, Henry Williams, had married Martha Gardner in 1852. Martha was the daughter of Richard Gardner, one of Grandfather Joseph's brothers.

The youngest of Nellie's sisters was Annie Gertrude, known universally simply as 'G'. She was living with Nellie and Ted and played a prominent part in the activities that took place in the house. It is clear that Gerald quickly formed an attachment to 'G'. "There is no doubt ... that G. became, and remained until her death, the closest friend he had in England".7 He even contemplated asking her to marry him, but his relative youth and economic situation put him off:

> *Gertrude was the life and soul of the party; played the piano and sang. He guessed that she would be about thirty, so bewitchingly vivacious did she seem. He had no money, though his hopes of rubber were good, but he "did not speak", however strongly he felt attracted to these truly delightful people. Later he was to find out that she was over thirty years older than he was.*[8]

That last statement is incorrect. In fact, she was *thirteen* years older than Gerald and I suspect some confusion in transcribing his verbal account.

When Gerald returned to Blundellsands, he asked his mother about the Sergenesons and about why she had never mentioned them and particularly why she had not mentioned that Nellie was his godmother. She explained that the Sergenesons were Methodists, and found it difficult to understand why Gerald did not think that a very good reason for not having any contact with them. It probably had something to do with 'Uncle Joe', who had been a Methodist during the period when he had quarrelled with the local Anglicans before making up with them again after quarrelling with the Methodists! Probably Gerald was

7. Bracelin, 121.
8. Bracelin, 120.

born and christened at a time when the Methodists were in favour and thus Nellie would have been an acceptable godparent!

Anyway, his mother's attitude did not put Gerald off visiting the Sergenesons on several more occasions during his time in England.

It sounds from what Gerald says that the Sergenesons' house was fairly hectic a lot of the time, with numerous individuals, some of them family members, coming and going all the time. It is perhaps little wonder that he got rather confused such that elements in the story that he tells become conflated:

> *Also of the circle were a doctor called Gardner, and his sister. Although they were often there, they were a little older than the others, and tended to stay near Nellie. Occasionally someone would tease them, asking whether they had done any magic recently; or if they had attended any good Witches' Sabbaths. Why should they have, Gardner wanted to know. Because, of course, their mother had been a witch. He was extremely intrigued by this. Who had their mother been? And why had they the same surname as he had? Were they relations?*

Gerald asked his brother, Bob, what was behind it all. He was told that his grandfather, Joseph, had not been happy in his marriage.

> *As a result, Grandfather reached the end of his tether, cut through it and freed himself. He stayed at home, but kept the lady somewhere up north. There is some doubt as to whether he really married her. At all events, he had a second and happier home, where there were strange goings-on.*

> *This Ann, the tale ran, had led him into wicked ways. She had been a witch, and had taken Grandfather Joseph up into the hills where secret meetings and horrible rites were held.*

> *Ann had witchpower, and she took Grandfather to meetings in the hills. Bob, of course, knew all about it; and he said*

Martha Gardner = Henry Williams   Maria Gardner = Robert Sergeneson

m. 1852

Henry Williams b. 1823 m. 1852

Maria Gardner b. 1832 m. 1856

Robert Sergeneson b. 1828 m. 1856 d. 1896

Annie Gertrude ('G') b. 1870 d. 14 October 1922

Eleanor ('Nellie') b. 1859 m. 1885 d. 1930 =

Edmund ('Ted') b. 1857 m. 1885 d. 1925

Eleanor b. 1865

Edith b. 1868

Maria b. 1860

Walter b. 1862

Also:

Martha Gardner Williams b. 1853
David Williams b. 1855
Henry Williams b. 1857
William B. Williams b. 1863
Mary E. Williams b. 1865
Harold Williams b. 1867
George H. Williams b. 1869
Richard Gardner Williams b. 1860 m. Annie 1893

Edmund Gardner Williams b. 1894, d. 1989
Thomas Sands Williams b. 1895
Ada Margaret Williams b. 1897., d. 1986
Richard Gardner Williams b. 1899

Sergeneson Family Tree

"Whenever your Uncle Jim is ill, he always sends for his half-brother". He laughed at the term Witchcraft, but showed some measure of knowledge: "Strange things go in the hills there, you know."[9]

Now, I don't think it's likely that there was any deception intended, either on Gerald's part or on that of anyone else, but the story turns out to be not quite as he thought. Firstly, the brother and sister called Gardner were Richard Gardner Williams (born 1860) and Martha Gardner Williams (born 1853). They were Nellie's brother and sister. Richard was certainly not a doctor. He was actually a broker's clerk. So, where did the idea of the doctor come from? There was a relative who was a doctor. His name was James Cardwell Gardner. His grandfather, Richard Cardwell Gardner, had been mayor of Liverpool in 1862/63. However, at the time Gerald was visiting in 1907, James Cardwell Gardner was practising in Amersham, Buckinghamshire, some 200 miles away. Also, the connection is really very remote indeed, common ancestors being back in the 17th Century. However, James Cardwell Gardner's father, also James Cardwell Gardner, who was a Clerk in Holy Orders, was born in 1835, the same year as Gerald's Uncle Joe. My guess is that they were at school together and that the coincidence of surname helped to re-forge links between the two branches of the family. The school was probably the Merchant Taylors' School in Crosby, which the later generations of Gardners certainly attended.

This does not, however, answer the question of why Gerald's Uncle Jim (James Edward Gardner) consulted James Cardwell Gardner on medical matters, even if they were old friends. Perhaps he frequently visited London on business and went out to Amersham on those occasions. Also James Cardwell Gardner probably came up to Lancashire to visit his aged father, who had retired to Fluke Hall, Pilling.

I had tracked down the Sergenesons to Freshfield Road, Formby in the 1901 Census. The name of that road rang bells in my mind and I remembered that in R.A. Gilbert's book, *The*

---

9. Bracelin, 122-123.

Golden Dawn Companion,[10] there is reference to a J. Knight Gardner being a member of the Golden Dawn, an occult Order which we shall meet again later in our story. In 1891, he lived at Trefoil, Freshfield Road, Formby. I had noted the name but not taken it any further. When I looked the name up in the 1891 Census, it was striking to notice that he was living with his parents at that address and that his parents' names were Joseph and Ann Gardner, the very names in the witch story! Could these have been the origin of the story that was told to Gerald?

This Joseph was actually grandfather Joseph's nephew, probably born in 1818. His father, Richard (grandfather Joseph's brother) was part of the Gardner family firm but had continued the original trade of blockmaking.

Ann was born Ann Jane Knight in 1824 in Boston, Lincolnshire, which is a county that has a lot of traditions of witchcraft, as I know from my own experience. So it is quite possible that Ann could have brought over magical practices from that county. Gerald says that she took Joseph to "the hills", a phrase that occurs three times. It suddenly occurred to me that rather than referring to the Pennine hills, the backbone of England, which were some considerable distance from Formby, it was actually referring to the sandhills, Formby Hills, locally referred to simply as "the hills". It all suddenly fitted into place. They were within easy walking distance of their house in Freshfield Road; there were plenty of nooks and crannies in the forested dunes where rituals could be held and even fires lit without being visible to others: it was the ideal location!

Recently, I came across the following account: *Formby Point is said to be haunted by several ghosts; one is a woman who dances on the sand dunes but disappears if approached, and the other is a mysterious cloaked figure that wanders along the dunes at night.*[11] Could this story have been started by someone who saw Ann and Joseph out one night performing their rituals?

Perhaps we may never learn more about Ann's type of witchcraft. She died in 1897, two years after Joseph. He is reputed to

---

10. R. A. Gilbert, *The Golden Dawn Companion,* (The Aquarian Press: 1986).
11. Julia Skinner (compiler), *Did You Know? Southport: A Miscellany,* (Francis Frith: 2006).

have been married three times, but it seems to have been true that they were never married to each other. But her Craft seems to have lived on in her son, James Knight Gardner, who, as has been mentioned, became a member of the Golden Dawn, and went on to be the Sub-Praemonstrator of the Horus Temple No. 5 in Bradford.

Some time between 1901 and 1911, Joseph Knight Gardner, his wife Rachel, their daughter Radha and son Arthur Godwin Gardner, emigrated to Canada, settling in Salmon Arm, British Columbia. Joseph died in 1937 and has a Masonic emblem on his gravestone.

⚜

On 21st November 1907, Gerald embarked on the *S.S. Derbyshire*, at Liverpool, on his voyage back to Colombo. He had made some very good friends during his time in England and had learnt skills which he hoped would be useful back in Ceylon.

Perhaps the contacts he had made and the stories he had been told on his visit had made Gerald curious about Freemasonry. I don't know whether his father and uncle were freemasons, but it took Gerald several years to take the step of becoming a freemason himself. In fact, it was not until 1910 that he made the first approach, which was to the Sphinx Lodge No. 107 in Colombo. There were nearer lodges, such as the Adam's Peak Lodge No. 2656 EC, which met in Hatton and the Nuwara Eliya Lodge No. 2991, but Gerald had to go into Colombo occasionally on business and he became familiar with the new Victoria Masonic Temple on Church Road which had opened in 1901. Several lodges met there and Gerald chose, or was directed towards, the Sphinx Lodge No. 107, which was under the Irish Constitution.

It was obviously important to Gerald to attend their meetings as it involved considerable effort and expense on his part. He had to arrange a weekend's leave, then walk 15 miles to the nearest railway station at Haputale in the company of a native servant carrying his dress clothes in a tin box, then the long and slow railway journey to Colombo, plus an overnight stay at the prestigious Grand Oriental Hotel, where he changed for the meeting.

One incident showed how strictly the Masonic dress code had to be adhered to:

Once, when he had arrived in the Capital and started to dress in the famous G.O.H. Hotel, he found that his boy had packed brown shoes with the evening suit. All the shops were shut. They had to be blacked, and ruined well and truly, before Gerald could show himself to the assembly.[12]

Gerald received his Entered Apprentice Degree on Monday 23rd May 1910. This was followed by his Fellow Craft Degree on Monday 20th June 1910 and his Master Mason Degree a week later, on Monday 27th June 1910. His Grand Lodge Certificate was issued on 18th May 1911 and it is noted that he resigned, but there is no date given for this.

I think Gerald had hoped that freemasonry would provide some sort of favourable environment for the encouragement of his spiritual leanings. It was clearly very important for him to have spent so much time and energy getting to the meetings, but, like many enthusiasms in the course of his life, his connection with the Lodge was short-lived, probably little more than a year, when he resigned, almost certainly because he was leaving Ceylon, as we shall see in the next chapter.

On the tea estate in the Kelani Valley where Gerald had ended up working, there was a small acreage of rubber, which had been planted mainly as a windbreak. Gerald had an inventive mind and plenty of time to use it. He started to look at ways of processing the rubber, involving rolling it on a table and drying it in the sun, which was not really very successful. Later it was found that smoking was the best method. Gerald did not give up, however, and was experimenting with various other methods but he couldn't take them very far because external factors intruded.

Gerald's father began to realise that the Atlanta Estate would be a drain on his resources for many years before it began to pay its way. He was reluctant to pay out regularly with no return and came to a decision to sell the property, perhaps back to Atkinson.

---

12. Bracelin, 35.

And so, in early 1911, he sold the land for roughly the amount he had paid for it some six years previously.

His father's decision to sell the estate gave Gerald the opportunity which he had been yearning for for some time - to leave Ceylon and go east. He began looking for jobs and saw an advertisement for a rubber planter in North Borneo (now Sabah). He applied with details of his relevant experience and he was accepted on that basis - no need for an interview in those far-flung regions!

CHAPTER FIVE

The Land Below the Wind

Some time early in 1911, Gerald travelled for the last time on the railway down to Colombo and embarked on a German ship bound for Singapore. As he approached the harbour, his senses were assailed by the sights, sounds and scents of Singapore and by the great mixture of races who had made it their home. He had booked a room in the prestigious Raffles Hotel, and the next morning went down to the harbour to enquire about ships to Borneo. He was directed to one and advised to get aboard quickly as it might leave the same day. He brought his things down from the hotel and was allocated a small cabin. He went to sleep.

The next morning he found on waking that the ship was still moored in the harbour. At first he could find out nothing, but finally he was told that it would not leave for another two days. He took the opportunity to explore Singapore, probably visiting the Raffles Museum that he would get to know so well in future years.

On the second day of waiting, other passengers began to arrive, including one individual with a "sunburnt, craggy, bruiser's face". He accompanied Gerald on an evening walk around the town. His reluctance to visit the 'red light' district was explained the following morning when it was revealed that his companion was Chaplain to the Bishop of Borneo, Robert Mounsey, who now came aboard himself. He had only been appointed in 1909 and for the first time his post had responsibility only for Borneo. He was enthusiastic about bringing Christianity to the native peoples. Gerald's intention was rather different: he wanted to meet and get to know and learn from them.

Borneo (known locally as Kalimantan) is the third largest island in the world. It is also known as "The Land Below the Wind" because it is beyond the range of typhoons and thus experiences a more equable climate. The northern part of the island was occupied at that time by the British protectorate of North Borneo (now Sabah).

It was towards this land that Gerald was heading. The first port of call was Victoria, on the island of Labuan. Gerald was impressed with what he saw, describing it as "ramshackle but attractive, its old colonial houses giving it a certain dignity, and its climate, tropical but cooled by the surrounding area, was delightful."[1]

However, when the ship docked at its final destination, the capital of North Borneo, Jesselton (now Kota Kinabalu) he was somewhat disappointed, describing it as "a huddle of bungalows, a dozen shops, a small harbour" and commented that it "looked as though it had been put together out of old soap-boxes". Beyond it, however, he could see, on the horizon, the jungle and this was what he had come for.

His musings were interrupted by a harsh voice enquiring if he were Gardner. This was R.J. Graham, manager of the Mawao Estate and a stalwart of the planting community, who would subsequently have a seat on the national Legislative Council as a representative of the West Coast Planting Community.

After a few words of introduction, he left Gerald in the hands of his "boy" with instructions to get to Membakut as soon as he could. This was a small town some 40 miles south of Jesselton and the obvious way to get there was by railway, which had been constructed about ten years previously. From Membakut it was another few miles by cart to the Mawao Estate rubber plantation,

---

1. Bracelin, 38.

where Gerald was shown to his quarters, which consisted of a small palm-leafed bungalow.

There was immediate conflict between Gerald and Graham that was never really resolved. From Gerald's description of him, Graham seemed to be too full of the sense of his own importance, expecting Gerald to take off his hat to him, for example, which Gerald resolutely refused to do. Perhaps more significantly there was a fundamental difference between the two men on the question of how the estate should be run. Graham wanted all the land cleared, whereas Gerald, based on his experiences in Ceylon, favoured clearing just those strips where the rubber trees were to be planted.

It sounds from this as if Graham was new to the estate and had not yet established a working practice, so that the arguments about alternative approaches were prolonged. There were certainly some underlying principles of human interaction with nature involved, Graham's approach to the jungle being that it was "a hostile army". In the middle of this conflict was the estate surveyor, Hofman, whom Graham rather looked down on because of his mixed race.

The pressure was to some extent taken off Gerald by the arrival of a new recruit, a Scotsman by the name of 'Dickie'. He was alcoholic and Bracelin recounts Gerald's attempts at keeping Dickie and the drink apart! The account reads very much like a Somerset Maugham short story and ends as tragically, for Dickie finally committed suicide.

The initial attraction of Borneo for Gerald had been the jungle – certainly the rich variety of flora and fauna which make up its abundant nature, but more especially the people living under its canopy. He really didn't know much about them, except that they were known as Dyaks and that they were headhunters. He suspected that there was a lot more to the native people's society and culture than that, and kept an eye open for any opportunity that might arise to meet them in their own environment. He didn't have long to wait.

It is not clear exactly which tribes of the native peoples Gerald made contact with. He describes them as Dyaks and, in a picture caption in *Gerald Gardner Witch*, identifies them as Iban. However, he also refers to visiting them in the *kampongs* or villages near Mawao, in which case they would be more likely to be Dusuns. In any case, initially he probably got to know those who were working on the estate at Mawao. This would have been on a casual social basis first, which sounds obvious but it was actually quite a rare thing amongst the Europeans living in North Borneo at the time, who tended to keep themselves to themselves. The people that Gerald got to know were lighter in colour than the coastal Malays, with jet black hair. They were friendly and talkative and had a great sense of humour, taking part in all sorts of games. They were prone to decorate their bodies with ornaments or elaborate tattoos.

Gerald had tattoos, including large ones on his fore-arms, which I suspect were obtained when he was in Borneo. If so, they would not just be for decoration:

> *The Dayak do not get their bodies tattooed for aesthetic reasons. For them, a tattoo is an expression of their religious beliefs, social status, heredity and initiation process. For them, a tattoo is an art form that has spirit, a living art. The Dayak believe the tattoo has deep meaning and an important religious sense. Tattooing their bodies is considered a holy act.[2]*

Gerald, being of the Common people rather than the chiefs, would have had a tattoo representing the underworld, which is usually a dragon, which in fact is what one of his tattoos appears to be.

Being who he was, their weapons interested Gerald, particularly the *sumpitan*, or blowpipe, which was a hollow tube some seven feet long from which darts, usually five to nine inches in length, were fired. Their design had been refined over possibly thousands of years and great accuracy and force was possible, which would have appealed to him: "The great secret in making the darts is to insure that they balance exactly, i.e., one-half must be exactly the same weight as the other. Under any other condi-

---

2. Edi Petebang and Theresia Game, "Sacred Dayak Tattoos Lose Their Meaning", (*The Jakarta Post,* 15 August 2000).

tions true shooting is impossible."[3] The author of this piece went
on to recount how they had seen a curled palm leaf being used as
a dart against a bird in a tree, such was the power of the device,
and continues:

> *The greatest adepts with the sumpitan, especially at the*
> *present day [1881], when its use is so surely dying out, are*
> *undoubtedly the Dyaks. From what I have heard, and from*
> *what I know from my own observation, a Dyak would shoot*
> *a dart a hundred and fifty yards to a certainty; and I should*
> *not care to bet very much against 200 yards being accom-*
> *plished by picked men. ... The small dart is, of course, not*
> *sufficient of itself to take human life, but the Dyaks poison*
> *their projectiles in warfare, when a slight wound anywhere*
> *is all that is necessary.*[4]

Gerald was very respectful of the power of the *sumpitan* for he
writes in *Witchcraft Today*:

> *In Borneo about fifty years ago I saw the terror raised by a*
> *... flight of arrows from blowpipes. They were about the size*
> *and length of thin knitting needles. A scratch caused paral-*
> *ysis in about thirty seconds; death followed in a few min-*
> *utes. I never ran so fast before or after; but I couldn't catch*
> *up with the others in my party.*[5]

In *The Meaning of Witchcraft*, Gerald gives an account of how
the native people had what seemed to be a very ancient method
of hunting:

> *When I was in Borneo fifty years ago, the Government had*
> *taken all the people's guns away, so they used to go out hunt-*
> *ing deer with a pair of horns set up on a pole. One man with*
> *these crept up to the right place, the rest of the party being on*
> *the other side of the herd. One of these would yell to startle*

---

3. "The Sumpitan, or Blow-Tube, of Malaya", from *The London Field*, reprinted in *The New York Times*, 3 July 1881.
4. Ibid.
5. G.B. Gardner, *Witchcraft Today*, (Rider 1954), 39.

the animals, then the man with the horns would put up the pole and run. The herd of deer, seeing horns moving, ran towards it and were led into a swamp, the man with the horns having previously laid some logs ready for himself to run on and escape. In the swamp the deer were easily speared. The country there was brushwood five or six feet high, so it was not necessary to wear skins as well as the horns.[6]

It is apparent that Gerald got to know the natives, probably first, in practical terms, those working on the Mawao Estate. This was in the area where the Dusuns were the most populous tribe and it seems likely from other evidence that it was members of this tribe that Gerald got to know, at least initially.

As he got to know them, Gerald became aware that, contrary to the sometimes expressed views of the Europeans that they "had no religion", they indeed had a religion and one that he could relate to. They had many local deities, something which attracted Gerald. They knew that magic worked and that there was part of them which survived death of the physical body.[7]

As he got to know them better, Gerald was soon to have a practical demonstration of these beliefs. This was what he describes as a 'séance' and he was invited to attend by a family whose daughter often acted as a medium. The Dusuns would probably refer to her as a *belian*. The meeting was held at the hut of the *pawang*, a shaman, otherwise known locally as a *dukun*, in a kampong (village) near the Mawao Estate. He was in his mid-30s and was a member of the Tutong tribe from Brunei and was related by marriage to the family that Gerald knew.

It sounds from Gerald's description as if the *pawang* had his own house which was large enough to hold the gatherings, rather than the traditional 'longhouse' which was largely communal. Bracelin describes the hut as being about 10 feet high, with walls of plaited palm leaves. As with all such huts, it would have been on stilts, for protection from a variety of dangers and to provide some shelter for the domestic animals. The floors consisted of slats of split palm, with sitting and sleeping areas solid, supposedly

---

6. G.B. Gardner, *The Meaning of Witchcraft* (Aquarian, 1959), 44..
7. Bracelin, 45.

to prevent intruders from thrusting their spears up from under the building. The *pawang's* tools and weapons were fixed to the wall, something familiar to Gerald, for he had a collection of his own!

He gave a vivid description of one of these sessions. The medium, or *pawang*, would sit at one end of the room and there would also be a small group of people, probably mostly his family. There would be jasmine incense. After informal chat, the *pawang* would start a chant, which might last an hour or so. He would then lay a girl down on a special mat, with a special square pillow, known as a *bantal,* under her head.

The pawang would then make passes above her until she went into trance. He would then start questioning her. She would eventually reply, in voices that were not her own, to various questioners. Occasionally, a hostile spirit came through, but the pawang usually managed to get it to leave.

At some point, things came to an end naturally. Gerald attended a few of these over time, gradually getting to know the people better.[8]

Nothing quite like these 'séances' is given in any of the contemporary accounts that I have read though recent accounts of the rituals of the Dusun tribe come fairly close, such as this account of a healing ritual by Kershaw:

> *The* belian *is so completely usurped by her guiding spirit that, for the onlooker, she appears to be following the spirit to wherever it wishes to go, and in whatever it deems necessary to undertake. The physical transparency of her undertaking is not matched by similar verbal clarity, however. It is the patient's, or his or her proxy's, duty to engage the belian in a discourse in order to elicit the knowledge she has thus gained. She will be unable to recall her experience, or the acquired insight, after the healing session.*[9]

The lack of contemporary accounts could be because Gerald was making it up or exaggerating some ceremony which he did

8. Bracelin, 47.
9. Eva Maria Kershaw, *A Study of Brunei Dusun Religion: Ethnic Priesthood on a Frontier of Islam,* (Borneo Research Council, 2000), 88.

see, but I don't think so. I think he genuinely had the sort of personality which encouraged people of all types to open up to him, and I can imagine that the native people that he met quickly began to trust him. An invitation to a 'séance' soon followed, something that most Europeans living in Borneo would never have even conceived let alone wanted and still less experienced. So it is perhaps not surprising that there are no contemporary accounts of such an event.

Towards the end of his time in Borneo, Gerald got caught up in one of the bouts of hysteria, rumour and counter-rumour that sometimes take over a community. It was centred around the town of Membakut, close to the Mawao Estate, but spilled over to the estate itself. There were rumours of headhunters in the vicinity, started by the finding of some scraps of paper on which someone had practised their writing. Someone then had a nightmare and screamed in his sleep, then everyone was running around with weapons looking for the non-existent headhunters.

The next night was worse, as no one would go to sleep. Gongs were beaten to keep the threat away, but about midnight many of the natives came to Gerald saying that there were men under the houses. They wanted him to shoot at them, but he would not shoot at what he could not see. He shone a torch under the houses and gradually the panic subsided.

But not for long! Soon there was a fresh panic: someone had seen a party of Dyaks in an abandoned house across the river. They would not respond to requests in any language. Gerald had brought his Winchester and was preparing to fire some warning shots when one of the native girls suggested calling out in the Besuia dialect, which had not been tried. When she did they slowly appeared. Apparently, they had hidden, thinking themselves that Dyaks were attacking. The rumours and panics gradually died down, but it was interesting to Gerald to see how these things start from nothing.[10]

On top of all the tensions of the job and, possibly to some extent exacerbated by them, Gerald fell victim to malaria. It seems as if the climate and other conditions of the area around

10. Bracelin, 48.

the Mawao Estate – low-lying and not too far from the sea – were just those which favoured the spread of the disease. Indeed, academic studies of the *Anopheles* mosquito have been based on fieldwork which was carried out in a handful of locations in Malaya, Sarawak and North Borneo, one of which was Mawao Estate, where a new species was discovered. This suggests that the estate was a very fruitful area for the study of such mosquitoes and thus, consequently, a place where a European such as Gerald, new to the area, would be more likely to contract the disease. The climate in Ceylon had been very different. Whilst nearer the equator, the altitude meant that the climate in the Highlands, where Gerald had been living, was more equable.

Gerald suffered from all the usual symptoms of the disease, including fever and shivering, and took to his bed, unable to work. It took some time to recover partially, by which time he had made a decision. The climate didn't suit him and he was increasingly unhappy with Graham as his manager. After less than a year in the job, he tendered his resignation.

Not quite knowing what to do next, Gerald took a short holiday. He was rather attracted by the neighbouring British colony of Sarawak, which had been a small state in north west Borneo ruled by the Rajah, Muda Hussein. The adventurer, James Brooke (b. 1803), visited the Rajah in 1839 and in time the two men developed a strong friendship. After Brooke had taken up arms on behalf of the Rajah against pirates who were causing trouble, the Rajah abdicated and handed his title to Brooke in 1841.

The Brookes ruled Sarawak within the British Empire for a hundred years and became known as the 'White Rajahs'. When James Brooke died in 1868, his nephew, Charles Anthoni Johnson (1829-1917) succeeded him and changed his name to Charles Brooke. He continued the fight against piracy, slavery and headhunting, whilst developing trade. He established the Sarawak Museum in 1891.

Gerald probably started his trip by returning to the island of Labuan, to which he had been so attracted on his initial voyage from Singapore. From there he would have got the local ferry to the town of Brunei (now Bandar Seri Begawan). This was a town more to his liking than Jesselton: he describes "graceful houses built on piles", now largely destroyed by the bombing carried out in World War II. He was impressed by the Kampong Ayer, a whole village built on stilts in the river and one of the many places known as "Venice of the East"!

Gerald then decided on a boat trip up-river. The price he was quoted sounded reasonable until he realised, when under way, that it did not include food. He hurriedly bought bread, bananas and tins of assorted fruit. Or so he thought! He found that the tins all contained lichees, whatever it said on their labels, which were "an imaginative whim of the Chinese manufacturers".

Uncharacteristically, Gerald felt that he learned little on this trip into the jungle. Perhaps he had still not fully recovered from his illness, for he describes "the monotony of tree and water". Perhaps he had little opportunity to converse with the natives. Or perhaps he was just suffering from an excess of lichees!

Bracelin says that Gerald then went on to visit "Sarawak proper" and to meet the second Rajah of Sarawak, Charles Brooke. This was at Brooketon (rather than "Brooketown" as Bracelin has it), originally known as Muara, at the mouth of the Brunei River. Coal started to be mined here in 1883, primarily for the use of steamships, by the Rajah, Charles Brooke, and the area became known as Brooketon. Although legally part of Brunei, the area was ruled by Brooke, who ran the police force and post office, and was effectively part of Sarawak at the time that Gerald visited. It is likely that Gerald did not actually visit Kuching, the capital of Sarawak and the Rajah's usual residence, for the description given by Bracelin sounds more like an account by the Rajah than a description based on Gerald's personal experience.

The Rajah was some 82 years old when Gerald met him. He had the reputation of caring deeply for the welfare of the people by abolishing the traditions of headhunting and slavery to which the people had been accustomed. Brooke had apparently heard that Gerald was visiting and asked to meet him. When the meeting took place, Gerald was impressed with Brooke's presence and an unmistakeable air of authority, though he wore a simple uniform with no badges of rank. He was interested to hear that Gerald had investigated the beliefs and practices of the Dyaks, as he had himself done the same, though he was regretful that so few Europeans were interested.[11]

Brooke told Gerald various tales about life in Kuching. One was that any newcomer was made drunk: if he behaved reasonably he was free to remain. Apparently convicts were allowed a lot of freedom in the town, as there were only two ways of escape – by sea, access to which was closely guarded, or into the jungle. Brooke had banned headhunting with one exception – if the victim was an escaped criminal. I have not been able to find confirmation of this: it might be true or it might be a story woven by either Brooke or Gerald. Nevertheless it is a good story!

After his short break, Gerald departed for Singapore, unsure what the future held. On the surface, his time in Borneo had been a dismal failure, contracting a chronic disease and constant conflict in the job. But in the things that really matter it had been a great success: he had made a deep contact with the local people and shared with them the experience of the "beyond" as a natural part of life. It would change him for ever and affect the rest of his life. As Bracelin puts it:

> *He had come to find the wilderness and he had found it, found it and penetrated a few of its secrets. He had come to know much of the lore and worship of the island's natives, had made many friends among them, had shared a small portion of their lives. Most precious of all, perhaps, he had learned to adopt their belief in the naturalness of the occult, had come to take for granted as they had some contact with those who had died, the possibility of developing faculties of concentration, mind and energy which in the West had fallen into general disuse. This was a development in his thinking which was to bear fruit many years later.[12]*

11. Bracelin, 53.
12. Bracelin, 54.

CHAPTER SIX

Towards the Sound of Gunfire

Gerald found a hotel in Singapore, perhaps the 'Raffles' again, intending to spend a few days sightseeing, doubtless spending more time in the Museum, before going on to Ceylon to find work.

He had put the word around that he was looking for a job. Someone had suggested one that they thought would be suitable: he applied, had an interview and got the job! It was assistant on a rubber plantation at Sungkai, in Perak, northern Malaya, over 300 miles from Singapore.

He took the train and was met by the estate manager, Brown, who was "tall, plump, rather shabby ... with a huge moth-eaten moustache".[1]

The area was a good one for rubber production and there were estates all round, for the demand for rubber was increasing every year. The estate that Gerald was to be working in had only been planted some seven years previously and had only recently been mature enough for tapping to start. Gerald's first task was to teach the necessary skills and procedures to those who would be doing the tapping. He felt confident about this and the subsequent supervision of the work.

---

1. Bracelin, 56.

Life did, however, have its exciting moments. One of Gerald's duties was to take the train every month to Ipoh, about 40 miles to the north, to collect money from the bank for the workers' wages. He usually came back by the same train, but one month he was delayed and returned by a later one. Travelling from the station back to the plantation, he came across the police, who were searching the surrounding bush. They explained that an American by the name of Cornwall who had come on Gerald's usual train had been attacked and robbed and had been taken to hospital, having been beaten and shot in his shoulder.

Gerald felt that it could easily have been himself in that situation and decided to visit Cornwall in hospital. He learned that he was a contractor employed to build factory and other buildings on the various local plantations. Gerald quickly became friends with him, and it was through Cornwall that he established close contact with the life of the local Malays.[2]

Gerald was to see the inside of the hospital again sooner than he thought, because very soon after the incident with Cornwall, he contracted a bad fever, with a very high temperature and accompanying trembling and weakness. He was also passing blood and from this and other symptoms he was diagnosed as having black-water fever, a complication of malaria. It seems to affect the immune system, causing a rapid destruction of red blood cells, consequent anaemia and the passage of dark red or black urine, hence its name. In the majority of cases it was fatal, and it is now known that quinine, given to combat malaria, can be the trigger that starts black-water fever going.

Gerald amazed the medical staff by managing to get to hospital somehow by rickshaw and train, and was put to bed. The doctor encouraged him, saying that he would be all right and that they sent someone home only the previous week who had been in a worse state than Gerald was when he was admitted. Privately, however, the doctor was not so optimistic and asked the matron to make sure she had the address of Gerald's firm so that if he died they could be sent the bill for funeral expenses![3]

---

2. Bracelin, 58.
3. Ibid.

But Gerald did not die, at least not for another 52 years! He gradually recovered, but it was several weeks before he was able to return to the plantation.

Things seemed to have deteriorated in his absence. Brown, the manager, was drinking heavily and had to be replaced: the company chose Gerald as his replacement!

It turned out that the job was really beyond Gerald's abilities. It involved dealing with the accounts, which he could never master, even when he had help and guidance from the company's agent, Freeman. Ultimately, there was nothing for it: the company had to dismiss him.

Looking for a job, Gerald thought about likely contacts. His notebook had the address of a character called Attenborough whom he had met on the train from Ipoh and got into discussion with about local customs and artifacts. He had a lot of Brunei brass and issued an open invitation to Gerald to visit him and view the collection.

Attenborough lived near Bidor, and Gerald decided to visit Cornwall at the same time, someone whom he found interesting and whom Gerald would like to get to know better.

Cornwall was somewhat shunned by the other Europeans because he had "gone native", as they would say. He was very suntanned, with a shaven head. He wore a sarong and a skull-cap. He had converted to Islam and had several Malay wives and children who lived with him.[4] It became clear to Gerald that Cornwall was a somewhat unorthodox Muslim, for he started to tell Gerald what he knew about the magic of the native peoples – the Malays, the Senoi and even those of Borneo.

Gerald, in turn, told him the family story that one of them, Joseph (Gerald always thought, mistakenly, that it was his grandfather), had been a witch. Cornwall certainly thought that witches had existed but had probably long since died out.

They talked late into the night. He invited Gerald to stay and, in fact, he stayed for a fortnight, during which time they had endless discussions about the occult, magic, beliefs and customs

---

4. Bracelin, 59.

throughout the world: they obviously got on together really well and it was probably one of the most important fortnights in Gerald's whole life.

On Cornwall's invitation, Gerald repeated the Confession of Faith of Islam (shahada): "La ilaha illa Allah wa-Muhammad rasul Allah" (There is no god but God, and Muhammad is the prophet of God).[5] It is difficult to know what to make of this. It was probably just a momentary enthusiasm on Gerald's part, but it certainly enabled him to enter more fully into the lives of the native Malays. However, in later life he never showed any particular interest in Muslim practices.

There were evenings when the Malays that Cornwall knew came and performed dances, including some with the keris, the magical dagger about which Gerald would subsequently become a world expert.

However, the time finally came for Gerald to leave and he made his way up to the address that Attenborough had given him. However, Attenborough had obviously completely forgotten him. He asked whether Gerald had come about the job. When Gerald told him that he had come to look at his collection of Brunei brass, Attenborough denied having any. Gerald showed him the address Attenborough had written in his notebook. He admitted that it was in his handwriting and then gradually the memory of their earlier meeting returned. He admitted that he had had some Brunei brass when he lived in Sarawak but had disposed of it.

The two talked for a while and Attenborough asked Gerald what he was doing. He explained that he was on his way to Ceylon where he hoped to get a job. Attenborough said that he had a job to offer him, the one he thought Gerald was after when he first arrived, which should suit him perfectly.[6]

This was a stroke of luck for Gerald. Attenborough worked for the Borneo Company, which operated a tin mine near Bidor. Things were not going well, because of the price of tin, and so some of their land, about 50 acres, had been planted with rubber

5. Bracelin, 80.
6. Bracelin, 60.

trees. Rubber was doing very well, so it was decided to expand on the 50 acres and the company wanted someone with experience to oversee the planting of the additional land plus supervising work on the existing acreage.

Gerald liked the sound of this and immediately decided to take the job. He described it as being the best that he ever had, though it was hard and he had little spare time. What time he did have he spent with Cornwall, his wives and friends.

Gerald was never one to follow fashion, but it did seem that quite a few of his colleagues were buying estates of their own, such was the profitability of rubber at the time. One of his co-workers, Hartley, had an estate and left at the end of 1912 to run it himself.

For once, Gerald followed suit. He bought an estate called Bukit Katho at Kampung Poh, "at the end of a cart track from Bidor". It was 450 acres, of which only nine had been cleared: the rest was jungle. He was only able to work there during the evenings and on Sundays, but he hired some native workers and they were soon clearing more of the jungle. Three of Gerald's colleagues bought into the estate and extra land was acquired, bringing it up to 600 acres.

❧

Unlike the Second World War, the First World War (1914-1918) went largely unnoticed in Malaya. Some went to join up, in many cases never to return. There was some social unease about the Germans who lived in the area: they tended to keep their heads down. Some left for Germany via Sumatra: the older ones tended to stay where they were.

As he had done in Ceylon, Gerald joined the local volunteers – the Malay States Volunteer Rifles, which had been formed during the Boer War (1899-1902) and had expanded considerably with the outbreak of war in Europe in August 1914. The volunteers had regular garrison duty once a month, but the only military action they saw was the following year when, in February 1915, occurred what has become known as the Singapore Mutiny.

When the war started, the King's Own Yorkshire Light Infantry, who had been stationed in Singapore, were ordered back to England before being sent to fight in France. They were replaced in Singapore by the Indian 5th Light Infantry, who were mainly Indian Muslims commanded by British officers.

Morale was low, particularly following a visit by those campaigning for Indian independence from British rule. The anti-British feeling became more intense after Britain declared war on Turkey, who had sided with Germany. The Sultan of Turkey was at that time regarded by many as the leader of the Muslim world and he issued a *fatwa* urging Muslims to oppose the British.

When they were ordered to sail to Hong Kong, many of the Indian soldiers thought that they would be ordered to fight against fellow Muslims and on 15th February 1915 they mutinied. Eventually the mutiny was put down by British and French forces, many of the mutineers being tried and some executed.

Gerald was a long way from all this action, although it was thought by the military authorities that the Malay States Guides might mutiny as well. They had been formed in 1896 and were mostly Sikhs, Pathans and north Indians. They were really Malaya's own regiment and had their headquarters in Taiping, to the north, and Gerald and his unit were ordered to hold the railway line in Ipoh and to disarm the Indian police. They refused to disarm unless the Malays also disarmed, so the rifles of all of them were confiscated. The next Gerald knew was that the police turned up for duty with seven-foot clubs!

In the end, the Malay States Guides did not mutiny, apart from 100 men of their Mule Battery in Singapore.

⚬

After the relative excitement of the mutiny, Gerald had time to think. He had seen the reserve officers go off to the war in Europe and he had seen the Germans do the same: he realised that he wanted to be a part of it himself.

It had been nine years since his last trip home. He arranged as far as he could for the plantations to run smoothly and then booked a ticket on the next ship calling at Penang that was bound for England. At least, he wanted to avoid the English winter, as he feared that it might bring on his asthma, from which he had suffered so much in his youth. So, probably some time in May 1916, Gerald arrived back in Liverpool to stay with his brother, Bob, in Blundellsands.

As soon as he arrived, he tried to enlist in the services. However, the Navy rejected him on health grounds, but reluctantly. Gerald always remembered the conversation: "It's a shame", the recruiting man said, "that anyone of your name shouldn't be able to get into the scrap". The possibility of working on an ack-ack unit near London, hunting Zeppelins, also didn't get anywhere because of his health.[7]

He eventually found employment as a V.A.D. (Voluntary Aid Detachment) orderly at the First Western General Hospital at Fazakerley, on the outskirts of Liverpool. However, he would not be needed for about another four weeks, so Bob, suggested a holiday.

He had booked a large house in Tenby, in south Wales and, as well as his immediate family (his wife, Louise, and sons Ralph, age 14 and Robert, age 11) there were his brother Harold's three daughters, Bobby (Muriel) age 18, Betty (Aileen) age 17, and Dorothy, age 13. Gerald mentions that several members of the Sergeneson family were also present. We do not know who they were, but could well have included, as well as 'G', age 46, her nieces and nephews, Ada, age 19; Edmund, age 22; Martha, age 17; and Thomas, age 21.

We are fortunate in that, in the Gardner family archives, there is a series of photographs of that family holiday. They show beach scenes with everyone in the characteristic swimming costumes and hats of the time, several including Gerald, usually with his arm around Bobby! There are also more formal shots, in front of the house they were staying in, and of trips out to Lydstep and Manorbier. Very few of the individuals in the photographs are identified, but they all have very distinct personalities, particularly Gerald who, at age 32, seems to be in his prime physically. They all look very much as if they are enjoying themselves:

---

7. Bracelin, 123.

To Gardner, looking back, this month seems almost an idyll. For the first time in England [sic. Actually, of course, he was in Wales!] he felt completely free. Although many of his friends were in uniform, or perhaps because of it, they all seemed gayer, more natural. Pretty girls seemed more attractive, dull ones were transformed, their hair allowed to go free, their figures shown off in that innovation, the new bathing dress. G., still happy, still teasing and laughing, was there too. Beset by war and even the chance of defeat, England seemed to Gerald Gardner for the first time a country worth living in.[8]

Such idylls do not last, however, and, towards the beginning of July 1916, Gerald returned to Liverpool and started his temporary job as a V.A.D. orderly at the hospital in Fazakerley. The contrast could not have been more striking, for the disastrous Battle of the Somme was in progress. On one day alone, 1st July 1916, the British Army sustained 58,000 casualties, one third of whom were killed: the worst day in its history. The injured were ferried back to England and dispersed to numerous hospitals throughout the land. Gerald started work just as the first casualties were arriving in the hospital trains. Seeing the injured made him wish even more that he could go and fight against those who had caused the injuries. The resources of the hospital were stretched to the limit, but Gerald and the other orderlies and nursing staff worked hard and long hours. This, at least, was something he could do to help the war effort.[9]

But, as summer passed to autumn, two things happened. He could not afford to be on leave from his plantation duties indefinitely, and the busy time of year was rapidly approaching. Also, the English climate got to him, he caught a cold and his malaria came back. The doctor prescribed quinine, but only two grains a day: Gerald had been used to thirty! The combination of malaria and the English cold meant that Gerald felt too unwell to continue to work in the hospital. He therefore had no reason to

8. Bracelin, 123.
9. Bracelin, 123-124.

remain in England and he knew that the only way to regain his health was to return to Malaya.

On 29th September 1916, he handed in his notice at the hospital: the Sister gave him a reference, which read:

> *Mr. Gerald Brosseau Gardner worked in this hospital as a VAD orderly in the wards and has given every satisfaction. He has assisted the nurses when the dressings were being done and also helped to look after the patients in many ways. We are sorry to lose him. Sister A. Rutherford, First Western General Hospital, Fazakerley.*

A fortnight later, on 12th October 1916, Gerald embarked in London on the P and O ship *Nankin* bound for Penang. As Bracelin says: "He went back to Malaya – but for the first time it was with reluctance and with a heavy heart."[10]

---

10. Bracelin, 124.

CHAPTER SEVEN

Malayan Customs

When Gerald returned to Malaya following his trip to England at the end of 1916, he took up the reins again, both in his job with the Borneo Company and on his own plantation, Bukit Katho. He spent what time he could with Cornwall and his Malay friends, getting to know and be trusted by them. He learnt Malay and took opportunities to find out about their culture, folklore, religion and what they actually believed.

Gerald's approach to the Malays and their magical practices was not academic or structured. He knew them as friends, was invited to rituals and had noted things that he had been told or experienced, particularly those elements which accorded with his own view of life. One of the rituals which Gerald attended was the 'Main Peteri', a dramatic performance the main purpose of which is therapeutic. It is intended to stimulate and set free the feelings of the person who is sick. Wright refers to the dance as being both a strategy for healing and a sign of health on the part of the patient who "signals re-entry into regular cultural life by ably joining the dance".[1] The ceremony "seeks to cure the symptoms by effecting the patient's reintegration into society". Gerald gives a very detailed

---

1. Barbara S Wright, "Dance is the Cure: The Arts as Metaphor for Healing in Kelantanese Malay Spirit Exorcisms", *Dance Research Journal*, Vol. 12 No. 2 (Spring-Summer 1980), 3-10.

description of a Main Peteri ritual which he obviously attended. Drumming, music and incense appear to be essential offerings.[2]

His interest in the magical practices of the Malays was centred on what was commonly called "the supernatural", a world inhabited by spirits who could be communicated with and who could provide information or help in various ways. There was a strong awareness of what we might call "the other world" or the world of faery, what Gerald called "the fourth dimension", and he found just the same legends as there are in other parts of the world about people who disappear, perhaps following beautiful women, who return, perhaps after a few days, perhaps many years, when time seems to have speeded up or slowed down. He found that they believed in two basic sorts of spirits, those who possess people and those who have an independent existence.

Some aspects of Malay magic remained mere curiosities to Gerald. Others took on a greater importance in his life as he started to become interested in the Malays' mystical weapon, the keris, as I relate in Chapter 10. One of the powers which seemed often to be linked to the keris was that of invulnerability. This was something which could be built up, as a sort of shield, but there had to be genuine need for it: Gerald told the tale of someone who was invulnerable to the stabbing of a keris, but when he was showing off to his friends, it didn't work and he died. There was a lot of bluff about this as well, of course, and Gerald tells the story of a Malay civil servant who was accosted in the street by a ruffian wielding a *keris*. The official challenged the fellow, telling him to put aside his weapon or he would only damage it because he was invulnerable. The fellow beat a hasty retreat.[3]

This power seemed to be linked to one theme underlying Malay magic which Gerald does not seem to have focused on: the concept of *sumangat* or *semangat*. Skeat writes that it is: "... the central feature of the whole system of Malay magic and folklore, from which all the different branches with their various applications appear to spring".[4] It is the vital principle which is present in all life, and the equivalent of that which has variously

---

2. Bracelin, 91-94.
3. Bracelin, 87.
4. Kirk Michael Endicott, *An Analysis of Malay Magic*, (Oxford, 1970), 34.

been called ch'i, mana, prana, the odic force, önd, wouivre and orgone energy. Later in his life, Gerald recognised this force as being identical to that which the witches used when raising the 'cone of power', so it is somewhat surprising that he did not seem to recognise that this underlay the Malays' magical workings.

Just as in England and much of Europe there is a veneer of Christianity over what are basically pagan beliefs and practices, so in Malaya there was a veneer of Islam, often primarily the use of Islamic names for the entities and powers that formed the subject matter of native rituals, which usually began with a prayer "seeking the pardon of the almighty for carrying them out."

As an example, a *pawang* confided in Gerald that he knew how to work magic to get good crops and weather but that whereas in his father's time, such workings would be permitted, now they were forbidden. He appealed to Gerald and asked him if he knew any spells to keep rats out of the rice fields. Everyone was blaming him. He could work magic with the aid of the gods, but the Imam had forbidden that.[5]

The Malays that Gerald got to know started to talk about really wild people who lived in the jungle. They knew little about them except that they used blowpipes. The opportunity of meeting and conversing with people that were more primitive than the Malays excited Gerald and he pressed them to effect an introduction. The people that Gerald wanted to meet were known as the Senoi, one of the tribes who made up the Orang Asli, or aboriginal peoples of Malaya. They were largely nomadic hunter-gatherers, though they did grow some tapioca. The Malays called them the 'Sakai', which means 'slaves' from the time when they were captured by the Malays and others and made to work as slaves. Naturally, they do not like this name as applied to their tribe.

The Senoi lived in groups of 20-50 people and tended to be very secretive and avoided being seen unless they wanted to be. Gerald discovered that if they heard a sudden noise or wanted to disappear, one of their techniques was to stand close to a bush, raising their arms as if they were branches, following the natural lines of the vegetation. Gerald speculated that this method might

5. Bracelin, 97.

have been used by the 'Little People', who were often supposed to
have vanished suddenly in old tales. The men were only 4ft 6ins
tall and the women even shorter. They lived on foods that they
gathered, like yams, bananas and wild fruits, and on animals that
they hunted, such as gibbons, wild boar and squirrels. For this
they used their blowpipes equipped with poisonous darts, the
poison coming from the resin of the upas tree, known as ipoh.

Gerald gradually gained their confidence by offering tobacco
and other small gifts in exchange for chickens. Each group
seemed to speak a different dialect, but he managed to make
himself understood by learning some of their language, using
some Malay and generally by making friends with them.

The Senoi had a reputation among the Malays for working
magic, and their help was often sought out for healing, prophesy
and finding things that were lost. It seemed to Gerald, as he got
to know them, that the whole community treated the working of
magic as something that was very down-to-earth: it worked and
they used it. However, he does not give details of their magical
rituals as he did with the Malays and I suspect the reason is that
they did not let him witness them, for those he did witness, such
as those of the Dyaks in Borneo, he describes in considerable
detail. All he says is that to perform magic, a group of women
would dance and sing, throwing herbs into a fire and "work
themselves into a frenzy".[6] They worked spells to drive disease,
which they believed was caused by demons, out of the body.

Gerald recounts an amusing, if sad, occasion when a film unit
arrived and sought his help in talking to the Senoi. It became
obvious, however, that they were not interested in what the Senoi
actually did. They had their own ideas of "strange rites". The
Senoi did what was asked of them but were very puzzled by the
time the film unit left. Bracelin makes the wry comment: "What
was the religion of the visitors, they wanted to know. Gardner
was not sure."[7]

---

6. Bracelin, 77.
7. Bracelin, 78.

In more recent times, the Senoi have been associated with the use of lucid dreaming to ensure happiness and mental health[8] but research has subsequently found that it was never particularly important in their lives.

⚜

The price of any commodity is a reflection of the interaction of supply and demand. The price of rubber had been high when Gerald first moved to Malaya in 1911 because demand, particularly for automobile tyres, was high, and increasing yearly, and rubber production, which took seven years from planting to the start of tapping, was inevitably lagging behind. So, in 1910, the price of rubber reached almost £1000 a ton, but by 1918 it had dropped to just over £200 – still enough to make a profit, however. But, the end of the war and the depression of 1920 caused a decline in demand, just at the time when rubber production in Malaya was at an all-time high of 300,000 tons a year. The price therefore dropped rapidly and by 1921 was only about £80 a ton.

This affected Gerald in two ways. His own plantation was only just establishing itself in full production and was really not making much, if any profit. And the Borneo Company, whose main enterprise was in mining, was not at all interested in maintaining a plantation on their land which was not providing an adequate return on their investment. They were threatening to get rid of the plantation altogether.

From the passenger lists, we know that Gerald made a trip to England in 1921 and that he stayed with his brother, Bob, in Leighton, Blundellsands. Whilst his other trips are faithfully recorded in *Gerald Gardner Witch*, this one is not mentioned at all.

Why not? Either he was pledged to secrecy or he was somewhat ashamed of it and didn't want to talk about it. I suspect the latter. At first, I thought that he might have gone to ask for a young lady's hand in marriage, but I don't think so, as he was clearly not in a stable position financially, and that sort of thing was particularly important in those days.

---

8. G. William Domhoff, *The Mystique of Dreams: A Search for Utopia Through Senoi Dream Theory*, (University of California Press: 1985).

Indeed, I think this provides a clue as to the real reason. Either Gerald was disillusioned with his work "out East" and wanted to return to England to live or, more likely in my view, he wanted to ask his father to invest money in his plantation. If so, it was not a good time to be asking, as the timber industry was going through an equally bad period. I think his father probably said: "Look at Harold. He's made a success of being a lawyer (and lawyers do well even when others are going bankrupt!) and Bob and Douglas are working hard in the timber industry and surviving. You're 37 years old! It's time you stood on your own feet!"

So I suspect that his father refused to lend any money to Gerald, who returned to Malaya disappointed and in rather low spirits. And I think he was still rather embarrassed about the whole episode almost 40 years later when he was telling the tales that would end up in *Gerald Gardner Witch*, so he just kept quiet about the whole trip! It seems the most likely possibility to me, anyway.

It was not the usual summer visit, at any rate, for Gerald left London on 27th May 1921 on the *Kalyan* bound for Penang. When he arrived back, his worst fears were realised: the Borneo Company had sacked him!

Gerald had to get through somehow. Bracelin calls it "sweating it out" and states that Gerald worked the plantation at Bukit Katho in a 'desultory' way. What income was coming in from the plantation he had to share with his partner, Bevan.

In order to survive, Gerald had to find additional employment. One organisation that he worked for was the Public Works Department, being in charge of workmen who were repairing public roads. This work was hard and unrewarding, but it probably helped him to obtain his next job, which was somewhat of a change in direction.

In September 1923, he applied for a Government post as an inspector of rubber plantations. Probably his experience both as a planter and for the Public Works Department stood him in good stead, for he got the job. The interviewer explained what the job entailed. Gerald was only too aware that the price of rubber had been at an all-time low. The government had intervened the previous year, as Mackay notes:

In 1922 a rubber restriction system was introduced and its enforcement was added to the responsibilities of trade and customs. Certain preventive officers were given powers to inspect the books of rubber dealers. In attempts to evade the new restrictions on exports there was large-scale smuggling of rubber to the Dutch East Indies, and the department had to muster fresh forces to tackle the illegal traffic. A preventive branch was established with a superintendent in each federal state. Extra staff was recruited, including European launch commanders to conduct sea patrols.9

The intention was to keep the price of rubber high by limiting its export. Each plantation was given a quota which they could not exceed. The size of the quota was determined by various factors, including the area of the plantation and previous yield.

This was what Gerald was employed to do and, following his calculations, to issue coupons to the various plantation owners without which they could not trade.

Gerald was given the job for a trial period and was told to report to the Government offices in Muar, in Johore. He set out for Johore, found the Muar River and was soon in a town called Bandar Maharani (Queen's Town). He enquired about the whereabouts of Muar and was told that this was just another name for the town he was already in.[10]

Gerald enjoyed the work very much. It involved going from plantation to plantation and checking that the area under cultivation was the same as that which was claimed. Very often it wasn't, because the owners were trying to get more coupons than they were entitled to, but this was all part of the job. It often involved several nights away from home, staying at the ubiquitous "rest houses" that he had been familiar with in Ceylon, but he enjoyed getting to know the places and the people.

One day, he received a visit from the honorable Dato W.N. Gawler. He was an influential member of the Planters' Association of Malaya, and represented the Association on various committees

9. Derek Mackay, *Eastern Customs: The Customs Service in British Malaya and the Opium Trade,* (The Radcliffe Press, 2005), 36.
10. Bracelin, 65.

such as the Standard Qualities Committee, which was concerned with the quality of rubber produced by the different plantations. He also seemed to have some official role, acting on behalf of the government.

Gerald was a bit apprehensive about what Gawler wanted. He asked Gerald if he knew that there were nine of them taken on for the job. Gerald confirmed that he did know, whereupon Gawler confided in him that there were now only two left. Gerald began to imagine all sorts of disasters that might have been responsible, but Gawler quickly explained that the others had taken bribes. He added that he knew that Gerald hadn't, so far, and advised him not to be tempted in future. Gerald gave Gawler the necessary assurances.[11]

Things seemed to be going really well when Gerald started to get pain in his knee, then severe pain, particularly when he moved it. The doctors at the hospital in Muar diagnosed synovitis of the knee and he was transferred to Singapore hospital. These days the condition can be treated with anti-inflammatory drugs, but in the 1920s the only treatment was heat and radiotherapy. Even this didn't go smoothly as, by mistake, he received too much heat treatment on one occasion which resulted in a severe burn on his leg. During the healing process his leg was kept bent by resting on pillows. However, when he came to try to straighten it, he couldn't! This worried Gerald quite a lot. Would he stay like that permanently? If so, he couldn't do his job. He was hoping to be back within six weeks and he was still "on probation".

One day, as he lay in bed indoors, he began to long for the fresh air and sunshine outdoors and, after some discussion, persuaded the nursing sister to wheel him out. He lay there for some time feeling strongly that the fresh air and sunshine was doing his knee good. Later, the sister came out to give Gerald's leg its regular massage. They were both amazed when his leg started to straighten. This practical demonstration of the beneficial effects of fresh air and sunshine stayed with him, eventually leading him to naturism. It can therefore truly be said to be a life-changing moment.

---

11. Bracelin, 65-66.

When Gerald came out of hospital, the Johore Government gave him an office job in the Lands Office while he recovered. Soon, he was fully fit and he found himself promoted to Principal Officer of Customs. He was made an Inspector of Rubber Shops. This involved checking the premises of merchants who had bought the rubber from the plantation owners to see whether there were the requisite coupons to authorise the sale. He had to look around in all corners of the warehouses, wharf areas and through files in their offices to find evidence of illegally traded rubber. Gerald remembers what seems to have been an exciting raid on one dealer. Everything seemed to be in order, except that they found a Customs seal hidden in a safe. This find meant that that particular company would not do any more business.[12]

Another exciting aspect of the job was going out on the off-shore patrol, which had the aim of trying to stop shipments of rubber over to Sumatra. The Dutch had no quotas and therefore there was quite an incentive to ship illegally-produced rubber over there. When the wind was from the east, the Customs officers knew there would be an attempt to smuggle rubber after nightfall. Bracelin gives a dramatic account of this:

> *The contrabanders, sails stiffened by the wind, would come swooping out of the Muar and Batu Bahat Rivers as night fell. Out in the deeper water the Customs launches would be waiting, almost invisible against the swell. They themselves could see the smugglers approach because of the silhouettes of masts and sails against the night sky. As the interloping boats came close, they would be hailed and asked to stop. Of this challenge they never took any notice. A shot would then be fired across their bows. If they still refused to heave to, the Customs launch would come in close, grapple with hooks, and send a boarding party in. Sometimes the smugglers would throw the hooks back, and there would be a sharp and ugly fight before the smugglers were overpowered and their craft taken in tow. Several Europeans and*

---

12. Bracelin, 69.

many Malays were killed in these sudden engagements
under the stars of the dark tropical skies.[13]

Occasionally, Gerald had to give evidence in court cases and it was while he was in Singapore for this purpose one day in 1926, that he happened to bump into his old acquaintance, Dato Gawler, who greeted him with the quip that he supposed they'd be having free 'smokes' thereafter. When Gerald asked what that was all about, Gawler was surprised that he hadn't heard. "You're to be in charge of *chandu* shops", he announced. He advised Gerald to go down immediately to the Commissioner of Customs, who was apparently getting increasingly concerned that he hadn't heard from Gerald.

Rather cautiously, Gerald visited the Commissioner, whose initial annoyance turned to resignation when he looked on his file and found not just the carbon copy of Gerald's appointment letter but the original as well![14]

Gerald really had no idea what the job involved, but quickly found out. *Chandu* was the Malay-Chinese word for opium, a substance with which the government had had a very mixed relationship over the years. The Malay states had traditionally derived considerable revenue from opium. In the 19th Century its collection was not carried out by the governments themselves, but "farmed out" to a variety of private individuals. In many ways this was not satisfactory and, at the start of the 20th Century, the Straits Settlements and Federated States Opium Commission recommended that such contracts not be renewed, and many expired at the end of 1909. There were calls for a total ban on opium, but, as Mackay points out: "... the difficulty of finding a suitable substitute for the revenue derived from opium ... was a major factor in the decision against a prohibition of the drug and to recommend instead a government monopoly."[15]

Opium comes from the poppy, *Papaver somniferum*. It has been widely used in the treatment of such varied conditions as diabetes, diarrhoea and heart disease, but is best known as an

---

13. Bracelin, 69.
14. Bracelin, 70.
15. Mackay, 31.

addictive recreational drug. A milky sap is extracted from the immature seed pods which is then dried, boiled and filtered to form a dark treacle-like substance: this is the chandu.

All the governments in Malaya were determined to eradicate the smoking of opium. So, users of opium were registered, such registration only being approved if previous use demonstrated the need or if, particularly with immigrants, there were medical grounds for inclusion. Only those who were registered could legally smoke opium, and this could only be bought legally at Government shops.

It was these shops that Gerald had to inspect, and right from the start he was aware that there were "irregularities". The first problem was, according to Mackay, that the ration of 40 *hoons* of opium for each user was far too generous. The average smoker only used 4 *hoons*, leaving 36 *hoons* to sell on the black market.

Gerald had to account for all the opium delivered to the shop, either as stock or sales money. Clerks had been fiddling the books by putting down non-existent sales, getting extra opium as a result and then selling it themselves privately. Every so often, one of these clerks would disappear, having made a small fortune in this way.[16]

Gerald gives a vivid picture of the opium shops and smoking saloons. The opium was in small twists of paper and delivered to the shops in locked tins, ten thousand twists to a tin. It was part of Gerald's job, tedious in the extreme, to count these.

A smoking saloon typically consisted of bunks for about twenty men, each having the obligatory lamp for heating the opium for smoking. The saloons were dimly lit with the overwhelming aroma of opium fumes.[17] The government was trying to phase out such 'smoking saloons' and by 1930 all such establishments in the Straits Settlements had been closed.

I have heard from three different sources that Gerald obtained most of the money that he had on his retirement from performing his duties as a Customs Officer less diligently than he should, in other words he took bribes to "look the other way" when illegal goings-on were happening. One usually reliable

---

16. Bracelin, 71.
17. Bracelin, 71.

reporter wrote that Gerald made his fortune by allowing the smuggling of opium. In return he was given the rubber shares out of which he made his money. An elderly member of Five Acres Club who knew Gerald told me the same story and I have heard it independently on at least one other occasion.

Could this be true? And, if so, how can we evaluate such a state of affairs? First of all, we know Gerald's attitude to opium: "There's a great deal of nonsense talked about opium", he says. "I never saw the shambling, broken-down old wrecks of propaganda and fiction, nor anyone even seriously the worse for it".[18] It was Gerald's opinion, based on what he had seen, that less than one user in ten thousand becomes addicted to it. Mostly, he considered that it had a positive effect, promoting relaxation and hard work, and that this had social benefits, as opposed to the effects of alcohol, which often fuelled fights. He also felt that opium could be a factor in the treatment of tuberculosis by inducing a placidity in the patient which aided recovery and in strengthened the immune system.[19]

Whether this view of opium is medically true or not, Gerald obviously believed it and therefore probably felt justified in helping to circumvent what he must have seen as an unjust law.

This attitude did not extend to all drugs. He saw the danger in *tai chandu*, the twice-smoked opium which was used by those who could not afford the real thing. The first smoking released poisons which remained in the residue. The Government recognised this and used to buy back the residue to try to prevent it being smoked. Gerald also considered hashish to be an extremely dangerous drug.

Having this attitude to opium, Gerald must have had an ambivalent attitude to his job. On the one hand, he had a good government post that paid reasonably well. On the other, he was the perpetual trickster, enjoyed subterfuge and, when approached, as he undoubtedly would have been, by those wanting to by-pass the system, he would certainly have been tempted by such a proposition, particularly with his known views on the benefits of opium.

---

18. Bracelin, 72.
19. Bracelin, 72-73.

CHAPTER EIGHT

Finding Spirits and Love in England

It was 1927. It had been eleven years since Gerald's last trip to England (ignoring the 1921 trip, which he had put to the back of his mind). He was doing well in his job, but he was not getting any younger. He rather liked the idea of marriage, and decided to have a trip to England. If, while he was there, he met some suitable young lady, then so much the better!

Whilst he had only been working for the Johore Government for four years, he was able to obtain compassionate leave because of the illness of his father, whom everyone thought was on his last legs, though in fact he lived another eight years. He seemed to be suffering from some form of dementia, for he rather frightened Gerald by talking about his mother as if she were still alive.[1]

The photograph of William and three of his sons was almost certainly taken at this time, for in November 1927, William took a ship to Teneriffe in the Canary Islands for his retirement, accompanied by his son and daughter-in-law, Bob and Louise. William never returned to England.

Being interested in natural phenomena, it is highly likely that Gerald had arranged his visit home to coincide with the total

---

1. Bracelin, 125.

eclipse of the sun on 29th June 1927, the only one to be seen in England during Gerald's lifetime. Moreover, the path of totality passed directly over Blundellsands. The eclipse was total at 6.23am. One can imagine Gerald and his family on the sandhills observing the spectacle, although the weather was described as 'hazy'. *The Daily Telegraph*, Gerald's favourite newspaper, reported that at nearby Southport:

> *..there was an unnatural fogging of the landscape ... It did not seem nature. It seemed like the death of nature. The world appeared ready and waiting for the end of all things. It would have fitted well into the picture had the dark sands begun to belch up sulphurous fumes.*[2]

Indeed, it may well have been a depressing time for Gerald, as things had changed significantly since he was last in England. Ted Sergeneson had died two years previously, and Nellie was still "heart-broken with grief". 'G' had died of ovarian cancer back in 1922 in Liverpool. And most of the young people with whom he had spent that enjoyable holiday in Tenby eleven years previously had grown up and got married or left home.

Gerald was very much open to suggestions, so when someone put forward the idea of going to a Spiritualist Church he felt "a twinge of curiosity". He still remembered the effect which reading Florence Marryat's *There is no Death* and other similar books had had on him, and he had since had practical demonstration of spirit communication when he was with the native Dyak people of Borneo. But, despite his interest in, and indeed acceptance of, a parallel 'spirit world', he had never attended a spiritualist meeting in England. So, ever one to try something new, Gerald went along to a spiritualist church near Liverpool. We don't know which one they went to, and, indeed, there were several in the vicinity at that time.

Liverpool had played a significant role in the British spiritualist movement. In 1873, following correspondence in the spiritualist press, a conference was held in the city which resulted in the

---

2. John Billingsley, *The Day The Sun Went Out*, (Northern Earth, 1999), 13.

formation of the National Association of Spiritualists. And in 1901 the World Spiritualist Conference was held in the city. Following the First World War, spiritualism received a boost from those wishing to make contact with loved ones who had died during the conflict such that by the mid 1920s the movement was in good heart.

Not that any of this impressed Gerald Gardner. The building was rather like a dingy chapel with a congregation of about fifty. After a short service, a medium appeared, sat facing the audience and soon appeared to be in a trance. Gerald was disappointed with the results, what he called "facile encouragement ... based entirely on the audience's will to believe".[3]

Despite this, Gerald suspected that there were better mediums around. He enquired further and was told that the best mediums tended to be in London, and one name came up more than once: that of James Hewatt McKenzie (1870-1929). He had been a writer and lecturer and in 1920 had founded the British College of Psychic Science. He had a very good reputation for mediumship.

Gerald intended to go to London to see him, but he was cautious - very cautious. He made determined efforts to ensure that no information about him should leak in advance to the medium. He made his plans. He told no-one that he was going to London. Instead he spread the word that he was going to stay with his old nurse-maid, Com and her husband, David.

Gerald had kept a rather loose contact with Com and David after he had 'escaped from her clutches' in Ceylon. In 1912, David and Com had moved to the Nilgiri Hills in southern India and had acquired several tea estates, including Ripple Vale and Ibex Lodge Hill, the most famous of which was the Nonsuch Estate, which still exists.[4]

David had retired at around the age of 50 in the mid-1920s and he and Com had bought a house in mid-Wales, 'Craigyllin', on the banks of the River Wye in the parish of Llanwrthwl, Breconshire, not too far from Rhayader and Llandrindod Wells. They also had a house at Seabourne, Fawley, near Hereford, and it was here that Gerald went to visit them, taking the train from Liverpool. He was

3. Bracelin, 126.
4. Letter from Gillian Hodges to the author, 5 May 2008.

met by David and Com, whom Gerald describes as being "an old lady". He only stayed with them two or three days, during which time Com confided in him that she didn't like living in Herefordshire and how she longed to be in London, or at least somewhere closer to what she thought of as being cultural activity.

Keeping up his subterfuge, he told them that he was going back to Liverpool, but in fact made his way to London. From Paddington Station he went to the Cromwell Road, where there were numerous hotels and, selecting one at random, he booked in: it was the Gloucester House Hotel (now the Cromwell Crown Hotel), 139/141 Cromwell Road. He seemed to be quite happy there since he stayed there for the whole of the time he was in London.

On arrival in London, Gerald did not immediately go in search of mediums, but on the morning of Thursday 28th July 1927, walked past the South Kensington museums, probably spending some time in the Victoria and Albert or the Science Museum, strolled across Hyde Park and up Oxford Street towards the British Museum, where he wandered through the various exhibition rooms.

He intended to make use of the world-famous library while he was in London and applied for a reader's ticket for three months. He gave as the subject of his research 'Basque and Welsh Folklore'.[5] However, future events were such that any plans that Gerald might have had for quiet research sessions in the famous British Museum Reading Room were not to be realised.

The following morning, Gerald continued his excessively cautious actions by leaving the hotel with nothing on his person by which he could be identified. Apparently he also put three letters in his pocket from someone to someone else that he knew, to lay a false trail for anyone who looked there.[6] I actually doubt whether Gerald went that far, but it makes a good story!

Anyway, Gerald did not go immediately to see McKenzie in Holland Park, but set off walking along Cromwell Road in the other direction, towards the museums. Just opposite the Natural History Museum, he felt drawn to walk down a side street, Queensberry Place. As he walked down, he noticed that no. 16

---

5. Email from Roger Dearnaley to the author, 6 December 1999, quoting email from John Hopson, British Library Archivist.
6. Bracelin, 127.

had a plaque on it reading "The London Spiritualist Alliance". He realised that this would be the place to go: even he didn't know he was going there until that very moment, so there was absolutely no opportunity for fraud.

Gerald went in and saw the secretary and asked to see a medium. She said that many were booked up several months ahead, but Gerald insisted. He asked who he could see immediately. She told him of one medium he could have in half an hour. He pressed for further sessions and, after resisting this as being unorthodox as he needed to rest and relax between sessions, she agreed to him seeing a second medium that afternoon and a third the following morning.

The first medium was something of a disappointment. Apart from seeing that he had been "out East", the medium told Gerald of two individuals, an Uncle John and a Cousin Anne, who were trying to communicate. Gerald denied that he had either an Uncle John or a Cousin Anne. His mother also came through, saying she was worried about Gerald's father, but she couldn't give her name. And that was that! Gerald left in disgust: there was very little to show for his money. He might have given up if he hadn't already paid for the other two sessions. At least he hadn't given away any information about himself, except that he hadn't got a Cousin Anne or Uncle John![7]

Anyway, he returned in the afternoon to see a medium who wrote down communications from the spirit world. Uncle John and Cousin Anne made an appearance again, together with the information that Anne had died of cancer four years previously. The writing then changed: it was Gerald's mother, but Gerald was sceptical. He asked for anything that would prove that she was his mother. She promised to describe the house they used to live in - the tower, the grass, the sea, and the hills in the distance. Gerald denied that there were hills until the medium suddenly spoke forcefully, reminding Gerald of the Welsh hills in the distance.[8] The medium then wrote down the names of Gerald's brothers and their wives and children, and also that of Gerald's old nurse, Elizabeth, whom he had not even thought about for years.

7. Bracelin, 129.
8. Bracelin, 130.

Gerald was much more impressed with this medium but thought that it might all be just telepathy. Nevertheless, he was quite eager for his third and final session the following morning. This medium went into trance and her 'control' was a doctor with a French accent. Uncle John appeared, but Gerald did not want to speak to him. He asked for his mother, but in fact Cousin Anne came through. The medium gave a few more details about Cousin Anne, saying that she had been dead for four years, that she died of cancer and that Gerald knew her very well. Realisation suddenly dawned on Gerald when the medium added that Gerald knew Cousin Anne as 'G'.[9] This was quite a shock to Gerald, as he suddenly realised who she was.

For the first time, Gerald spoke to 'G' directly through the medium. She called him a 'bloody fool', saying that she had been trying to contact him for ages. In his mind he could see her face and hear her voice. He relaxed and started chatting to her. She issued him orders. He was to contact a relative of hers who was not leading the sort of life that she should be. He was to talk to her, to "give her hell" and get her to change what she was doing. She then gave Gerald a hint that something nice was about to happen to him shortly and that he wouldn't get back to his work until Christmas.[10]

'G' then spoke about Gerald's father. He would have some sort of crisis in his health in November, but if he survived that then he would live for several years. She added that he had been signing legal papers for a man called Thomas, though Gerald did not at the time see the significance of this remark.[11] Gerald confirmed later that his father had indeed been signing papers for a man named Thomas, but that only Gerald's brother, Harold, had known it at the time.[12]

Gerald was finally convinced: he knew that he had been speaking to 'G' and this had a profound effect on him:

---

9. Bracelin, 131.
10. Ibid.
11. Bracelin, 132.
12. Letter from Gerald Gardner to Louise Gardner, 18 September 1960; and Bracelin, 136-137.

In a sense, this seance was a watershed in his life. He had almost always believed in spiritualism, and in the existence of a spirit world. In Borneo, he had seen impressive confirmation of this certainty. But never before had this touched him directly, nor had he ever been able to prove, to his own satisfaction, the truths of his beliefs. Now he had done so; from now on he had a personal, as opposed to a merely intellectual, conviction that life survives what is called death.[13]

It was, in fact, a very short time indeed before "something nice" happened to him. In fact, it happened that very evening.

❧

London can be a very lonely place if you don't know anybody, and Gerald took any opportunity he could find to meet people. Before Gerald left Blundellsands, his brother Harold and his wife, Edith, had given him the address of Edith's sister, Ida Rosedale, who had been living in London following the death of her husband, William Elitto Rosedale, five years previously in 1922.

Gerald arranged to meet Ida for lunch and, in the course of their conversation, she told Gerald that she had been William's second wife, and that he had had three children by his first wife, Annie, who had died in 1916. One of them, Dorothea, was working in London as a Nursing Sister at St. Thomas' Hospital, Lambeth. I think there was a certain amount of match-making going on on Ida's part, probably prompted by earlier correspondence with Edith and Harold. Anyway, it was suggested that a theatre trip be arranged for that evening, to which Dorothea, usually known as 'Donna', was to be invited. Immediately Gerald saw her, he knew that this was the woman he would marry.[14]

He invited Ida and Donna to tea the next day, at Kew, probably in the Refreshment Pavilion in Kew Gardens, the world-famous botanical gardens and research establishment. One can imagine Gerald leading them through the Palm House, with its

13. Bracelin, 133.
14. Bracelin, 133.

tropical environment, telling them all about the plants with which he was so familiar from his time out East. He could not really say what he wanted to to Donna, but surreptitiously he gave her a present of a silver cigarette case. Whether it had a message inside we can but speculate!

The following day, Gerald set off in the morning and walked through South Kensington, past Victoria Station, from whence he had set off with Com those many years ago on his first trip abroad, past the Houses of Parliament and over the River Thames on Westminster Bridge. Over the river, he turned right and found the main reception desk in St. Thomas' Hospital and enquired as to when Nursing Sister Dorothea Rosedale would finish her shift. He waited, quite a long time.

Then, she was there, accompanying Gerald for a walk beside the river, along the Albert Embankment. He then told her: "You are coming back to Malaya with me, as my wife." As Bracelin says: "She had no good arguments to offer against this proposal; nor the desire to use them if she had."[15]

However, there were practicalities, and Gerald's leave was nearly up. They would have to get married quickly. Gerald suggested a Register Office, but Donna would have none of it: it would have to be a church wedding. After all, her father had been a clergyman!

Gerald hadn't realised that, so Donna gave him a brief outline of her family's history. Her grandfather was William Lewis Rosedale. He was born in Germany in about 1821. His family was Jewish and the surname was originally Rosenthall. At one time he was intending to become a Rabbi, but, for some reason, things changed and he spent some time in America. At some point he became a Christian minister and, by 1853, he was Vicar of Short Heath, Willenhall, Staffordshire.

His two sons, William Elitto Rosedale, Donna's father, and Honyel Gough Rosedale, also became Ministers of the Church of England. William Elitto, having graduated from New College, Oxford, held a variety of posts in Essex, London and Monmouthshire, becoming Rector of Canton in the suburbs of Cardiff

---

15. Ibid.

William Lewis Rosedale
[formerly Rosenthall]
b. 1818
m. **Caroline Ann**
d. 28 Apr 1904

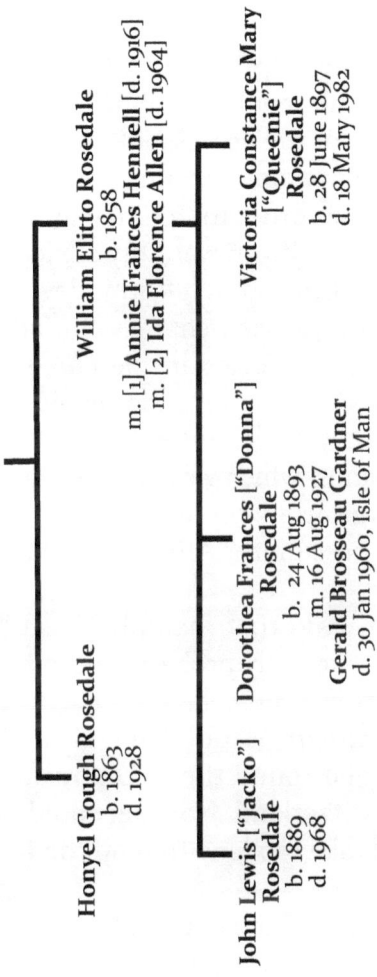

Honyel Gough Rosedale
b. 1863
d. 1928

William Elitto Rosedale
b. 1858
m. [1] **Annie Frances Hennell** [d. 1916]
m. [2] **Ida Florence Allen** [d. 1964]

John Lewis ["Jacko"] Rosedale
b. 1889
d. 1968

Dorothea Frances ["Donna"] Rosedale
b. 24 Aug 1893
m. 16 Aug 1927
Gerald Brosseau Gardner
d. 30 Jan 1960, Isle of Man

Victoria Constance Mary ["Queenie"] Rosedale
b. 28 June 1897
d. 18 Mary 1982

Rosedale Family Tree

in 1889 and where Donna (Dorothea Frances) was born on 24th August 1893. In 1894, when Donna was only a year old, the family moved to Willenhall, where William became Vicar of St. Giles Church, near where Donna's grandfather had been vicar. Donna did not have fond memories of her father or uncle, however, although it would be several years before she revealed the reason to Gerald.

First thing the following morning, Gerald set out trying to find a church where they could get married. On Cromwell Road he asked a policeman for the nearest church. He added: "I want to get married, and I have not got much time". The policeman directed him round the corner to Collingham Road, adding as an aside the wry comment: "If you want my advice, don't!"

Gerald easily found the church - St. Jude's - a large Victorian building in the Gothic style. He went up to the adjoining office and asked for the vicar, who rejoiced in the name of William Ewart Beamish Barter. He was out, however, so Gerald spoke to one of the staff, who said that they could certainly marry him, but it would involve calling the banns, which would take several weeks.

Gerald was downhearted: his leave ended in a couple of days. Was there no other possibility? After all, St. Jude was the patron saint of lost causes!

Then they told Gerald that the only possibility would be to get a Special Licence, actually probably more accurately a "common licence", which he would have to get from the Bishop of Kensington, John Primatt Maud. They gave him the Bishop's address and he hurried round there. Unfortunately, the Bishop was on holiday in Switzerland. Nothing could be done until his return, and it would take too long to send the relevant forms and get them returned.

Gerald did not know where to turn. He had heard the rumour of a church where one could get married without all the formalities. He took the Underground, intending to visit it, but he didn't hold out much hope: even if they were able to, he suspected that Donna would not agree to it, if it was at all unorthodox.

Opposite him in the carriage he noticed a friendly-looking clergyman. Gerald spoke to him and told him that he wanted to get married quickly. After establishing that Gerald knew that he needed to get a common license but that the Bishop was away, he gave Gerald the address of the Bishop of London's private solicitors, who, he thought, should be able to help. Gerald got off the train at the next stop and immediately went to see the solicitors. His visit was successful, for he obtained the required licence the following morning.[16] He then cancelled his ticket on the ship that was to leave imminently for Malaya: now it would leave without him!

Donna introduced Gerald to her brother, John Lewis Rosedale (1889-1968), known as Jacko, who was also working at St. Thomas' Hospital as a biochemist. She had told Gerald something about Jacko, which explained why her memories of her father and uncle were not so fond. Apparently, Donna's father had wanted Jacko to follow the family tradition and become a clergyman, so he sent him to a theological college. This was not in any way Jacko's choice and he ran away, but his father "forbade him the house".

This was in 1916 and Jacko enlisted in the Army. He called at the house to say goodbye to his sisters. His father discovered them and told them all to leave. The girls sought refuge at the house of their uncle, Rev. Honyel Gough Rosedale, but when he discovered that their father had thrown them out, he threw them out too. Eventually they found accommodation with friends, Donna got a nursing job and her younger sister, Victoria (Queenie), got work in a school.

After Gerald and Donna obtained Jacko's approval to the marriage, the next obstacle was her matron at the hospital. Although Donna was 33 years old, the matron seemed to have some power over her. I think she felt a certain responsibility for Donna, as neither of her parents were still alive and that she felt almost that she had to act 'in loco parentis'. Anyway, she refused Donna leave to get married.

Gerald confronted her: she proved to be formidable. She asked to see Gerald's papers, but this was clearly not sufficient for her. She told him that he should go back to Johore and make a nice home for Donna: in a year or so she would let her go out.

---

16. Bracelin, 134-135.

Gerald told her that wasn't good enough and that she was going to leave with him right then. After confrontation with the matron, Gerald's determination won through, and the matron allowed the marriage to take place.[17]

The marriage of Gerald Brosseau Gardner and Dorothea Frances Rosedale took place on Tuesday 16th August 1927 at St. Jude's Church, Collingham Road, Kensington, officiated by the vicar, the Reverend William Ewart Beamish Barter. The witnesses were Donna's sister, Queenie, and Ida's brother, Arthur C. Allen. Donna's matron was also there, having been won over, to give her blessing. Gerald's brother, Bob, may well have attended, though it is doubtful whether Harold and Edith came to the ceremony, since she had "expressed a pious horror at the speed of the courtship". It is likely that photographs were taken, but I have so far been unable to track them down.

One of the first things Gerald did after the ceremony was to send off a cable to his employers in Johore informing them that he had just got married and requesting the two months' unpaid leave to which he was entitled. Then, Gerald and Donna took the Underground to Waterloo station and boarded the train to Portsmouth Harbour, whence they took the ferry over to Ryde on the Isle of Wight, where they stayed for a few days on a short honeymoon. He knew Ryde from the holiday he had taken there with Com many years before. The only thing Gerald mentions that went on during the honeymoon is that he taught Donna to shoot with a pistol, presumably a very useful skill to possess in a tropical country!

After the short honeymoon, they went up to Blundellsands. They did not, however, stay with Harold and Edith, since they were still disapproving of the marriage, but with Bob and Louise. After a hectic few weeks, Gerald was at last able to relax. He told Bob his experiences with the mediums in London. He told him that whilst some of the information he received was really accurate, some was completely wrong, like the ubiquitous 'Uncle John'. Bob replied that Gerald definitely had had an Uncle John, but that he died when Gerald was very young.[18] The fairly

---

17. Bracelin, 135.
18. Bracelin, 136.

detailed information which I have for the Gardner family does not indicate a John, but it is possible that he was Gerald's mother's brother, though I have so far failed to find him.

Gerald then showed Bob the automatic writing that was supposed to have come from their mother. Bob went over to his desk and brought out a letter from her. They compared them: the writing was identical!

The following day, Gerald went into Liverpool to meet G's "wayward relative" and passed on to her the message that G had given him. When she heard that it had come from 'Cousin Anne' she burst into tears and said that this was confirmation to her that the message was genuine, as it was only to her mother that 'G' had ever called herself Anne. Her full name was Anne Gertrude Williams, but Gerald had not known that.[19]

The same day, Gerald received a cable saying that his extra leave had been granted. Rather than book a ship directly from Liverpool or London, he thought that a trip through France and Spain might be a more interesting way of spending his extra leave, so this is what they did, picking up the ship at Marseille. They eventually arrived back in Singapore harbour on Christmas Eve, thus fulfilling G's prediction.

---

19. Bracelin, 137.

CHAPTER NINE

Digging for Knowledge

G erald and Donna settled into a bungalow at Bukit Japon in Johore Bahru, together with his ever-growing collection of weapons which were displayed on the walls.

There was, however, the matter of the ghost of a Scotsman who appeared from time to time. They tracked him down in the nearby cemetery and either told him in no uncertain terms to go away and leave them in peace or else learned to accept the occasional disruption to their lives which he caused.

In 1927, Donna's brother, Jacko, applied for and obtained the new post of Professor of Biochemistry at the King Edward VII College of Medicine in Singapore. It rather looked as if he had moved half way round the world to keep an eye on Donna: perhaps he didn't quite trust Gerald, at least initially. I would imagine that Donna was quite pleased to have her brother within easy reach, as it is likely that Gerald would not have wanted her to work and she would probably spend many hours in the bungalow, engaged in quiet womanly activities like reading and sewing! Or perhaps she didn't! Bracelin describes her as being a "talented amateur actress" in 1938, so she may have found an outlet for those talents during her time in Johore Bahru. Jacko stayed as Professor of Biochemistry in Singapore (with a break back in his old hospital in England in 1930) until his retirement to London in 1941, just before the Japanese occupation.

Gerald's job involved regular trips, several times a month, by river launch into the jungle to the towns and villages where the opium shops were, sometimes accompanied by Donna. The work part of these trips involved visiting the opium shops, checking their stock and collecting the necessary dues. There was also a good deal of socialising at each stop, so progress was slow.

Between stops, Gerald had plenty of time to be alone in the jungle and to think. Not only was he able to assimilate the knowledge obtained from his contacts with the native people from a variety of cultures over many years, but he became gripped with an enthusiasm for finding out about the history of that land. Not only did he start to read what had already been written, but he explored the land itself, looking for clues as to its past, which was still very much wrapped in mystery.

One site that he passed frequently was Johore Lama (Old Johore). It had been the capital of the Johore Sultanate in the 16th Century but fell into ruin following a succession of battles with the Portuguese. At its height, it had been a major fortress with a significant settlement adjoining.

When Gerald first looked at the site, there seemed to be a few earthworks still visible through the jungle which had grown back in the 400 years since the destruction of the fort and settlement. Those earthworks excited him and he was determined to find out more. No one seemed to know anything: he would have to investigate things for himself. His first visit proved fruitful. There was little to be seen from the direction of the river, but he had a walk round and found what turned out to be four miles of earthworks. As he was climbing up a hill, he suddenly realised that it was artificial, one of a series of fortified embankments. He was sure that he was looking at the walls of a fort.[1]

At the next opportunity, he visited the Raffles Museum in Singapore and excitedly told them of his findings. The response was, however, disappointing, to say the least. They had it on reliable authority that there was nothing there. They were not prepared

---

1. Bracelin, 103.

to go all that way to have a look when they knew there was noth-ing there. In the face of such prejudice, Gerald gave up with the authorities for the time being: he would have to collect the evi-dence himself, and that meant excavation.

This put him in something of a quandary. He knew he ought to get permission from the Sultan of Johore before digging. But he had heard that the Sultan might not approve, so that rather than risk a formal rejection, he decided to go ahead and plead igno-rance if necessary. He started by going to the local village and recruiting some of the children as being less conspicuous than adults would have been. They proved very willing workers, enabling Gerald to excavate larger areas.

He probably started excavating about 1928 or so and contin-ued until at least 1932 and possibly longer. But being the sort of person he was, Gerald was not content with just excavating one place. He claims, in addition to Johore Lama, to have identified the site of the ancient city of Singapura, from which Singapore takes its name. He got to know the gravediggers in the Royal Cemetery in Kota Tinggi and they let him have some of their finds. He also did some excavations further upstream at the old settlement of Sayong Pinang.

With the limited resources at his disposal and his initial lack of experience at excavation techniques, he did not try to reveal the plan-form of the original buildings on these sites. Rather, he concentrated on smaller items which could, nevertheless, be revealing of their date and history. His emphasis was on looking for items in two main categories: coins and beads. On one occa-sion he also found the remains of a ship. Each of these caused him to think and interpret.

The first things he found in any number were coins. He tells the story in an article which appeared in 1933.[2] When Gerald first found gold coins during his excavations, he took them to the Raf-fles Museum in Singapore, but they did not know any more than he did about them. Nor did the Dutch museums. On his visit to England in 1932, he submitted some of the coins he had found to

2. G.B. Gardner, "Notes on Some Ancient Gold Coins, from Johore River",- *Journal Malayan Branch Royal Asiatic Society*, Vol. XI, Part II (1933), 171-176.

the British Museum. They had three of their own, but no other information about them. In the article, Gerald gives drawings of the coins, some of which are eight-sided. By referring to the names of the sultans represented on them, he was able to date some of them, primarily to the 16th and 17th Centuries. They were frequently found in cemeteries, but Gerald was convinced that this was merely tradition, that they were not just designed to be thrown during a funeral, but were real money. He cites references from the 17th Century to Johore gold coins being used in trade.

The second main category of item which Gerald found was beads.3 During his excavations he had collected a large number of beads and gemstones. The gemstones, about 800 in total, seemed to be early Indian, and about 20% of the 600 or so beads seemed to be from the Roman Empire. The question Gerald tried to answer in an article was how and when did these Roman beads get there. He concludes:

> Goods are usually traded in the period of their manufac-
> ture, and there is a mass of evidence bearing on Roman
> trade with India and the East, which it is needless to repeat
> here. It is, however, worthy of special note that traders from
> the Roman Empire took glass, among other things, into
> India ...4

Gerald began to realise that there was a flourishing sea-trade between India and Malaya in ancient times, which explained the presence of the beads and other objects. There was considerable evidence of trade by sea between India and Java, so it was quite feasible that there had been trade with the Malay States as well. Gerald concludes:

> The Malay States have always been famous for their gums,
> incense, and spices, and the Roman demand would encour-
> age this trade, presumably through Indian middlemen, who
> would have gems, stones and Roman products, including

3. G.B. Gardner, "Ancient Beads from the Johore River as Evidence of an Early Link by Sea between Malaya and the Roman Empire", *Journal Royal Asiatic Society*, 1937, 467-470.
4. Op. cit., 468.

beads among other things, to send in return. Thus the Roman beads found by me on the Johore river, in conjunction with ancient gem stones or stone beads, were probably part of this early overseas traffic between Malaya and India, and thence to the Roman Empire.[5]

And then, in the course of his excavations at Johore Lama, Gerald uncovered the keel of a large boat – confirmation, or so he thought, that such vessels had existed in ancient times. He was intrigued and wanted to find out precisely what sort of vessels they were. He searched in vain for any drawings of such boats locally and was inclined to give up his search when he heard about the carvings of ships in the ancient 9th Century Buddhist temple of Borobudur in Java. As soon as he could, he went there to investigate. When he saw the carvings, Gerald realised that they were not Indian ships, as they had outriggers. He had to ask himself the question as to whether they were imaginary or whether they had actually existed.[6]

There certainly weren't any ships around now, Gerald realised, but in his reading, he had learned that the Dutch had destroyed all sizeable boats when they had invaded and had prevented the building of any more, in order to keep all trade in their own hands. The reliefs of the ships on the wall at Borobudur were supposed to represent a fleet of Indian ships which invaded Java about 70 CE. These weren't like any Indian ships of the period, which puzzled Gerald until he realised that they must have been a representation of the ships that were around when the sculptor carved the reliefs in about 800 CE.

He decided that the best way to take things further would be to make a model, so, with photographs of the Borobudur reliefs and by examining the surviving Malayan tradition of boat-building, Gerald began to construct a scale model of how he imagined the old trading-vessels would have looked. It was a two-masted ocean-going vessel which was, as nearly as Gerald could make it, an accurate reconstruction of an ancient trading ship of the Malays.

---

5. Op. cit., p 469.
6. Bracelin, 110.

Gerald took the model to the Raffles Museum in Singapore, expecting another rejection, but they seemed genuinely interested and, indeed, wanted it for display. He gave it to them: the tide was beginning to turn.

Gerald soon began to realise that there had been an ancient Malay culture which had substantial buildings, gold coinage and ocean-going ships. He was determined to prove it, but he met scepticism when he approached the authorities. However, as Bracelin put it: "...in the end, Gardner was to prove every one of his contentions, and change the story of prehistory in the Malay Archipelago."7

It was only in 1953 that Gerald was partially vindicated. In that year, there were excavations at Johore Lama by a team of archaeologists from Cambridge. They were able to excavate far more than Gerald some twenty years previously, including three boats and the remains of gun platforms.8 One of their conclusions was that the boat that Gerald excavated in part was in fact Chinese rather than Malay and no more than 100 years old.

⚜

The 1931-1932 period was a time of change for Gerald in several ways. There had been no Masonic activity in North Borneo when he had moved there in 1911 and it seems likely that it was not until he moved to Johore that he became active in freemasonry again. He became a member of the Johore Royal Lodge No. 3946 but retired from it in April 1931.

This was about the time when a change was beginning to take place in official attitudes towards his findings, from disbelief to interest. One factor in this was the appointment of Sir Richard O. Winstedt as General Adviser to Johore in 1931. Winstedt (1878-1966) had a distinguished career in various fields, including making the first systematic approach to Malayan history and setting up an education system specifically for Malays, establishing a teacher training college in 1922. He became aware of Gerald's

---

7. Bracelin, 101.
8. G de G Sieveking, Paul Wheatley and C A Gibson Hill, "Recent Archaeological Discoveries in Malaya", (1952-53), "The Investigations at Johore Lama", *Journal of the Malayan Branch of the Royal Asiatic Society* Vol. 27 pt. 1 1954, 224-233.

investigations, visiting Johore Lama on at least one occasion, and was supportive and helpful in many ways. In his book on the keris, Gerald expressed his indebtedness to Sir Richard for his friendly interest, advice and help extending over many years.

A change of climate also came with the appointment of a new Director of the Raffles Museum in March 1932, Frederick Nutter Chasen (1896-1942). He had been born in Norfolk, where he had acquired a life-long interest in birds, which was his specialism at the Museum. Yet he seemed to be more sympathetic to Gerald's theories and to have a more positive approach to his researches than his predecessor. His assistant, the anthropologist, Hubert Dennis Collings (1905-2001) was very helpful to Gerald. He had been born in Southwold, Suffolk and was a life-long friend of Eric Blair (George Orwell), in fact marrying Blair's former girl-friend, Eleanor Jacques. He was also to become a life-long friend of Gerald's.

From that time on, with the encouragement of Winstedt, Chasen and Collings, Gerald began to think of himself as an archaeologist and anthropologist. He had no formal qualifications, and if that didn't matter to those whom he talked to and asked advice of, then it certainly didn't matter to him. As Bracelin put it: "... the time when he had been wholeheartedly planter or civil servant was almost over; more and more the folklorist archaeologist in him began to take over."9

Gerald's archaeological work in Johore led him to write articles for the journals of varied learned societies and to his application for membership of those societies. I think Gerald rather liked the imagined prestige which he felt that membership of Royal Societies gave, for he was elected a Fellow of the Royal Anthropological Institute in 1936.10

Chasen was also Hon. Secretary of the Malayan Branch of the Royal Asiatic Society and may have been influential in electing Gerald to membership in 1932. That was also the year that Gerald was entitled to several months' leave, which he decided would be largely devoted to archaeology and anthropology. He would visit

---

9. Bracelin, 74.
10. Letter from Beverley Emery, library representative of the Royal Anthropological Institute to the author, 4 October 2001.

his family in England, of course, but also attend an international conference and do quite a lot of digging as well!

One of the most mysterious statements in the whole of the Bracelin biography about Gerald's 1932 trip home is as follows: "... he finally returned to England. Here he learned that his father, whom he had meant to visit in the Canaries, to which he had retired, had finally died."[11] Death and probate records show that William Robert Gardner died on 5th August 1935. Gerald's brother, Bob, visited him there several times until 1931 but not beyond that year. Perhaps William had become so ill with dementia that he no longer recognised his family and they decided it was not advisable to visit him any more. They would therefore probably have suggested to Gerald that it might be best not to visit his father. Perhaps Gerald felt subconsciously as if his father was dead already and this may have influenced his memory when he was recounting his story for the biography.

Gerald had heard about the forthcoming inaugural International Congress of Prehistoric and Protohistoric Sciences to be held in London on 1st to 6th August 1932, and decided to attend, but he intended to stop off on the way.

One of the most prominent archaeologists in the world at that time was Sir Flinders Petrie (1853-1942), who was carrying out a dig at Tell el-'Ajjul in Gaza. He was one of the pioneers of more systematic excavation as opposed to what had been little more than "treasure hunting". He wrote: "Nothing is so poor as not to have a story to tell us. The tools, the potsherds, the very stones and bricks of the wall cry out if we have the power of understanding them." and "I believe the true line of research lies in the noting and comparison of the smallest details." Gerald decided to call in on Petrie on his way to London to see how things were going and to offer his help.

Some time, probably in May 1932, Gerald and Donna took the ship from Singapore, but whereas Donna continued all the way to England, probably to stay with her sister, Gerald "jumped ship" at Port Said on the Suez Canal and spent a week in Egypt looking at

---

11. Bracelin, 139.

some of the remaining splendours of its past civilisations. He then arranged transport to Gaza, where he arrived at dawn.

Tell el-'Ajjul lay on the northern bank of the Wadi Azza, about four miles south-west of the ancient city of Gaza and about half a mile from the sea. It was the site of an old city covering some 30 acres with its origins dating back to 2300 BCE. It has more recently been identified as the biblical Sharuhen.

The camp seemed to be just a group of mud huts near the river, one of which was occupied by Sir Flinders and his wife. There was a low hill beyond, which was the site of the dig. Although it didn't seem to be anything significant to Gerald, this was the site of the ancient city of Tell el-'Ajjul.[12]

Sir Flinders came to meet him and got him settled in. Gerald gave him a letter of introduction from Macalpine Woods, an archaeologist that he had got to know.

Then Sir Flinders showed him round the dig. At first, Gerald was disappointed with all the trenches: they didn't seem to make any sense. But Sir Flinders brought it all to life, pointing out the foundations of the outer wall on a steep escarpment: Gerald could see how this would be almost invulnerable.

As he got to know the dig and the people, various items of interest were revealed, one of which was a mile-long secret passage, which excited him, perhaps reminding him of the old passage made of barrels which his ancestors had supposedly constructed below the streets of Liverpool. He was also interested that they had found Irish gold on the site, of which strips had been soldered and then twisted together.

I don't know how long Gerald worked for Petrie at Tell el-'Ajjul, probably several weeks, but before he left he had a talk with him about the difficulties which he had had in getting his discoveries in Johore recognised by the authorities. Petrie was supportive and encouraging: "Archaeologists are the most jealous people in the world ... But you must butt on. You've found the beginnings: you've proved that there really was a Malay civilisation. Now others can follow the trail."[13]

12. Bracelin, 137.
13. Bracelin, 139.

I think Gerald would have liked to have stayed longer working for Petrie, whom he obviously admired, but Sir Flinders emphasised the importance of what Gerald was doing in Malaya, so he left on the next stage of his journey to England, taking the ship from Port Said to Marseille, where he disembarked and travelled overland through France, visiting the famous prehistoric cave paintings en route.

The First International Congress of Prehistoric and Protohistoric Sciences opened in the Great Hall of King's College, London on the afternoon of Monday 1st August 1932. Over 600 people attended the numerous sessions during the following five days. Most of the well-known figures in the fields of archaeology and anthropology were present and Gerald probably made contact with several of them. Petrie was there and he may well have introduced Gerald to various people. Certainly such individuals as P.V. van Stein Callenfels and Professor A.W. Brøgger of Oslo were later to become acquaintances of Gerald's.

He got to know Alexander Keiller, the archaeologist and marmalade manufacturer, who had made a name for himself by carrying out excavations at Avebury and Windmill Hill. One of Keiller's interests was witchcraft, particularly the study of 16th Century witchcraft in Scotland, though he disagreed with Margaret Murray's findings. He sounds an interesting person, for his biographer, Lynda Murray, writes: "... in the 1930s, one Halloween night found him leading a small group of associates out into the garden of the Manor at Avebury. He carried before him a phallic symbol, and bowing three times before the Statue of Pan, he chanted 'witchlike' incantations."[14]

Gerald could not possibly have gone to all of the lectures, but there are at last two lecturers whom he contacted and made reference to later.

The first is Miss V.C.C. Collum, who spoke on "The Discovery and Excavation of an allée couverte with sculptured supports, containing a burial of the Early Iron Age, at Tressé, Ille-et-Vilaine, Brittany." She referred to double pairs of human breasts sculptures in relief on part of a burial chamber. She said that "the work

---

14. Lynda J Murray, *A Zest for Life: the Story of Alexander Keiller* (Morven Books 1999), 23.

is realistic and beautiful in its sensibility, for the two pairs on the transversal stone are the pointed breasts of a young girl and those on the western stone are the full breasts of a mother."[15] She considered that they represented the worldwide cult of the Great Mother – the Cult of the Female Creative Principle:

> *That goddess was the Great Female Principle (comprehending a Male Principle), both in its unmanifested aspect as Potential Creatrix, and its manifesting aspect as Woman the Lover-Bride and as the all-nourishing Mother, whose cult was widespread in Asia Minor, Syria, Central Asia and NW. India, Mesopotamia, Babylonia, and Egypt. This Cosmic cult can be demonstrated both in the archaeological remains of Gaul and Great Britain, and in the occult poetry and religious epics of Ireland and Wales and in Gaelic hymns surviving orally in the Western Isles of Scotland. ... The peculiar symbolism of double pairs of human breasts was probably suggested by knowledge of cult statues of Artemis Ephesia of the Graeco-Roman period and of the esoteric Tantric and ancient Kabbalist doctrine of the twofold Mother-Bride as potential and active Creatrix and Reabsorber of all life at death. ... Such esoteric teaching was probably first introduced by the poet-seers or 'druids'... The questions raised by a study of these sculptures are so important that a fresh examination of Gaulish religious remains, and of folk-lore in formerly Celtic-speaking countries, is urgently required, together with a wider and deeper comparative study of the Cosmic cult associated with the Mother Goddess.*[16]

Gerald, if he did attend her lecture, would undoubtedly have been much affected by the subject matter, much of which he later wrote about in his own books.

The other speaker who undoubtedly influenced him was Dr. Porphyrios Dikaios, Director of the Cyprus Museum in Nicosia, Cyprus. He spoke about "Early Bronze Age Cults in Cyprus as

15. V. C .C. Collum, *The Tressé Iron-Age Megalithic Monument* (Oxford 1935), 53.
16. op. cit., 113-114.

revealed by the Excavations at 'Vounous', Bellapais". He also spoke about the Cult of the Mother Goddess. The summary of his talk reads in part:

> ... *there already existed in Cyprus, in the Early Bronze Age, a well-developed cult of the Mother Goddess, associated with the Snake God and the Divine Bull, with separate temple-sites and organized ceremonies including dances, disguises, masques and sacrifices. ... The notion of a sacred marriage associated with the symbolical dove was extant, and among the sacred symbols there appear the 'horns of consecration'.*[17]

Gerald probably made contact with Dikaios at that time: he certainly met him when he visited Cyprus in 1937.

Keiller introduced Gerald to his sister-in-law, Dorothy Liddell, who was attending the Congress but who was also carrying out an excavation at Hembury Hill in Devon. She had started in 1930 and much was being discovered. She, or Keiller, or both, persuaded Gerald to spend some of the rest of his time in England helping the excavations at Hembury Hill. By this time, Gerald had made contact with Donna again and they both went down to Devon to help with the dig. Lady Aileen Fox and Mary Leakey, subsequently to become well-known archaeologists, were among those who were helping.

Bracelin also refers to "digs ... in other parts of the country"[18] so I would imagine that the Gardners only spent a few days at each site.

Gerald was certainly back in London in time to make considerable further investigations into spiritualism. Most of his appointments were disappointing, to say the least. A trance medium, when asked about the history of the *keris majapahit*, could give no answer. A finely-adjusted typewriter was supposed to convey messages, but that which Gerald received was, in his own words, "completely pointless". And then there was the individual who came through claiming that he had met Gerald at school. Gerald decided

---

17. *Proceedings of the First International Congress of Prehistoric and Protohistoric Sciences* (Oxford 1934), 185.
18. Bracelin, 140.

that he had come to the wrong person since he had never been to school. Bracelin reports: "During this leave, too, he finally went to see Hewart Mackenzie ..."[19] If so, it must have been via another medium, since McKenzie had died in 1929!

Gerald enjoyed mixing with the big names in the archaeological world, and receiving genuine appreciation for his work in uncovering the advanced nature of early Malay civilisation as well as a deeper and more thorough understanding of the character and qualities of the native keris.

As an interesting aside, I have accumulated over the years various photographs of Donna, both as a young girl and following her marriage to Gerald. What struck me was that in the photographs of her on the river-boat with Gerald in *Gerald Gardner Witch* and the one wearing the bandana, she clearly has a very large nose. On the photograph of her in the Johore bungalow, also in *Gerald Gardner Witch*, and other more recent photographs, she has a short snub nose.

The only explanation which I can suggest for this is that she must have had what is colloquially known as a 'nose job'. The only possible time and location for this to be done would be during the 1932 visit to London. Cosmetic plastic surgery was coming in during the 1920s and 1930s, particularly for Hollywood film stars, and there were undoubtedly practitioners in London who could undertake such an operation. Gerald could certainly have afforded it and it seems at least possible that they both wanted such an operation.

I had been somewhat swayed against this theory when I saw that the photographs demonstrated that her nose when a child was not large, but I was recently talking to someone who told me that when she was in her teens her own nose started to grow - a family characteristic.

Gerald and Donna boarded the *S.S. Comorin* in London on 30th September 1932 for the voyage back to Singapore.

In 1934, Gerald had another period of leave and he decided to visit China. It was the year of Mao Zedong's "Long March" and there

19. Bracelin, 141-142.

was much unrest between the Nationalists and the Communists, as he would find out. Taking a ship from Singapore to Saigon (now Ho Chi Minh City) in what was then French Indo-China, he went on to Phnom Penh in present-day Cambodia, where he visited the Silver Pagoda, locally known as Wat Preah Keo Morokat (Temple of the Emerald Buddha). This was built in 1892 to house the ashes of the royal family and is now a repository for cultural and religious treasures. Gerald noted the floor, which was solid silver, containing over 5000 tiles. There were statues of the Buddha, including a life-size gold figure, encrusted with over 9000 diamonds.

Gerald continued by train into China, visiting the historic city of Hangzhou (Hangchow). Marco Polo, visiting at the end of the 13th Century, described it as "the City of Heaven, the most beautiful and magnificent in the world" and it is today considered by many the loveliest city in mainland China.

Gerald then took the train on another hundred miles or so to Shanghai, from where he was due to take the boat back to Singapore. The railway journey was eventful, however. He was rather apprehensive to note that the ticket collectors were accompanied by eight bodyguards with pistols. There had been a rumour that an attack was to be made on the railway, so, despite the timetable, the train made a non-stop run to Shanghai, even though each station they passed was packed with disappointed passengers. Gerald embarked on the ship back to Singapore with perhaps a sigh of relief.

Until about 1930, archaeologists in south-east Asia didn't seem to talk to each other, although there had been a conference in Hanoi in 1932. I think that Gerald had probably missed this, so he was determined to attend the Second Congress for Prehistoric Research in the Far East, which was to be held in Manila from 6th to 12th February 1935. Chasen and Collings were there from the Raffles Museum, and Gerald renewed his acquaintance with such delegates as Dr. Th. van der Hoop, Director of the Java Museums, and Professor van Stein Callenfels.

The Congress was organised by H. Otley Beyer (1883-1966). He was head of the Anthropology Department of the University of the Philippines and founded the university's Museum and

Institute of Archaeological Ethnology. Gerald recalls an amusing incident when he went to see Beyer before the Congress when he was researching Malay weapons. Beyer said they had some relevant literature in their library, but when sent for it turned out to have been written by Gerald himself!

Gerald made the acquaintance of the archaeologist, Madeleine Colani (1866-1943) while at the Congress. She was the representative of the École Française D'Extrême Orient (the French School of Asian Studies). She had found beads similar to those which Gerald had found and had come to similar conclusions about long distance trade routes.

Gerald's ideas about his finds seem to have been taken more seriously by the time a conference was held in Singapore in December 1935:

Several years ago Mr. Gardner found what appeared to be ancient beads and pottery near Kota Tinggi and at several other sites along the Johore River.

Nobody could be persuaded to take any interest in these finds, and indeed so little value was attached to them by Malayan savants that a sawmill was actually permitted to be built over one of Mr. Gardner's most promising sites, with the result that the evidence still buried in the soil at that spot will presumably never be available.

But Mr. Gardner's revenge came when prehistorians from all over southern Asia gathered in Singapore last December. His despised potsherds were then examined by experts, while his beads were submitted to the world's greatest authority on ancient beads.

The result is that we now know that that pottery found on the bank of the Johore River is at least 1,600 years old, having been exported from China during the Han dynasty, and that the beads were made anywhere between 700 B.C. and 300 A.D.[20]

20. *The Malaya Tribune*, 28 April 1936.

Gerald was not very impressed with most of the speakers at the Manila conference: either they gave the impression of knowing it all or else were very cautious and uncertain. His own attitude, what I have called "intelligent speculation", was largely absent. This was a sign of growing confidence on his part - he was turning into someone who could stand his ground with the best archaeologists and anthropologists. This is best seen where his interests in magic and weapons combined in the study of the Malayan *keris*.

CHAPTER TEN

The Mystical Weapon

It was perhaps inevitable, with Gerald's interest in Malay native culture and magic and his almost lifelong enthusiasm for weapons, that his attention should eventually be drawn to that Malay magical weapon 'par excellence': the *keris*.

He had acquired his first *keris majapahit* in the wake of the attack upon Cornwall and found that it engendered a lot of respect. This caused him to become interested in the numerous stories of the magical keris that abounded amongst the Malays. And yet there was very little written about them. What there was merely dwelt on their characteristic shape: their claimed magical properties were completely ignored.

Gerald was not satisfied: he felt strongly that he must learn from the native Malays, so he asked Cornwall to invite a few Malays to show him their knives, to dance the old keris-dances which he had heard about, and, he hoped, to tell some of the old stories about the keris. He had no academic qualifications, in either archaeology or anthropology, or, come to that, anything else. Whilst there are definite disadvantages in this lack of formal recognition, it does sometimes, and certainly did in Gerald's case, allow for a certain freedom of thought, an independence of ideas which allows a breakthrough in understanding which may be denied to those whose learning has occurred under a more formal structure.

Characteristic of this is the spelling 'keris', for both singular and plural, which Gerald uses. It is the Malay version of the word which is generally transcribed as 'kris' in English. It is, perhaps, typical of Gerald to use the native form of the word. The *Museums Journal* in its review of Gerald's book, *Keris and Other Malay Weapons*,[1] sums it up: "The Keris (pl. Keris) is, of course, our old friend the kris, and our still older friend the creese."[2] In Gerald's book the 'e' in keris is indicated with a 'breve' accent, a mark like the lower half of a circle, above it. It generally indicates a short vowel and, whilst there are no formal accents in written script in Malay, it is probably there to indicate that the 'e' is not stressed at all. This is probably why the Europeans have generally adopted 'kris' as the usual spelling, because the 'e' is so little stressed.

Anyway, Gerald was determined to find out exactly what the keris was, its origin and functions, and to allow his speculative faculties full flow. *Keris and Other Malay Weapons* starts boldly: "The keris is undoubtedly the distinctive Malay weapon."[3] This is, however, only partly true, as Frey remarks: "...among all weapons the kris is unique in that its principal function has long been that of cultural association rather than an extension of the hand for doing harm to others."[4]

It is interesting and not perhaps a coincidence that the witch's athame has a similar role. Perhaps it is also more than a coincidence that the witches' Book of Shadows says of the athame, "This is the true witch's weapon ...",[5] an echo perhaps of Gerald's pronouncement quoted above.

The keris is a form of dagger or short sword. It has a blade which is usually thin and sharpened on both sides. Where it is used as a weapon, it is used for thrusting in personal defence. One characteristic is that the blade widens on one side towards the hilt: this is known as the *ganja*. Whilst the older blades were

---

1. G. B. Gardner, *Keris and Other Malay Weapons*, (Progressive Publishing Company, 1936).
2. *The Museums Journal*, Vol. 36, 320.
3. Gardner, (1936), 8.
4. Edward Frey, *The Kris: Mystic Weapon of the Malay World* (Oxford University Press, 1986, 3rd Edition, 2003), 2.
5. Janet and Stewart Farrar, *The Witches' Way*, (Robert Hale, 1984), 20.

straight, many have a characteristic wavy profile, often dama-scened with coloured patterns introduced in the forging process. These are often now made specifically for the tourists, who prefer them to the older design.

The keris is thought to date back to at least the 14th Century CE. Its exact origin is unknown, but Gerald had his own ideas about that, as we shall see. He also began to understand the magical nature of the keris, manifested particularly in the qualities of what was generally considered to be the oldest form of the keris, one of the rarest but also one with a profusion of magical legends attached to it, the *keris majapahit*. These were made of iron, all in one piece, usually fairly small with a thin blade and with the hilt as a human figure.

Gerald attributes one quality to them: "All agree that they are very poisonous, the usual saying is, 'the depth of the white of a nail is enough to kill with a *majapahit*'. It is said that the poison is in the iron and that the keris does not need to be poisoned. It is possible that 600 years' rust is in itself poisonous."[6]

He then goes on to give some of the legends, beliefs and superstitions associated with the keris, and in some cases gives his own explanation as to how they may have come about. There is a strong belief that all old things have some indwelling spirit (*semangat*). By this means the keris is supposed to be able to kill at a distance. They are therefore kept tightly sheathed. In addition, Gerald remarks, a keris should always be:

> ... *pointing upward or downward; as otherwise the evil influence will do harm and cause sickness, in the direction in which it is pointed, even though in the sheath. How much the modern Malay believes I cannot say, more than he admits I think. That older people believe in it I had proof, when a highly educated Malay lady screamed and nearly jumped out of her chair, because a sheathed keris majapahit I was showing was inadvertently pointed at her.*[7]

6. Gardner (1936), 43.
7. Op. cit. 59.

Gerald always seemed to try to find a mundane explanation, however unlikely, for seemingly magical properties. One such is the belief that someone could be killed if their footprints were stabbed with a particular type of keris, the keris bertuwah:

> *This is capable of explanation. If a pawang stabbed a man's footprints with a k. bertuwah having taken the precaution of putting a slow poison in his rice the night before, the inference would be that he was killed by the stabbing of the footprints. After the trick had been known to work several times, a man might well die of fright, if he heard that his footprints had been stabbed with that keris. Similar power would then be attributed to other ancient keris, and so the story would grow.*[8]

However, he gives no material explanation for one power that the keris is supposed to possess:

> *Another queer superstition is that a certain keris can draw fire; that is, if the house is on fire and the keris is pointed at the fire and moved to one side the fire will leave the house and follow the keris. I have an old Malay friend in Muar who only eight months ago when the next house to his caught fire, brought out a special keris and held it pointing between the burning house and his own. He triumphantly asserts that although sparks were flying all round and another house caught fire the keris stopped the fire from harming his house. I asked why he did not try to save the burning houses, by drawing away their fire, and he ingenuously replied: "They weren't my houses".*[9]

Gerald was not content with just describing the many varieties of keris or chronicling the folklore and legend associated with them. As would be repeated many times in the course of his life, he would make his own contribution by speculating on the origins of things. By 1933, he was sufficiently confident to put

---

8. Gardner, (1936), 61.
9. Ibid.

some of his thoughts together into an article.[10] One of these varieties was the keris pichit, which Gerald describes as follows:

> *Their special feature, from which they take their name Pichit (squeezed), is the round depressions on each side of the blade, which appear slightly raised on the other side, exactly as if someone had taken a strip of clay and squeezed it between the tips of his fingers. Or as if he had taken a red-hot blade, and squeezed it out with tongs shaped like the tips of his fingers.*

Gerald then brings his imaginative faculties into play:

> *The only explanation I can suggest of the story of these keris is that they are made in the ordinary way by some Pawang (Witch Doctor) the finger marks being hammered into the red-hot iron; then, at night, in the presence of witnesses, with much ceremony, the handle is heated red-hot, and the pawang, with well oiled fingers, quickly pinches along the blade, and when it is cold shows the finger-marks as proof of his powers. I have been told of many Pawang who could make these Keris Pichit, but it is always in the next district, and when I enquire there, the Pawang is always unknown, or dead! ... The finger marks may be simply put on with a hammer, but the weapons are so rare that I think there must be some basis for the story.*[11]

This is typical of Gerald's approach to things: to feel himself part of the whole exercise and to imagine how people, not too dissimilar to himself, might have felt and acted. Indeed, he is probably best known for his ideas as to how the keris came about in the first place, by making connections between similar forms and functions. Countering the theory that the keris came from India, Gerald put forward the idea that it originated locally - in Malaysia. He had noticed the similarities of the oldest, most primitive, keris to the sting of the *ikan pari*, the sting-ray. After

---

10. G.B. Gardner, "Notes on Two Uncommon Varieties of the Malay Keris", *Journal Malay Branch of the Royal Asiatic Society*, Vol. XI, Part II, (December 1933), 178-182.
11. Ibid.

noting that it had been recorded that a young man had fainted following the prick of a ray sting, Gerald speculated:

> ... *it must have occurred to some primitive man, that this would be a fine thing to stick into an enemy. The ray sting is barbed down the sides and anyone who held it like a knife and stabbed would poison his own hand and reduce the length of his reach and he would probably break the sting; but if held between thumb and finger, with the butt against the base of the thumb it could be used with safety and this is the way to hold a small* keris *majapahit. A refinement would be the tying on of a bit of bark cloth ... I made an experiment and found that when the cloth handle is grasped like a keris it resembles the* k. *majapahit* hilt. *The wielder of such a weapon would not be trying to reach the heart or other vital spot, he would jab and withdraw. His enemy would be paralysed with pain and could easily be finished off.*[12]

He noted that the ray stings had been found five or six days' journey from the sea, which seemed to demonstrate that they had a definite use.

As Gerald got more and more knowledgeable about the keris and as his collection grew, ultimately to 400, he began to realise how he could remedy the lack of a book on the subject: he would have to write one himself! He had certainly had experience in getting articles published and, whether he had the initial idea himself or was encouraged by others to undertake the enterprise, he was certainly given help from a variety of friends and colleagues, including Chasen and Collings, Dr. A.N.J. Thomassen, A Thuessink Van Der Hoop, Secretary of the Royal Batavia Society and Curator of the Batavia Museum, Dr. P.V. van Stein Callenfels (1883-1938), also of the Batavia Museum, and Cyril Blair Cooper. Gerald also had a lot of help from the native Malays and it is characteristic of him that he acknowledges them first in the Foreword to his book. He had shown a copy of the draft to van der Hoop, who was most encouraging: "Publish at once. We do not know

---

12. Op. cit., 11.

half of what you have written, and this knowledge is dying out"
he told Gerald.[13]

⚜

Gerald's life began to change in 1935. First, he heard that his
father had died in August of that year and had left him a legacy of
getting on for £3000. This was one of the things that started him
thinking about retirement.

It seems as if the job allowed Gerald to take a long leave every
four years to visit England. He started the job in 1923 and, as we
have seen, he took leave in 1927 and again in 1932. Bracelin takes up
the story: "In 1936 he was due for leave. It was discovered that if he
came back from that, he would only have eighteen months left to
serve, and it was therefore decided that he should retire at the
same time as he went on leave, losing none of his pension rights."[14]
I am not sure precisely what the regulations were, but a piece about
him in a local paper of the time states: "Although Mr. G.B. Gardner
is past the age at which Europeans usually retire from this country,
his departure a few weeks ago means that a very real loss has been
suffered by those branches of local scholarship which are concerned with Malay history, traditions and customs."[15]

He would really have liked to have remained in Malaya, but
Donna wanted to go back to England. Indeed, she insisted on it.
The climate had never really suited her and she had an ominous
feeling that "something might happen in Malaya". The Japanese
invasion a few years later showed that this foreboding was justified. So Gerald gave in to Donna's wishes even though he had
doubts about whether he could cope with the English weather.

On 29th January 1936, Gerald Gardner retired from his post
with the Johore Civil Service. He was 51 (the same age, incidentally, as I was when I retired from my job in local government to
become a full-time writer and researcher into the life of Gerald
Gardner!).

---

13. Bracelin, 109.
14. Bracelin, 142.
15. *The Sunday Times*, 17 May 1936.

The setting of a retirement date provided the impetus necessary to complete his book and arrange for its publication. But how to find a publisher? Even in Malaya, the book would have limited appeal, so he decided to pay the costs of production himself.

Gerald had always had difficulty in writing in a form suitable for publication, primarily a problem in organisation of material and in spelling, a skill which he never did master fully. Perhaps this was the result of his lack of formal schooling coupled with his mercurial personality. Certainly he continued to mis-spell even common words throughout his life. It has been suggested by some that he may have been dyslexic. Whilst I make no claims to be an expert on the condition, it does not seem to me that Gerald displayed any of the characteristic features of dyslexia: it's just that he couldn't spell! More precisely, he tended to spell words phonetically, as if the aural sense was stronger than the visual in his mind.

The idea that Gerald might have been dyslexic seems to have originated in a statement by Aidan Kelly that he was "marginally dyslexic".[16] However, he goes on to say: "That is, despite his intelligence, which I do not propose to underestimate, and his avid reading and collecting of books, he could not spell or punctuate well enough to meet even minimal standards for being published ..."[17] Kelly has more recently[18] stated that a better description would have been "marginally illiterate", though more open to misinterpretation.

Whatever the reason, Gerald couldn't spell, and therefore needed the services of an editor to get his manuscripts into shape for publication. Betty Lumsden Milne would appear to have been an ideal person to help Gerald in this respect. There is more than a hint in the review of the book in the Straits Times that she did a considerable amount of editing, a function which had to be fulfilled for each of Gerald's four future books:

> ... the layman is aided by the arrangement of Mr. Gardner's book, which is most satisfactory; what might easily have

---

16. Aidan A. Kelly, *Crafting the Art of Magic: Book I: A History of Modern Witchcraft 1939-1964* (Llewellyn Publications, 1991), xv.
17. Ibid.
18. Gardnerians_all message board, 30 April 2007.

been a mass of indigestible material is set out clearly and attractively and in proper sequence. For this result full credit is due to the editress, Mrs. Lumsden Milne, and to the publishers.[19]

The reviewer may well have had "inside knowledge"!

Betty may have been related to William Milne, who was instrumental in setting up what became the Malaya Publishing House. It was certainly that organisation that published her first book, *Malayan Scouts' Song Book*, in 1935.

It would certainly appear that she had a close hand, not just in editing Gerald's book but in publishing it as well. The book was published by the Progressive Publishing Company of 150 Killiney Road, Singapore. Whilst there was a Progressive Publishing Company operating in London in the 1880s issuing socialist, secularist and freethinking titles, and perhaps two American publishing houses of that name producing books in the early 20th Century, there is no evidence that they had any connection with the company that published Gerald's book. Indeed, I can find no record of any other book published by the Progressive Publishing Company of Singapore, and it looks very much as if it was an entity established solely for the publication of *Keris and Other Malay Weapons*. It seems as if some of the early complimentary copies of the book were sent out on behalf of the author from A.L. Milne, Milne and Company, 150 Killiney Road, Singapore, who is likely to be a relative of Betty's, possibly her husband.

The book was published in two editions. The first was a Limited Edition of 150 copies, numbered and signed by the author, which appeared in March 1936. Now, this is rather strange, in that Gerald was on route between Singapore and London during the whole of March. Yet, I have seen a copy of the Limited Edition which is certainly signed by Gerald. I think the most likely explanation is that the unbound copies were signed before Gerald departed, the copies being left with Milne and Company, who arranged to get them bound.

The book contains a large number of illustrations, including photographs of some 350 items and an almost equal number of

---

19. *The Straits Times*, 11 May 1936.

drawings. This is probably the reason why the text, of slightly under 24,000 words, has been set double-spaced, in order to accommodate the 57 pages of illustrations in a book of 138 pages overall. This means that the font size is rather small and gives a slightly amateurish feel to the whole production, but perhaps that is what was to be expected of a book of its time and place.

The price was set at $2, or $10 for the Limited Edition. The equivalent prices in England were 6s 6d and £1 4s od.

I think the idea of the Limited Edition was in the main so that Gerald could present copies to various dignitaries, libraries and academics in the field.

It was mid-April 1936, by which time Gerald was back in England, when complimentary copies of the book were sent out, at his instructions, to various people. Some were to dignitaries to whom he obviously felt that it was the "right thing" to send copies. These included His Excellency the Governor of Singapore and the Sultans of Johore and Perak. Some of the main museums of the world also received copies, including the Nederlansch Museum, the American Museum of Natural History, the Metropolitan Museum of Art, the Museum of Fine Arts, Boston, Mass., the Royal Ontario Museum of Archaeology and the University Museum of Archaeology, Cambridge.

Those who had helped him and encouraged his research also received a copy. These included Frederick Chasen and Dennis Collings at the Raffles Museum. Chasen was the first to reply, on the day that he received it. Gerald had given an accommodation address in London (c/o Midland Bank, Pall Mall), so Chasen replied there. He wrote: "It is a wonderful effort and you must be proud of it. Such a book was badly needed".[20] He proceeded to order four copies for the Museum and Library.

He also had some disappointing news for Gerald, who had decided once his retirement had been confirmed that 400 keris were too many to take to an as yet unknown destination in England and so he enquired as to whether the Museum would acquire most of them from him. Chasen was keen on this idea and asked for extra money to purchase them. He had been hoping that

---

20. Letter F .N. Chasen to G B Gardner, 24 April 1936.

money would be made available to buy a large proportion of Gerald's collection of Malay weapons. However, he continues:

> *To my surprise my application for a special vote to purchase your collection, now in my hands, was turned down and I was told by Govt. that I had to find the money by reducing expenses elsewhere! This is a tall order even for such a notorious juggler in finance as myself and had caused me to think a lot. The only way out seems to be to go easy for the next few months, saving all I can, and then, when the end of the year is in sight, examine the Departmental budget with a view to sending you a cheque. I hope this course will prove agreeable to you. I am sorry to keep you waiting but you know that I have little money to play with. I did not for one moment anticipate that my application for a special vote would be unsuccessful. A sign of the times I suppose.*[21]

Dennis Collings did not reply until June, when he gave an update on the acquisition of the collection:

> *The finance people will not let Chasen buy your collection yet, but he is determined to do so eventually, but till then I'm afraid you will have to wait for the cheque. The committee apparently agreed + then somebody made a fuss + put a stop to it. In the meanwhile I have arranged it all upstairs, each case being labelled "G.B. Gardner Loan Collection.*[22]

He also liked the book: "Your book is a great success, + an excellent piece of work. I have heard no adverse criticisms, and I think is selling fairly well among the people I know."[23]

Review copies were also sent out to newspapers, including the *Malaya Tribune*, the *Times of Malaya* and the *Straits Times*. Reviews were generally very complimentary, praising the book as a major contribution to the literature on what was still a relatively little known national native weapon. *The Malaya Tribune* writes:

---

21. Ibid.
22. Letter H. D. Collings to G. B. Gardner, 6 June 1936.
23. Ibid.

Mr. G.B. Gardner ... has rendered valuable service by publishing this treatise on the Malay weapon. He has made a life-long study of the matter, and his own collection of keris is almost unique. Here in this book you will find all the necessary information to give you a real knowledge of the subject.[24]

The *Straits Times* refers to the book as:

... quite the most comprehensive thing of its kind ever done in the English language. One is indeed thankful that in our time, while there are still Malays living who remember when the kris was not an anachronism, this famous weapon should have found so devoted and authoritative a historian. [25]

In a longer review, the *Straits Times* states:

Mr. Gardner ... is perhaps the only European in this country who has made a specialised study of Malay weapons. Other men have included the kris and its peculiar etiquette in their study of Malay life, and have made fine collections of these weapons, but none has concentrated on this subject quite as intensively or as comprehensively as Mr. Gardner has done. The kris has always fascinated him; one might almost say that it has been a hobby carried to the point where it becomes an obsession; and his collection of 400 of these weapons is a very fine one, including as it does almost every type of kris known in this country. But there have been many enthusiastic students of the kris before. Where Mr. Gardner's book is unique, so far as we know, is in the ramifications of his hobby, so that he has been able to give a complete picture of the Malay as a fighting man.[26]

The reviewer in *The Sunday Times* gives a more personal portrait of Gerald:

... independent of conventional social distractions, he loved exploring the historic Johore River, re-discovering its

---

24. *The Malaya Tribune*, 28 April 1936.
25. *The Straits Times*, 6 May 1936.
26. *The Straits Times*, 11 May 1936.

forgotten forts, and illuminating the dark places of Johore history by means of the tales and legends preserved by the Malays around him. There was no more charming host and conversationalist than Mr. Gardner when he had a visitor who really shared his interests. A friend of mine who once spent three hours talking with him and looking at his collection of Malay weapons tells me that he looks back upon that experience as having been worth years of interminable gossip of the pahit-party variety.[27]

The only real criticism is with the presentation rather than the contents, when *The Museums Journal* comments: "As regards illustration, quality has been subordinated to quantity, and in most cases the fascinating detail that characterizes so many Malay weapons is entirely lost".[28]

Gerald put the marketing of the book in the hands of the long-established booksellers, Bernard Quaritch, Ltd., of 11 Grafton Street, New Bond Street, London, who agreed to put it in their regular catalogue and also sent out a card announcing the book to a large number of people. He may have chosen the firm because he was familiar with the work of Dr H.G. Quaritch Wales, who had discovered ancient Indian cities on the Malay peninsula, and who later became a member of the board of Quaritch's.

Later that year, they indicated that they expected to sell all the copies that they had received on sale or return. It is clear that nevertheless the sales were not great, though they agreed with Gerald that: "... sales, up to the present, have not been disappointing as you say, especially when it is remembered that this type of book appeals only to a very small number of people. The Summer season interfered with the sale of the book and we have not yet had time to include it in one of our catalogues."[29]

---

27. *The Sunday Times*, 17 May 1936.
28. *The Museums Journal*, Vol. 36, 320.
29. Letter Bernard Quaritch Ltd. to G. B. Gardner, 20 October 1936.

PART II

Potent Seed

CHAPTER ELEVEN

The Year of Three Kings

1936 was not just a year of change for Gerald, but for London and, indeed, the British Empire. King George V died on 20th January 1936. He was succeeded by his son, David, who became Edward VIII, only to abdicate on 11th December of that year in favour of his brother, Bertie, who became King George VI.

It was to such a city that Donna Gardner arrived, alone, in early March. She probably stayed initially with her sister, Queenie, but she needed to find some sort of accommodation by the time Gerald arrived in England later the following month.

He had planned to leave the ship at Port Said, to make his way at a leisurely pace on to England after working on an archaeological dig in what was then referred to as Palestine (now Israel). He had probably met James Starkey (1895-1938) and his assistants Olga Tufnell (1905-1985) and Lankester Harding at the 1932 Conference in London, and he would therefore certainly have heard of the work they were doing under the auspices of the Wellcome Archaeological Research Expedition.

This was the excavation of Tell el-Duweir, which they believed to be the site of the ancient city of Lachish, which is approximately 25 miles south-west of Jerusalem in the Shephelah Hills about 20 miles inland from the coast. Petrie had provisionally identified Tell el-Hesy, some 10 miles to the west, as being Lachish, during his excavations there in the 1890s, but it is now acknowledged that Starkey was right in his identification of Tell el-Duweir. He and his assistants had started work in 1932 and, by 1936, were uncovering some remarkable things. Lachish is now generally recognised to have been one of the most important cities in the old kingdom of Judah, and that it was occupied from ancient times until the 6th Century BCE, when it was destroyed by the Babylonians.

The site of the city was a hill in the middle of a wide valley. Gerald noticed particularly a scarped defence around the hill, with chalk beaten in. He could still see where attackers had piled wood against the limestone walls and set fire to it, causing the stone to change to a powder. He speculated that during the process most of the inhabitants would have suffocated.

Gerald was quickly put to work excavating a pit and then the gate fortifications. It was here the previous year that the so-called "Lachish Letters" were discovered: clay tablets ("ostraca") which had ancient Hebrew writing on them in ink, some of the earliest known.

Another discovery that particularly interested him was that of a temple to both Yahweh and Astaroth: the god and goddess. He also noted that clay figurines of the goddess Astaroth had been found throughout Palestine, showing that she had been revered for a considerable period.

Gerald was probably at Lachish for not more than a month. It was the end of the 1935-1936 season and, before leaving, he arranged to help with the excavations for the next season. He then made his way overland to London via Amman, in what was then Transjordan, the ancient city of Petra, back to Jerusalem for the Easter ceremonies in the middle of April. He then visited Ismir and Istanbul in Turkey, Athens, Belgrade, Budapest, Vienna, Nuremburg and then finally to England.

Meanwhile, Donna had found a flat right in the centre of London, at 26 Charing Cross Road, a street known then, as it is now, for second-hand bookshops. Flat 10 was in a block which extended from Charing Cross Road through to St. Martin's Lane and which was a mixture of commercial property and living accommodation. It was not ideal but at least it was somewhere to stay and fairly central. If Gerald wasn't happy with it when he arrived, he could always start to look for somewhere better.

No sooner had Gerald arrived than he was off again, this time to Denmark. He had already made contact with others interested in historic weapons, including Holger Jacobsen, a leading light of the Vaabenhistorisk Selskab, the Danish Arms and Armour Society. Jacobsen was particularly interested in knives and in Gerald's work on the keris.

So Gerald had been invited to attend a meeting at the old Royal Castle in Copenhagen, Christianborg, on 25th April 1936 at which he spoke. He enjoyed himself tremendously with the other enthusiasts, including Jacobsen. Gerald gave talks on the Malay keris and the Scottish dirk. There were also sessions where the weapons were demonstrated. He remembers a flintlock being fired 175 times in succession perfectly until everyone got tired of it![1] I enquired of Peter Rasmussen of the Vaabenhistorisk Selskab about this and he said that the firing of the flintlock was just the sort of thing that Jacobsen would get involved with.[2]

Gerald and Jacobsen were obviously interested in the same sort of weapon and aspects thereof, and clearly helped each other with their researches. I am sure that Gerald provided him with information about the Javan keris that Jacobsen used in an article the following year.[3] And in 1938, in the same journal, Jacobsen published a Danish translation of Gerald's article on the Cypriot dagger.[4]

Commenting on this visit, Bracelin says that Gerald found that his book on the keris was used in the museums of Denmark. I think this is unlikely, as the book had only been published the previous month. It may have been that Jacobsen had spread the word and ordered some advance copies, but I think it more likely that that comment actually refers to Gerald's next visit to Denmark, in 1951.

⚜

1. Bracelin, 152.
2. Email Peter Rasmussen to the author.
3. Holger Jacobsen, *Den Javanske Kriss*, (Våben Historisk Selskabs Årbøger I, 1937), 83-103
4. George [sic] B. Gardner, Problemet: Det Cypriske Svaerdfaeste, (Våben Historisk Selskabs Årbøger II, 1938), 145-151.

There is a poignant passage in Gerald's novel, *A Goddess Arrives*, which gives a revealing insight into his state of mind as he came back to settle in England:

*It was as though some experience of which he had no recol-lection had left its indelible stamp upon him of an antithe-sis of life as he now knew it, heightening his instinctive delight in natural beauty. Such a feeling might come to one who, having left his native land in early youth, had kept vivid in his mind its picture, always with the intention to return and who, returning in old age, finds that memory has retained some quality of the place which no longer exists in the original. Through the passage of time he has become alien to his place of nativity. He has voluntarily abandoned the situation of his life's activity and a curious state of suspension follows in which he can establish no real contact with his immediate past or his remote past. He is an alien in time and cannot rid himself of a loneliness of spirit transcending mere description in words.*5

It is clear that the English climate did not suit Gerald, as he tells in *A Goddess Arrives*, where, referring to the hero, Denvers (recently retired from work in Malaya and clearly based on him-self), he says: "Long years in Malaya had thinned his blood and made of these English winters a torment."6 Gerald caught "the usual cold" which "hung about him".7

He registered with a doctor, Edward A Gregg, of 14 Oakley Square, London, N.W.1., who was a prominent local dignitary, being an Alderman and former Mayor of the Borough of St. Pan-cras in 1925-26. Amongst his clients was the poet, Dylan Thomas. On visiting him, Gerald received the following advice: ""I could suggest something that would cure you, but I expect you will refuse to do it". It was a visit to a nudist club. "I'll die there", said Gardner, but the doctor was adamant that it would help him."

Now, this is rather strange, since four years earlier, during his trip in 1932, Gerald had enquired about the existence of nudist

---

5. G. B. Gardner, *A Goddess Arrives*, (Arthur H Stockwell: 1939), 111.
6. Op. cit., 10.
7. Bracelin, 151.

clubs as he had previously realised the benefit of nude sun-bathing in helping to cure his synovitis. So why Gerald should have thought visiting a naturist club would kill him I really don't know. Perhaps he was having second thoughts in an England which was still cold compared with Malaya. And it is certainly true that the first naturist club he visited was an indoor one – the Lotus League. Michael Farrar, Archivist for British Naturism, writes that it:

> ... operated from early 1934 to 1939 at Cardrew House, 92 Friern Park, Finchley, London N12. ... there was a garden, entirely screened from public view, open to members from 9am to sundown every day except Wednesday. This included a lawn, 50ft by 100ft for sunbathing and a hard court for games such as badminton, deck-quoits etc. All meals were served outside when weather permitted. Inside the house, which had 20 rooms, there were three large public rooms for the use of members including a beautiful dance floor with parquet floor, a pleasant lounge with coal fire in cold weather and a games room with ping-pong table. ... There were physical culture classes in the dance room, and an ultra-violet lamp.[8]

This was a straightforward journey on the Northern Line for Gerald, an easy walk from Woodside Park station. It certainly cured his cold, and he made many friends there. However, the Lotus League was not the only naturist club within easy reach of London. Indeed, it was somewhat unusual being largely indoors. After a working life in the tropics, Gerald was used to being out-doors and, as it was the height of summer when he joined, he took note when the other members told him of other naturist clubs centred around Bricket Wood, in Hertfordshire, particularly Fouracres, which they thought would suit him.

The origins of Fouracres lay in the earliest naturist site in Eng-land, in Essex, known as "The Camp", set up in the early 1920s, but which had to close because of neighbouring housing devel-opment. Members began searching for an alternative location at

---

8. Letter Michael Farrar to the author, 22 June 1999.

a price they could afford, but it was to be 18 months before they found a site near the village of Bricket Wood. Members of the group looked at the land in January 1927 and bought it with financial assistance from a supporter, Major F.R. Griggs of Derbyshire. The club opened on 16th May 1927. It still exists and is the longest established nudist club in England.

Fouracres developed a very distinctive ethos, as Cottie Burland confirms:

> The little group at Four Acres flourished in their wild patch of woodland. They happened to be a companionable crowd of people who did not want to tame the woods and fields. They camped, built a very pleasant club house with a lawn in front of it, and talked philosophy a great deal. The membership was never up to fifty, but there was a quality about the club which made it a centre of opinion. It did not advertise its ideas, but its members were people who were nudists by conviction. Their conversation spread the idea widely.9

As a result of an attack on nude sunbathers on private land at the Welsh Harp reservoir in North-west London in 1930, there was an impetus for wanting the protection that the naturist clubs offered, as Reginald ('Rex') Wellbye, writing as 'Ancton Tuqvor', recounts. Wellbye (1873-1963) had been a leading light from the very early days of naturism. He was a pioneering sociologist and wrote a series of touring, or 'Roadfaring' guides, mainly for cyclists.

> Among them ... was a West End doctor. He looked round for something more secure, discovered Fouracres, joined with his charming wife, and soon brought in doctor friends and their wives, until before long the Club had no less than 11 members of the medical profession, including two women.10

It was rather unusual at that time for a doctor to be recommending naturism and it seems possible that Gerald's doctor was

9. Cottie Burland, "Time Will Tell," (manuscript in archives of British Naturism, 1963), 2.
10. 'Ancton Tuqvor' (Rex Wellbye), "The Story of Nudism IV: How it Spread", (Verity, March 1950), 32.

a naturist himself. If so, he may have been one of the 11 medical practitioners who were members of Fouracres. It would also make it more likely that Gerald, as well as being a member of the Lotus League, would have joined Fouracres as well. The distinctive Fouracres philosophy could well be the origin of Bracelin's statement about Gerald:

> *... he felt that he met people in this way whom he did not know existed in England; interesting people, prepared to talk, argue and discuss. Many had a faint occult interest; fortune-telling, palmistry, astrology, vague spiritualism. He felt healthier, too, and liked the lack of class-consciousness which naturism brought.*[11]

Activities included "periodical gatherings for folk-dancing, communal suppers and discussions". A member's impression is of: "Sitting round the lawn in groups, many are the interesting discussions that can arise from quite a casual remark, and sometimes startling is the contrast of opinions revealed, which open up new fields for the thoughtful."[12] The emphasis certainly seemed to be on the intellectual side, as Iseult Weston remembers that the swimming pool was really just a muddy hole in the ground and that, unless you were first in, it got very muddy. To climb out you had to use a rope ladder.

The club stayed open all year, as opposed to some which closed in the winter. An advertisement for the club, dating from this period, states:

> *It seeks to be the gathering place of people possessing, besides sociable and genial dispositions, moderately culti- vated minds, or at any rate serious interests, people of some character and independence of outlook, who will converse freely and interestingly, and work and play together the more congenially by reason of the basis of their association being wider than nudism alone.*[13]

11. Bracelin, 155-156.
12. "The Fouracres Club: A Feminine Member's Impression", *Sun Bathing Review*, (August/September 1936), 73.
13. Advertisement in *Sun Bathing Review*, (Spring 1936), 25.

Another way of looking at this is that the club had something of a reputation for exclusivity, as a report in 1937 concludes:

That spirit of communal activity and friendliness is the most delightful feature of Fouracres; natural as it was in the early days of the club as a private group of friends, its persistence into our larger growth is mainly due to the fact that the club is not run for profit; membership is limited and prospective members are welcome, not for their subscriptions, but for their ability to fit into the Fouracres atmosphere. Yet in spite of, or perhaps because of, our reputation for "exclusiveness", applications continue to arrive, and we are glad to make room for newcomers.[14]

The club's circular, sent to enquirers, used to state that "an atmosphere of intimacy has been maintained ... by keeping membership limited and selective" and a report in 1939 defined the character of the Club as being "an intimate atmosphere among a company of interesting people". There were suggestions that the selection basis for members was largely class-based, a criticism which was vigorously denied by the Committee.

Naturist clubs, particularly in the late 1930s, tended to be rather secretive: it wasn't considered acceptable to be a naturist among general society. And now, seventy years later, we really don't know who was a member of Fouracres. Certainly no membership books have survived. But we have a few clues and we can make a guess as to whom Gerald was friends with and talked philosophy with from the time he joined the Club, in summer 1936 to the time he moved away from London in summer 1938, a period of two years.

One clue is the membership list of Fouracres' post-war successor, Five Acres, which does survive, plus the people from other fields that Gerald was friendly with who also happened to be naturists.

One individual with whom Gerald was undoubtedly acquainted and who later became a friend was James Laver (1899-1975). He was born in Liverpool and, in 1922, was employed in the department of engraving, illustration, design and painting at the Victoria and Albert Museum, of which he became Keeper of

---

14. "The Fouracres Club" in *Sun Bathing Review*, (Spring 1937), 34-35.

Prints and Drawings in 1938. In order to date pictures accurately, he had to become expert in costume, and it is for this that he became best known, developing his Laws on the Timetable of Style, where fashions are considered indecent and shameless before their time, dowdy and hideous after their time, eventually becoming charming and beautiful many years later.

Laver was very likely a naturist by at least the early 1930s, for his novel *Nymph Errant*[15] contains a chapter set in a naturist establishment in Germany. He also wrote articles for naturist magazines.

He was interested in magic, and he knew and visited the occultist, Aleister Crowley. In 1942, his book on Nostradamus and his prophecies was published.[16]

Laver wrote the Foreword to *Gerald Gardner Witch*. In it, he suggests that he first met Gerald in his office in the Victoria and Albert Museum. Perhaps it was just not done to admit that they met in a naturist club! He wrote of Gerald:

> *... he was one of the sanest men I ever met. It is true that he talked of strange things but he did so in a natural and humorous way that soon convinced me that I was in the presence of a man of a scientific and scholarly mind. ... But there was something else. It was impossible to meet Gerald Gardner without realising that he was a great human being. He radiated friendliness and understanding. In spite of the screaming headlines of the sensationalist press, he was quite plainly and obviously a good man.*[17]

Cottie Arthur Burland (1905-1983) was Curator of the Department of Ethnography at the British Museum. He was also a member of Fouracres. He wrote over 40 books, on anthropological and cultural themes, particularly on pre-Columbian America, including ancient Mexico, the Aztecs and Incas. He also wrote on Ancient Greece, Egypt and China. He was an acknowledged expert on Primitive Art. His books also reflect an interest in what

15. James Laver, *Nymph Errant*, (Heinemann, 1932).
16. James Laver, *Nostradamus, or The Future Foretold*, (Collins, 1942).
17. Bracelin, 6.

we might call pagan themes, with titles including *Echoes of Magic: a study of seasonal festivals throughout the ages; Beyond Science: a journey into the Supernatural; Myths of Life and Death; The Arts of the Alchemists; The Magical Arts: a short history* and *Secrets of the Occult.* He was a member of the Fellowship of Isis and helped Adam McLean to establish *The Hermetic Journal,* contributing articles to it.

One can imagine Cottie and Gerald having many discussions about matters of mutual interest. They became life-long friends. 'Dayonis' describes Cottie as being a nice man whom she liked a lot.

It is likely, but by no means certain, that Gerald met Harry 'Dion' Byngham during his time at Fouracres. If so, he would undoubtedly have had an influence on the development of Gerald's ideas. Byngham (1896-1990), a journalist from Catford in S.E. London, was a member of the London Healthy Life Society and the Eutrophia Society. He started writing articles advocating naturism as early as July 1921 when his article 'A Tirade' (against clothes) appeared in Edgar Saxon's magazine, *The Healthy Life.* This was followed in 1922 with 'Dithyrambos', on Greek mysticism and phallic worship.

Vitalism became a key life principle for Byngham. Henri Bergson (1859-1941), the French philosopher, was one of its chief exponents, and postulated that the vital force was pure energy and lay behind all organic evolution and creative action. Perhaps the greatest influence on Byngham, however, was the German philosopher, Nietzsche, who had also criticised modern civilisation and contrasted it with a life-affirming philosophy which he called 'Dionysianism', after the Greek god Dionysos, son of Zeus, who, with his followers, lived a life of savage wildness in the mountains of Macedonia. This was underlined by the work of Jane Harrison, who postulated that Dionysos was the Greek personification of Bergson's 'élan vital'. Byngham was inspired by the 'Dionysian Spirit' which he saw as being uninhibited and full of joy, energy and passion, attuning to the animal side of our nature. He wanted a new society in opposition to what he saw as repressive forces such as Christianity. He also started to call himself 'Dion' Byngham in honour of the Dionysian ideal.

If the two had met and had long discussions at Fouracres, then undoubtedly Gerald would have been enthused by Byngham's Dionysianism, with the incorporation of the feminine aspect of divinity; recognition of the 'life force' and its use of sexual energies; the nude seasonal rituals and the worship of the sun.

⁂

Having attended the first International Congress of Prehistoric and Protohistoric Sciences that was held in London in 1932 during his period of leave in England, Gerald was keen to attend the second such congress, which was to be held in Oslo from 3rd to 9th August 1936 (not 1938 as Bracelin suggests).

Bracelin says that Gerald: "...read his authoritative paper on the prehistory of the kris before one of the world's most distinguished audiences."[18] I have examined the programme for the Second International Congress, and I have to say that there is no mention of Gerald or his paper in that programme. There was great emphasis laid on lecturers keeping to time, so I don't think Gerald's paper would have been "slotted in" at the last moment. So it is likely that Gerald's claim to have read his paper was exaggerated to say the least. He did, however, renew his acquaintance with Alexander Keiller and met such luminaries as Jacquetta Hawkes and Abbé Breuil.

Geoffrey Swinford Laird-Clowes (pronounced 'clues') (1883-1937) of the Science Museum in South Kensington, London, had somehow got to hear about the model of the ancient Malay trading ship which Gerald had made, probably via contact with Chasen and Collings at the Raffles Museum in Singapore. Laird-Clowes was an expert on the history of sailing ships and had over the years accumulated a collection of models, which were on display in the Museum.[19] He wanted a model of the ancient Malay ship to display.

---

18. Bracelin, 156.
19. G. S. Laird-Clowes, *Sailing Ships: Their History and Development as Illustrated by the Collection of Ship-models in the Science Museum*, (HMSO, 1932).

When he learned that Gerald was living in London, he contacted him and arranged for a room to be made available for Gerald to make a copy of the model which was in the Raffles Museum. All materials would be provided. Gerald spent quite a lot of time there and completed the model by the end of the year. The model is still in the possession of the Science Museum, but is currently not on display. The description given by the museum is as follows:

> This model has been copied from the bas-reliefs of ancient ships which remain on the walls of the ruins of Borobudur in Java.
>
> The vessel was of considerable size but had to rely for its stability on elaborately constructed outriggers, one on each side, and it is interesting to note that after more than a thousand years double-outriggers, some of them of very similar construction, are still in common use over an area which extends from Java northward through Celebes to the Philippine Islands.
>
> The ship was fitted with two bipod masts each hoisting a square sail, which was used as a fore-and-aft sail, as is still common in Malaya, while a bowsprit supports a sprit-sail, most unexpectedly European in appearance and almost exactly like the "artemon" of the Roman sailing-ships. She was also propelled by means of long oars worked inside the outriggers.
>
> The hull probably consisted of light upper-works built up on a large hollowed-out log, but on this point the original sculpture is not very explicit.
>
> The curve of the mast-heads towards the stern is still typical of many of the vessels of the Malays.[20]

---

20. Science Museum inventory no. 1936-654.

Laird-Clowes died in July the following year, but Gerald continued to work on other projects until he moved out of London in 1938.

Towards the end of 1936, Gerald was beginning to find the flat at 26 Charing Cross Road somewhat cramped, as Donna had suspected, and he began to look for more spacious accommodation.

He found it in 23a Buckingham Palace Mansions, on the opposite side of Buckingham Palace Road to Victoria Station. This was a large block of flats, five storeys in height, built in 1888 by the aptly named Middle Class Dwelling Company. It had an elaborate facade and, from some evidence, elaborately panelled interiors. One of the residents in the 1920s had been Sir Arthur Conan Doyle.

To mark the occasion, Gerald gave Donna a copy of J.B. Priestley's *They Walk in the City*[21] subtitled 'The Lovers in the Stone Forest', which had just been published, and inscribed it "Donna with love from Gerald to celebrate the new flat".

The electoral register and the telephone directory, however, only give Donna as living there: Gerald clearly did not want his name included. Now, he was a habitual trickster – confusing and giving people the wrong impression was second nature to him. However, I think the most likely reason for his reticence was that he had been taking bribes during his time as a Customs Officer in exchange for allowing the smuggling of opium and he didn't want to risk the authorities finding out where he was now living.

---

21. J B Priestley, *They Walk in the City*, (William Heinemann 1936).

CHAPTER TWELVE

The Arrival of a Goddess

As winter drew on, Gerald began to dread the cold weather and the effect which it would have on his health. After all, he had not been in England over winter since he was a very young boy. He therefore began to prepare for a pattern of wintering abroad that continued, apart from the war years, for the rest of his life.

For the winter of 1936/37, he planned to go to Cyprus. The reason for choosing that island dated back some time. For several years Gerald had had a succession of dreams which gradually built up into what seemed to him a very real life. It was set in ancient times, in a hot country, and Gerald was in charge of having a wall built to repel invaders. As well as being the designer of the wall and supervising its construction, he was also responsible for organising the melting down of bronze cooking utensils for making weapons.

He probably suspected that these were memories of a previous lifetime, though not as coherent or detailed as those brought through by Joan Grant, whose memories of a life in ancient Egypt were to be published as the novel, *Winged Pharaoh*.[1] These dreams did not engage Gerald's attention unduly. He felt that

---

1. Joan Grant, *Winged Pharaoh*, (Arthur Barker, October 1937).

they might be a real place, and that it might be somewhere in the Middle East, as for some years he had had the strange feeling of "belonging" to that area.

The extent to which Gerald's novel, *A Goddess Arrives*,[2] is an account of a former life which he remembered is uncertain. We have, for example, the unequivocal statement in *Witchcraft Today*: "… I must say that, though I believe in reincarnation, as most people do who have lived in the East, I do not remember any past lives, albeit I have had curious experiences. I only wish I did."[3] Yet, six years later, Bracelin certainly implies memory of a previous lifetime.[4] Probably the truth of the matter is that Gerald did have a series of dreams but they were never so clear or detailed that he could be sure that they were memories of a previous lifetime: he just suspected that they were, and was frustrated that he could not bring them into focus.

I think Gerald somehow recognised that the place that he was having dreams about was probably Cyprus. Certainly it was worth a visit, and, as he needed to go to a Mediterranean climate over the winter anyway, Cyprus it was.

His interest in, and knowledge of, ancient weapons provided a focus for the trip. He may have been put on the track of Cypriot weapons at the gathering in Denmark in April 1936. It may have dated further back, to the 1932 conference where he heard the talk given by Dr. Porphyrios Dikaios on early Bronze Age cults in Cyprus.

When Gerald arrived in Cyprus, probably in early 1937, he went straight to the Museum in Nicosia, by which time Dikaios was Curator. He set Gerald a challenge. He knew that Gerald was interested in weapons and wanted to know how the ancient Cypriots hafted their swords. He gave him a sword to look at: it had a very thick mid-rib and a very short tang with a hook on the end. Gerald suggested various possibilities, such as the use of cement, or splitting, carving somewhere for the tang and binding ferrules. But there had been no trace of either cement or ferrules.

2. G. B. Gardner, *A Goddess Arrives*, (Arthur Stockwell, 1939).
3. Gardner, (1954), 18.
4. Bracelin, 153.

Gerald decided to allow his intuition into play. He said that "suddenly and extraordinarily my hands felt as if they knew". He asked for an old blade and the sort of tools which the original makers would have used.5

> *My hands told me what to do. Next day I brought the sword back, hafted. They tried it many ways and found it good, and then they said: 'Take it out, and show us how you did it'. And it would not come. We had to get an axe and split it to get the haft off.*
>
> *I had bored a hole at an angle for the tang and another across it. Putting the chisel in this I cut a hole to take the hook. A saw cut took the sharpened shoulders and kept it from twisting. A wedge of wet wood locked the tang in position, and a plug of hard wood took the end of the hook, and stopped the blade from creeping up the hilt when thrust against bone. Now to do this I had to make the hilt a curious shape, and they said: 'Why did you make it that shape?' I said I had felt that it must be so. 'But you are right. We have found clay models, and they are just like that. The blade is for thrusting, not for cutting, and it makes it slip between the ribs'.6*

Gerald subsequently wrote an article entitled "The Problem of the Cypriot Bronze Age Dagger Hilt". As far as I know, this was never published in English, but he did send copies to the Journal of the Société Prehistorique Française, who translated it and published it in their Bulletin No. 12 in 1937 as "Le Problème de la Garde de l'Epée Cypriote de l'Age du Bronze". He also sent it to Holger Jacobsen, who translated it and published it in the Transactions of the Vaabenhistorisk Selskab in 1938 under the title of "Problemet: Det cypriske svaerdfaeste".

Bracelin suggests that Gerald's first trip to Cyprus was in 1938, whereas it is clear from the 1937 publication date of the French article, it must have been earlier, and I would suggest that this points clearly to it having been in the winter of 1936/37.

5. Bracelin, 153-154.
6. Ibid.

I suspect that it may have been the experience with hafting the blade that made Gerald think that he might have been a sword-maker in Cyprus in a previous lifetime. He would then probably have made the connection with the dreams he had been having, and would have come to the conclusion that they were indeed related to a previous lifetime in Cyprus.

⁂

Gerald probably spent most of the summer of 1937 at Fouracres, interspersed with periods of research at the British Museum. He did not renew his 1927 six-months Reader's Ticket, but I cannot believe for one moment that he could have lived in London so close to the Museum and be interested in all the things he was interested in without having a Reader's Ticket. I suspect that the answer lies in a false name, probably 'John Gardner', for the same reason that he kept his own name out of the street and telephone directories, though I understand that the records of readers at the British Museum are incomplete.[7]

In September 1937, Gerald applied for, and subsequently received, a diploma bestowing on him the degree of Doctor of Philosophy. Thereafter, he is referred to as "Dr. Gardner".

However, this is not what it appears at first glance. The institution from which he obtained this diploma was known as the "Meta Collegiate Extension of the National Electronic Institute", an organisation that is not recognised by most academic institutions. Indeed, it is specifically listed by a variety of well-respected bodies, including the University of Alaska, as being an organisation which supplies invalid academic degrees, and it is specifically not accredited by the Maine Government, the State of Michigan and, most significantly, the U.S. Department of Education.

I have not been able to find out more about this organisation. Certainly it doesn't have a website, which seems to confirm that it no longer exists. It is described as being "Incorporated in Nevada" and I understand that in many cases this is because that state offers corporate directors and shareholders a lot of protection against personal liability.

---

7. I am indebted to Gareth Medway for this information.

The full wording of the diploma reads:

"Let There Be Light". Meta Collegiate Extension of the National Electronic Institute, Incorporated in Nevada. Nature. Science. Mind. This Certifies that G.B. Gardner, having meritoriously and honorably passed the requisite qualifications of this institute, is hereby entitled to this Doctor of Philosophy (For completion of course and published works) Diploma. Therefore, the undersigned confer upon him the degree of Doctor of Philosophy (Ph. D.). In Witness Thereof, we herewith affix our official signatures this 21st day of September, in the year A.D. 1937. Ernest J. Stevens, MSc, PhD, MAAD, President; J.F. Lynes, MA, Vice President, E.G. Hill, MD, Secretary, A.G. Pappas, MP.[8]

Gerald had never had any formal education: he never went to school or college. Indeed, he probably always felt as if he had been living in the shadow of his father's achievement of being "second in all England", and that he needed to rectify things somehow. I think that when he started to meet archaeologists and anthropologists at conferences where he was talking with them about his excavations at Johore Lama and his work on the keris, he began to feel as if he ought to have the formal qualifications that the others had. And after the genuine praise he received following the publication of *Keris and Other Malay Weapons* he felt he deserved such qualification and in particular a PhD (Doctor of Philosophy).

Ronald Hutton, Professor of History at the University of Bristol, is quite definite when he writes that *Keris and Other Malay Weapons*: "... would certainly not satisfy the requirements for a British doctorate of philosophy, either now or in the 1930s or 1940s. It is a catalogue of information rather than a thesis, badly written and with virtually no intellectual content. As a collection of data it certainly has value, but it would not earn a higher degree in this country."[9] However, he states that American standards for such degrees have always been lower such that an American MA is only the equivalent of a British BA:

8. This diploma is in the Toronto collection.
9. Letter from Ronald Hutton to the author, 24 May 2007.

Britons who have wanted the title of a Doctor of Philosophy to boost their standing, and have not been up to the British mark, have regularly obtained it from American colleges by submitting sample work and paying a fee; sometimes just the latter. In practice, only the lowest-ranking American institutions of higher education would do this, and the Meta-Collegiate one is certainly in this category. Hence, having obtained the degree, Gardner would have felt able to style himself a doctor, but he would never have been accepted as such by any British body of scholars.[10]

I suspect that, to start with, Gerald submitted the book to various universities after he returned to England in 1936, but his request for a PhD was politely declined: it just did not meet their criteria.

So Gerald turned to what he must have recognised as being a poor second-best. He had obviously read somewhere about the Meta Collegiate Extension of the National Electronic Institute. They probably advertised in likely magazines in England: degrees available in exchange for so many dollars. It was probably not quite as crude as that, as there is mention of both course work and his published work.

Gerald clearly felt that it was important to get some sort of qualification, however dubious, for it was only after he received his diploma that he started calling himself "Dr. Gardner". He certainly knew that it wasn't worth very much, since he was rather evasive, as John Yeowell writes:

When I asked Gardner about his doctorate he became visibly agitated. As I had no reason to doubt that it was genuine I persisted over several months, asking which university he had attended. At last he stormed out of the room when I asked him for what was to be the last time, muttering something about 'an American seat of learning' or words to that effect.[11]

---

10. Ibid.
11. Letter, John Yeowell to the author, 12 September 2002.

After he received his certificate through the post, Gerald felt at least in part that he could hold his head up amongst his fellow archaeologists. He had already arranged with Starkey to go back to Lachish to help with the continuing excavations. However, just before he was due to go, word came through that Starkey had been murdered on 10th January 1938, apparently by 'highwaymen' in the Hebron Hills on the track leading from Beit Jibrin to Hebron, while he was on his way from Lachish to Jerusalem to attend the inauguration of the Palestine Archaeological Museum (the Rockefeller Museum).

Without Starkey to direct them, the excavations seem to have been abandoned and the site looted. Later, excavations were resumed under Olga Tufnell and Lankester Harding, by which time Gerald had made other plans. He was clearly both shocked and disappointed with this news. But he needed to escape from the English winter quickly, so, on an impulse, he arranged to go back to Cyprus. This was on a slow orange-boat, which took a month to get there.

On the eve of his departure he had another extraordinary dream "about a man who found that he was not wanted at home: so he dived into the past, seemingly with ease - where he was wanted."[12] Whether this was in some way to do with his relation-ship with Donna I do not know, but I suspect that this dream was one of the series which Gerald wrote down and which formed the basis for his novel, *A Goddess Arrives*.

On the boat, the other passengers seemed intent on drinking and playing bridge, which didn't interest Gerald at all, so he made a decision at that time to write the novel based on his dreams. I think he probably guessed that he would find the landscape of those dreams when he reached Cyprus, and so it proved to be.

Gerald was keen to try and find the site of some of the locations which he remembered from his dreams sufficiently clearly to have reasonable hope that he would be able to identify them. He particularly wanted to locate a small round hill at the mouth of a small river.

---

12. Bracelin, 153.

He went to Famagusta and met a "wild-eyed semi-Mexican woman who said that she was English". Bracelin said: "He hired her to look for the dream-place which he had found the previous winter."[13] Why it should be necessary to hire someone to find somewhere that he had already found, I do not know. Perhaps he had forgotten where it was. Anyway, he was directed to a site on the southern coast of the Karpas or Karpasia peninsula, which forms the north-eastern extremity of the island. Here was a hill known locally as Stronglos or Stronglas, upon which had been built the Castle of Gastria by the Knights Templar in the 12th Century. It was at the mouth of a stream known as the Argaki tou Kastrou. It is a very good defensive position since the hill descends steeply on its eastern side into the sea. To the west is an area, now dried up, but which had been a marsh through which the stream, now silted up, winds to the sea. There is a sheltered harbour at the mouth of the river where ships would be hidden from view by the hill itself.

All this was familiar to Gerald, apart from the castle, presumably because it dated from an era later than that of his memories. He identified the area of former marsh and a ravine, between which he thought he had had to build a wall in a previous lifetime. He recognised the various older earthworks and stones as well as their orientation.[14]

Now that he knew for sure that his dreams were memories of real places, he became more convinced than ever that he had the pieces of a real lifetime lived in ancient Cyprus. And it had been lived in the landscape that he was now in.

On an impulse Gerald bought some land here with the intention of building a house on it, but the war intervened and nothing came of the project. Cecil Williamson gave a few more details but, as with all his stories about Gerald, his account needs to be taken with a very large pinch of salt:

> ... *he had made plans to set up his retirement home together with a GODDESS CULT TEMPLE. ... with a degree of diplomatic skill he actually managed to purchase a plot*

13. Bracelin, 156.
14. Bracelin, 154-155.

*of land complete with the Ruins of an ancient Greek Stone
Temple set on a spur of land jutting out into the sea. A wonderful site.*

*Gerald Gardner had a habit of being a little more than eco-
nomical with the truth. So it was some time before the local
Island authorities woke up to exactly what Gerald Gardner
had in mind to do to one of their Historic sites. When they
found out the truth, they promptly gave Gerald his march-
ing orders and he had to quit the Island at short notice, so
that he had to leave before he could dispose of the land and
Temple complex by sale.[15]*

Gerald could possibly have had in mind the erection of a
retirement home or even a temple to the Goddess, but the "ruins
of an ancient Greek stone temple" seem to be a figment of
Williamson's very fruitful imagination, as does the idea that Gerald was ever long enough on the island to do anything very much
about the land that he had acquired. Gerald's niece, Mimi, said
that he had a Crusader's castle that he started to rebuild, that he
tried to get the government to fund the rebuilding but that they
refused.[16] What the truth of it all is I am not sure, but I doubt
whether Gerald had time to do very much work on his land.

From the time he returned from Cyprus, probably in April
1938, until summer 1939, Gerald was busy writing his novel,
which was to be entitled *A Goddess Arrives*. It is a very competent
first work of fiction, in many ways better written than his next
book, *High Magic's Aid*, which was published ten years later. It is
certainly a long book and I think it almost certain that Gerald
paid the costs of publication, as it seems highly doubtful that a
publisher like Stockwell would otherwise have been interested in
a first novel running to over 380 pages.

A Goddess Arrives is important because its writing spans the
roughly two and a half years from Gerald's retirement in January
1936 to his claimed initiation into the witch cult in September
1939. It may therefore reveal something of his thinking during

---

15. Cecil Williamson, "The Wonderful World of Wicca," (unpublished article in the Boscastle Museum of Witchcraft archives).
16. Telephone conversation between Mimi Gardner and Morgan Davis, 12 July 2001.

that period. Certain themes, for example, may have been added in later revisions of the text as new ideas occurred to him. As an author myself, I appreciate how this is a natural and expected part of the process.

So, what were the raw materials from which Gerald fashioned the pages of his novel? First, as I have mentioned, there were memories, both vague and precise, of a previous lifetime in Cyprus. He probably used these as a starting point and read up all he could about the history of the island, using the resources of the British Museum.

In outline, the book tells of the Egyptian invasion of Cyprus in 1450 BCE and of the legend of Venus emerging from the sea. As Gerald says:

> *In Cyprus, Venus (Aphrodite) is a very real person. She was a Goddess, yes; but she commanded armies, and won great victories over hordes of black troops. She rose from the sea at Paphos, where her great Temple is, but she built castles and palaces, many of which still remain. She made laws, she buried treasure; the place where she was stoned to death and the site of her tomb are still shown, and of nights she is still sometimes seen at the head of her ghostly armies.*
>
> *She evidently was a real person, who made a great impression on popular fancy, and on whom legends were fastened, as with King Arthur.*
>
> *How it would be possible for a woman to be received as a Goddess, rising from the sea, I have endeavoured to show.*[17]

As Ronald Hutton states: "It is, in fact, a rationalist and sceptical work. The whole plot is based upon the premise that the cult of the goddess Aphrodite owes its origin to the appearance of a human woman who deludes the Cypriots into taking her for a divinity."[18]

The novel starts in the London of the 1930s. Robert Denvers, the hero, obviously based on Gerald, is concerned that his wife, Mina (short for Domina) is having an affair with his former boss,

17. Gardner (1939) Special note, p v.
18. Ronald Hutton, *The Triumph of the Moon*, (Oxford University Press, 1999), 223.

Hank Heyward. He finds some comfort in a bronze snail which he had acquired from somewhere and which had resurfaced in a drawer after several years.

> *When he was in the presence of any object of genuine antiq-*
> *uity he had a curious sense of complete familiarity with it,*
> *as though, through its medium, he could recreate the life*
> *which had surrounded it from its inception.*[19]

Whether this is based on a technique which Gerald himself adopted, I do not know, but it is interesting that Joan Grant used exactly the same technique, in her case an Egyptian scarab, to bring through the memories that were subsequently published as her novel, *Winged Pharaoh*. It was a long time after *A Goddess Arrives* was published that Joan Grant revealed that this was what she did and that her stories were far-memory, as she called it. It has certain similarities to the technique used by the hero of H. Rider Haggard's *Allan and the Ice Gods*,[20] who goes back in trance to a prehistoric life following the ingestion of a specific drug.

Denvers gradually drifted into a sleep which, to all outward appearances resembled a cataleptic trance. Inwardly he was able to re-live, in great detail, the most exciting part of one of his previous lives, as Kinyras, a citizen of Karpas, in Cyprus in the 15th Century BCE.

Kinyras, the hero through whose eyes the story is seen, and his brother Zadoug, are convinced that their land of Karpas, the north-eastern promontory of Cyprus, is in danger of invasion by the Khemites (Egyptians), who have already attacked the neighbouring kingdom of Aghirda, killing Damastes, the king, and capturing its princess, Dayonis. Some of the Carpasians, including Hange, argue against believing that the Khemites would invade, but Kinyras and others win the people round.

The book was being written in the 1937-1939 period, one that was crucial in the history of Europe. The rise of Nazi Germany and its threat to the stability of the whole of the continent was something of which everyone in England was fully aware, not least Gerald, who experienced some of it first-hand in Germany

---

19. Gardner, (1939), 33.
20. H. Rider Haggard, *Allan and the Ice Gods*, (Hutchinson, 1927).

on his way back to England. He was highly critical of the policy of 'appeasement' which was typified by Chamberlain's 'Munich Agreement' with Hitler in September 1938. This is certainly reflected in certain passages in the book, such as that from the soon-to-become leader of the Karpasians, Erili:

> *I am here, Karpasians, to guard you from disaster, but I know from my spies that Khem is mustering a great force against you, determined to conquer you once and for all. They are formidable warriors, they live by fighting, their engines of war are many and modern to the last degree, their troops are hardy and indomitable, their generals, men of great experience and much ability. Against such an army my own men are inadequate, being but a small force. If Karpas is to resist invasion by my aid, then Karpas must be prepared to make sacrifices.* [21]

The opposing viewpoints are made very clear in a subsequent exchange of opinions:

> *I would remind you that there IS NO WAR and to prepare for war is the very way to bring it about. ... On the contrary, the country which is prepared is the country immune from attack.* [22]

Erili is given the powers of a dictator and he orders the hero of the novel, Kinyras, to design and have built a defensive wall across the land which separates the Kingdom of Karpas from the rest of the island in order to defend it from the much greater force of the Khemites.

Whilst Kinyras is both brave and practically minded, he does have an unusual skill, which is to see into the future and to bring through designs for new weapons and things of that sort. He saw in detail the plan of a fortified wall in a dream and sets everyone to work to build it in as short a time as possible. One of the most useful visions is of a weapon called the *staveros*, which turns out to be a form of cross-bow, albeit getting on for 1000 years earlier

---

21. Gardner, (1939), 40.
22. Gardner, (1939), 43.

1. *William Robert Gardner -*
Gerald's father

2. *Louise Burguelew Gardner -*
Gerald's mother

3. *John Jay Ennis -*
Gerald's maternal grandfather

4. *Gerald aged about seven*

5. Uplands

6. Holmside

7. *The Glen*

8. *The Glen with Ingle Lodge, Gerald's birthplace, in the background*

9. David Elkington's Bungalow,
Ladbroke Estate, Maskeliya

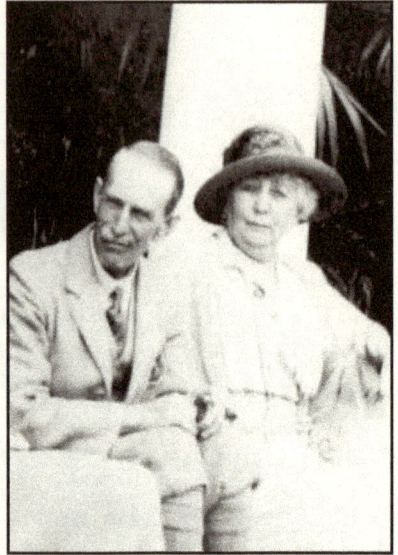

10. David Elkington and his wife,
Georgiana ('Com') in India, 1920s

11. Gerald with his niece, 'Bobby',
at Tenby - Summer 1916

12. William Robert Gardner (bottom
left) and three of his sons, Gerald
Brosseau (top left), Harold Ennis
(top right) and Robert Marshall
(bottom right) - Summer 1927

13. Donna (Dorothea Frances Rosedale), her father, William Elitto Rosedale, and her brother Jacko (John Lewis Rosedale) about 1900

14. Donna Gardner, late 1920s

15. Gerald's model reconstruction of an ocean-going Malay ship

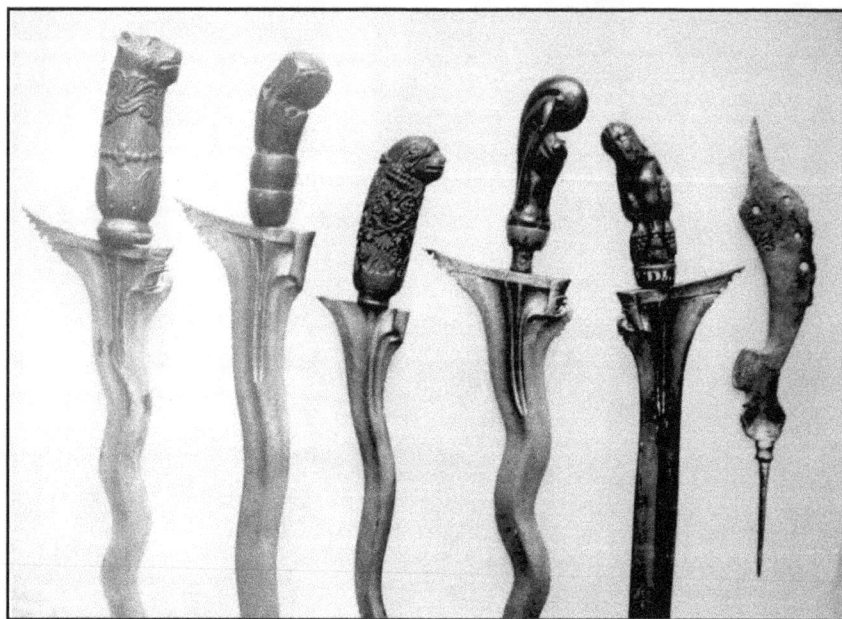

16. Malay keris from Gerald's collection

17. Portrait of Gerald Gardner: late 1930s. The photograph is inscribed 'To Dafo. With all love. G.B. Gardner'

18. Edith Woodford-Grimes ('Dafo') September 1949

19. Gerald (left) outside the Nelson Inn, Mudeford, following the wedding of Rosanne Woodford-Grimes and Cecil ('Tommy') Thompson (third and fourth from left) 17 August 1940

21. *Four Generations of the Mason family. Standing: Ernie Mason, Susie Mason and Arthur Fudge. Seated: Rosetta Fudge, Rosetta Mason and Edna Fudge. The child is Judith Ann Fudge. Beechwood Hall, Osborne Road, Southampton - January 1935*

20. *Rosanne and 'Tommy'*

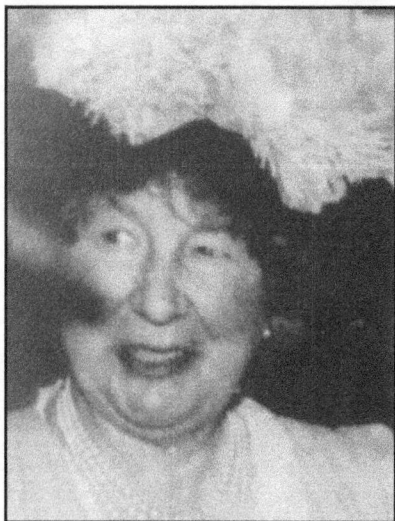

23. *Katherine Oldmeadow (in centre with wide-brimmed hat)*

22. *Dorothy St. Quintin Fordham (née Clutterbuck)*

than the period when they are presently known to have existed in the Mediterranean. It had the advantage of being capable of use by someone with little training and still have great strength and accuracy.

Gerald included 'love interest' into the story in the character of Dayonis, Queen of the Aghirda tribe who, escaping from capture by the Khemites, fights naked alongside Kinyras and subsequently becomes his lover and wife. Dayonis was some sort of ideal woman as far as Gerald was concerned, perhaps even a 'dream woman', not at all like Donna in personality. In fact, the individual whom she most closely resembles is Rosanne Woodford Grimes, who we shall meet in Chapter 14 and who, from all accounts, was outgoing and adventurous and popular with the opposite sex.

Now, at one level, Gerald was attracted by naked young ladies and to introduce one into his story is probably to be expected. However, whilst in some respects Dayonis conformed to societal expectations of the time with regard to her behaviour and attitudes, in other ways she certainly did not.

The plot of the story is complex, with many attacks, counterattacks, spying and other treachery. Dayonis escapes from her captors and, after being found by Kinyras and helping him defeat an attack by the Khemites, is brought back to his house to rest. An attempted invasion by sea by the Khemites is defeated.

Kinyras is married to Dayonis at an underground temple in her own land. There is a vivid description of a series of large underground caves reached through a fissure in the ground from which vapours emerged. This was the dwelling-place of their god, Jaske. The cave formations as described by Gerald are largely imaginary, although based on the so-called Hot Cave north of the village of Agirdag (Agirda) on the southern slopes of the Kyrenia Mountains (Pentadaktylos Range). It is described as a partially collapsed natural formation from which warm air emanates, which can be felt from a quarter of a mile away. It is interesting, in view of the later development of the Craft, that Gerald did not focus on the Mother Goddess cult centred on Vounous, less than six miles away from the cave, which Dikaios had spoken about back in 1932.

The climax of the book is set near Paphos, the site of Venus' legendary emergence from the ocean. Two religious factions are in conflict with each other. The Tamiradae, who were wool-merchants and owned dye-works, abhorred the sight of the naked human body and worshipped Hera. The worshippers of Ashtoreth, the more ancient goddess, loved nakedness.

Dayonis, having escaped capture a second time by diving naked into the sea, swam ashore where she was identified as Ashtoreth/Aphrodite. The Tamiradae were defeated.

Meanwhile, Hange is unmasked as a traitor. It is learnt that the Khemite king, Thothmes, is dead and the Khemite troops are withdrawn and return to Khem because it is seething with rebellion about his successor.

Back in the London of the 1930s, Heyward forces the snail from Denvers' grasp. Having slept for a fortnight, Denvers wakes up, realising that Heyward and Hange are the same person. His wife, Mina, realises how much she loves him and wants to stay with him. The book ends with Denvers telling his wife about Steiner's theory of group reincarnation.

That, in outline, is the story. It is a good one and an accomplished one for a first novel. It was Gerald's first published novel. Whether it was the first one he wrote is open to some doubt. He may well have spent the tropical evenings after a long working day not just reading avidly but writing as well. We know that he did not socialise as much as many of his compatriots and he was an abstemious drinker at most, so it is at least reasonable to suppose that he gained his skill at writing fiction during those hours. No manuscripts from that period have been found among Gerald's papers but he may have had short stories published, either under his own name or a pseudonym, during his working life from 1901 to 1936. It is at any rate possible.

Certain themes in the story have later echoes in the Craft. The existence of a secret society, a theme with which Gerald, with his Masonic background, was familiar, is introduced by Kinyras in which the mingling of blood, secret signs, swearing oaths and nakedness all feature.

Nakedness is a frequent theme, particularly of Dayonis. Whilst this may be an indication that Gerald was already familiar with, and active in, naturism during this period, it must not be forgotten that nakedness, particularly when fighting, was quite usual in the Mediterranean area during the period in which the book is set. One particular passage is very striking, where Dayonis escapes from her captors on board ship:

> *For some brief seconds Dayonis saw a clear passage to the stern. It was now or never. She was naked, her hair was hidden and she had her sword for attack. If she sped lightly, in the rush she might escape recognition and it would be difficult to snatch at her naked body, which she had taken the precaution to oil well.*[23]

The idea that it is difficult to capture someone in the nude whose body was well oiled, also occurs in *Witchcraft Today:*

> *... they found that the soldiers would usually let a naked girl go, but would take a clothed one prisoner. The slippery oiled bodies also made them hard to catch hold of.*[24]

It is important for us is to look at Gerald's references to witchcraft, how he saw it at that time, and other themes which would prove important in his later writings. It is clear that Dayonis is presented as being a witch, although this is rarely stated unambiguously. Kinyras' brother, Zadoug, had been spying on Dayonis and her captors and says:

> *She passed most of the time at her witch-tricks. ... It was well known that she was a true Cabire and had invoked these Lords [of Fate] and acquired mighty powers. I discovered that the Cabire were a secret witch cult.*[25]

This statement unambiguously suggests that Dayonis was a member of a "secret witch cult". The use of the term "witch cult" is interesting, as Gerald uses it right through until *Gerald Gardner*

---

23. Gardner, (1939), 349.
24. Gardner, (1954), 54.
25. Gardner, (1939), 100.

Witch was published in 1960. It was, of course, the term which Margaret Murray used in *The Witch Cult in Western Europe*.[26]

The Cabeiri or Cabiri were in fact Greek deities who were worshipped in a mystery fertility cult or cults on the Greek island of Lemnos and Samothrace. So, they were the gods rather than a cult, but we must remember that *A Goddess Arrives* is a story and therefore does not have to be historically accurate.

Gerald attributes healing qualities to Dayonis and it is clear from the context that these are derived from her being a witch:

> *As she bathed with slow, rhythmic gestures she began to chant in a curious low croon, "Hail Hecate! Goddess, Ruler of the Night, Hail! Aid me, who thy dread secrets share. Help me staunch this flowing blood, banish pain - cool this fever with thy breath. By all the worship I have given thee, grant this man be made whole."*

> *Kinyras listened with the utmost gravity as she chanted these words three times, unable to determine whether it was some magnetic quality in the slowly droned words, or some healing in the touch of her fingers which made the pain gradually leave him. The blood had stopped oozing and as he gazed the surface dried, looking like a healthy wound three or four days old.*

> *"You must be a witch!" he exclaimed, making a snatch at her fingers, which she avoided, laughing in a teasing way.*

> *"Well, cannot a witch have her uses sometimes?"*[27]

In other words, Dayonis is not confirming his statement, but implying its veracity. She also says: "I have the gift of sight from the Old Ones." Later, she reveals other magical techniques to Kinyras, who in turn reveals his own techniques:

> *"I do nothing but leave my mind open for what will be put into it. I come and I go, up and down Time according to my need, sometimes without voluntary effort."*[28]

---

26. Margaret Alice Murray, *The Witch-Cult in Western Europe*, (Oxford 1921).
27. Gardner, (1939), 133.
28. Gardner, (1939), 136-137.

She, by contrast, makes a dense smoke and the gods speak to her out of it. It is clear also that she makes sacrifices, both human and animal, as part of her magical workings. For example, she slaughters a jailer, not directly in order to escape, but as an offering:

"I knew that to obtain real power I must have a human sacrifice, but I always hated to do it. But when I was a helpless prisoner, and my country lost, it was another thing. And he was a beast of an enemy. So I did what was needful, and it worked, for the very next day Ammunz broke through the wall and led me to freedom." [29]

There is a vivid description of a ritual which Dayonis performed on board ship:

The great cabin in the ship's stern was cleared of furniture, only two chests being retained with which she prepared two altars. Upon these were placed several big, shallow bowls. She next drew a large circle upon the floor with red paint, setting the smaller altar with a brazier in the centre, the larger outside, and ringing the circle with little lamps set a foot apart. When the time drew near she summoned her assistants and the sacrifices were driven in.

"We must cast away our clothes," she announced in a hushed voice, as she slipped deftly from her one garment and her sandals.

Silently the two men obeyed her, while she took the sacred stone from her neck and laid it on the smaller altar. Prayer, in an unknown tongue, followed next and a command to her assistants to hold the black sheep. Midnight was now approaching and, with her sword in her right hand and holding a magic wand in her left, with one blow she severed each head from the animals, whose bodies were placed on the outer altar. The wand, the sword and a small figure of herself as enchantress, rested on the inner altar and her

---

29. Op. cit., 148.

*assistants were bidden to enter the circle with herself.
Holding the two severed heads she marked both herself
and the men on breast and forehead with blood, devoting
them to Jask.*

*With the bloody necks of the slaughtered sheep she
marked out a broad, inner circle round the celebrants and
placed the heads on the small altar. Then, with a fire drill,
she lit the lamps and kindled a fire, chanting all the while
in her secret language and pacing the circle in antithesis
to the progression of the sun. Next, lighting the brazier,
she cast into it many roots and herbs. A dense, choking
and stinging smoke arose while, unheeding its discomfort,
the two men knelt clasping hands, one each side of her,
with instructions not to lose contact until the ceremony
was over. Dayonis then knelt between them with her arms
on their shoulders, bidding them to support her body with
their arms. So with the circle complete, she explained
that, as she went into the trance she would bend over the
smoke and breathe it in, bidding them breathe no more
than was possible and to guard her from falling face for-
wards into the fire.*

*"Mark well what I say and lose not contact else shall I
waken ere the magic be complete. Remember, every spoken
word has its meaning."*[30]

I have quoted this passage at length because, if one disregards
the animal sacrifice, there are several factors which are later
found in Gerald's own description of Craft rituals, including the
ritual circle, nudity, sword, wand and incense.

Nevertheless, the hero, Kinyras, who is clearly based on Gerald's idealised view of himself, clearly disapproves of much of
Dayonis' activity, as we can tell from the passage where she wants
one of Kinyras' men as a human sacrifice, to which he replies:
"Have done, lady. Human sacrifice is an abomination, of which I
will have none".[31] And following the ritual, Kinyras remarks:

---

30. Gardner, (1939), 212-213.
31. Op. cit., 212.

"Hark ye, mistress, it's the last time ye play these tricks aboard my ship. I'll have none of it."[32]

꧁꧂

What conclusions can we draw from an examination of *A Goddess Arrives?*

In this context, the date of publication becomes particularly significant. There is no date in the book and the records of the publishers (Arthur H. Stockwell Ltd.) were destroyed when their premises in Ludgate Hill, London were bombed during the war. The firm moved out to Ilfracombe in Devon and is still in existence. However, the British Library received their copy on 6th December 1939. Under the Copyright Act 1911, publishers have to send copies of all new books published to the British Library, and this is obviously likely to happen shortly after copies have been received from the printers. It was not unknown for publishers to omit the date of publication around the end of the year "so as not to make their work seem quickly out-of-date".[33] This might well apply to *A Goddess Arrives*, particularly as it was being published not just towards the end of the year but towards the end of the decade as well. We can, I think, with reasonable confidence, give the date of publication as the very beginning of December 1939.

We have another clue. A review of *A Goddess Arrives* appeared in the *Christchurch Times* of 27th January 1940, presumably as the result of a review copy sent by Gerald. Assuming that the review copy was sent out shortly after he received it and giving the reviewer time to read the book thoroughly (which he obviously did) the above publication date seems reasonable. Gerald therefore probably submitted the book to the publishers no later than the summer of 1939.

It is clear that he had been interested in many of the main themes of the book for some years – weapons and warfare, reincarnation, secret societies and magical powers, not to mention naked young ladies!

32. Op. cit., 215.
33. Letter, Richard Price, British Library's Curator of Modern British Collections to the author, 27 October 1998.

Perhaps it is not surprising that the heroine of his story is made a member of a witch cult but it does mean that by the summer of 1939 at the latest he was writing confidently about a witch performing naked rituals in a circle ringed with lamps, with an altar upon which were bowls, holding a wand and sword, with circumambulation, incense and anointing, all of which would form part of the rituals which Gerald wrote about in *High Magic's Aid* following his initiation.

I think by this time Gerald had read the Key of Solomon and other magical texts, and all these elements could have been obtained from such sources.

Indeed, it was not primarily a book centred on witchcraft as his next book, *High Magic's Aid*, was. It was about warfare and love in ancient Cyprus and about how the legend of Aphrodite rising from the waves may have originated. The psychic or occult element is present in the actions of both hero and heroine but the role taken by witchcraft plays a relatively minor role: it is certainly not a book extolling its virtues or advocating its use.

It seems to me a book by someone interested in witchcraft as one of several interests, someone who had read about it but who had misconceptions, for example about the place of animal sacrifice. Indeed, Bracelin says as much about Gerald's initiation: "Until then his opinion of witchcraft had been based upon the idea that witches killed for the purpose of gaining or raising power, and he had thought the persecutions of them fully justified."[34]

---

34. Bracelin, 166.

CHAPTER THIRTEEN

To the New Forest

Like most other people, Gerald was well aware that war was coming. He had seen evidence of that on his way through Germany back to England in April 1936. From his early and continuing interest in weapons, and in his experience in the Legion of Frontiersmen, the Planters' Rifle Corps and the Malay States Volunteer Rifles, Gerald was keen to play his part. He had been rejected for enlistment in World War I on health grounds and now, at the age of 52, he was too old to join up, however much he might have wanted to. So, when, in April 1937, the Government decided to create an Air Raid Wardens' Service, Gerald, back from Cyprus, readily volunteered and trained as a warden.

Active duties only really got going as war became imminent, but in the meantime Gerald got involved with the digging of shelter trenches in Hyde Park. They were initially just simple trenches with wooden sides and wooden planks laid on top and covered with earth. Gerald bought a pair of Wellington boots and went down there. It appeared that there were insufficient volunteers for this activity, and the local authorities were allowed to finance paid workers to carry it out. For Gerald, this proved something of a problem initially, since they didn't want volunteers 'queering the pitch'. However, he sorted it out: "... a couple of halfcrowns settled that, and I was free to dig as much as I liked."[1]

The reason that Gerald moved from central London to High-cliffe on the Hampshire coast in 1938 is not entirely clear. He claimed that it was the threat of government requisition of his flat because of its proximity to Victoria Station, but I suspect that there was some other reason, as I am sure he could have acquired another flat somewhere else in central London. The most obvious reason was the threat of war and of air raids, and that somewhere out of town would be safer. However, there may be another subsidiary reason, which a Highcliffe resident who knew Gerald told the local historian, Ian Stevenson:

> *He lived in a haunted house in London when he first came back to England. And he said it was a complete nuisance because they would keep turning lights on and opening doors, and he'd go to bed and at two o'clock in the morning his bedroom door would swing open and then the light would go on on his landing, and he'd have to get up and switch the light off and shut the door again, and in ten minutes he'd hear someone walking along the landing and the light would go on and his door would open again! ... He accepted it for exactly what it was: a haunting ... I think it unnerved his wife a little, and this was one of the reasons why I think he moved. Because I don't think she understood, or could come to terms with it. She was nervous of being in the house on her own.[2]*

Bracelin says that: "The only place in England where he had friends was the region of the New Forest ...".[3] The New Forest lies roughly half way along the south coast of England. To the east lie the cities of Portsmouth, home of the Royal Navy, and Southampton, seaport and ocean liner terminal. To the south lies the Isle of Wight, popular as a tourist destination since Victorian times. And to the west is Bournemouth, a large seaside holiday town, but

---

1. Bracelin, 159.
2. Interview Ian Stevenson and 'MD', 8 April 2005.
3. Bracelin, 159.

also very much a retirement spot, as is a lot of the south coast. Between these lies the New Forest, which is itself relatively unpopulated. This is mainly due to the sandy soil, which is not good for agriculture, and was probably the reason William I declared it a royal preserve for hunting, where the penalties under the game laws for killing a deer were most severe. Whilst the New Forest does contain considerable areas of woodland, these have mostly been planted, and the more usual landscape is that of open heath.

At the time, David and Com were living in retirement at East-cliff Mansions, 25 Grove Road East, Bournemouth. They were probably the friends that Gerald was referring to.

There is a possibility which has been suggested that Gerald met someone at Fouracres who lived in the New Forest area and who became very friendly with him. He certainly knew her later, after he moved to the New Forest area: her name was Edith Woodford-Grimes, as we shall see. However, this is all very much speculation and there is no clear-cut evidence, though I suspect that she may have been the 'Feminine Member' to which I refer in Chapter 11, as the writing style is very similar.

Whatever the reason, Gerald came down to the New Forest area some time in Spring 1938 to look for somewhere to live. At that time the threat of invasion was thought much less likely than bomb and gas attacks on major cities, so the New Forest area, though close to the coast, was thought to be a lot safer than places like London and Southampton. His friends at Fouracres would undoubtedly have told him about a naturist club in the area that he was wanting to move to – the New Forest Club.

This had originally opened in 1934 on an inland site in Dorset, but in April 1936 it had reopened on a four acre site at Rushford Warren, Mudeford, on the shores of Christchurch Harbour. There was a large 24-room former hotel on the site which had a general club room, dining room, games room and sun lounge as well as accommodation for visitors. The grounds were naturally wooded with views out across the Harbour to Hengistbury Head and the Isle of Wight.

As the club had accommodation for members to stay, it is quite likely that Gerald went down and made the club his base while he went out and tried to find somewhere to live, taking the train down to Christchurch some time in June 1938. He had probably already arranged accommodation at the club, and one of his first actions would very likely have been to walk in to Christchurch and buy himself a bicycle. Whether he had ridden before, during his time 'out East', I do not know, but it was the only really practicable way of getting about looking for houses he could rent or buy.

Bracelin writes:

> It was the end of the year; the naturist club which he had joined was closed for the winter, and he was thrown upon his own resources. On one of his long cycle rambles, Gardner came across a curious building in Christchurch. Cut in the stone the legend said: THE FIRST ROSICRUCIAN THEATRE IN ENGLAND. Later he was to find out what this meant. This was the discovery which led to his recruitment into the cult of the witches ...[4]

Now, there is something wrong with this statement. It implies that Gerald first came across the theatre building in the winter, yet we know that he only moved to Highcliffe in July 1938 and he attended a performance in the theatre in August of that year.

Bracelin writes as if "long cycle rambles" were a regular activity on Gerald's part. Whilst they were more in the nature of exploration for its own sake after Gerald had found a house, initially they were probably more focused on "house hunting". This would undoubtedly have involved cycling down suburban roads looking for likely houses for sale.

If I am right about Gerald having temporary accommodation in the New Forest Club while searching for a house, then it is more than likely that he would have come across the unusual theatre building while cycling down Somerford Way, which is only about a mile from the New Forest Club, and which is a likely

---

4. Bracelin, 159.

route to take to get onto the main Somerford Road, which led east to such places as Highcliffe, where Gerald finally ended up.

The fact that Bracelin uses the phrase "the First Rosicrucian Theatre in England" makes it clear that Gerald had noted down the wording on the foundation stone of the theatre, which read, in full:

> THIS FOUNDATION STONE
> WAS LAID BY
> ALEXANDER MATHEWS
> ON MARCH 13TH, 1938
> TO COMMEMORATE THE FIRST
> ROSICRUCIAN THEATRE IN ENGLAND.
> PAX VOBISCUM

Bracelin did not mention that the building was under construction, merely that "Gardner came across a curious building ...",[5] which sounds as if it were complete, at least externally, which fits in with the suggested June 1938 date.

Gerald had heard of Rosicrucianism. It did not reside within any one organisation. Rather it was a movement which formed part of the Western esoteric tradition. It had its roots in Gnosticism, kabbalism and several other strands. It really started with certain documents which were published in Germany at the beginning of the 17th Century. The anonymous 'Fama Fraternitatis' explained how the Order of the Rosy Cross was founded by a mysterious figure known as Christian Rosenkreutz, who was born in the 14th or 15th Century. The movement spread throughout Europe, including England, and many have claimed that Francis Bacon (1561-1626) was a member. There is a belief, popular particularly amongst Rosicrucians, that Bacon was the author of the Shakespeare plays. Christopher McIntosh, however, points out that Bacon was actually not very sympathetic to the occult and that his writing style was very different from that of Shakespeare.[6] There were probable links with Freemasonry from the earliest days, and certainly by the mid-18th Century there were specific

---

5. Bracelin, 159.
6. Christopher McIntosh, *The Rosicrucians: The History, Mythology and Rituals of an Esoteric Order*, (Weiser 1997).

Rosicrucian Masonic degrees. In 1865, the Societas Rosicruciana in Anglia (SRIA or Soc. Ros.) was founded, reputedly based on old documents found in Freemasons' Hall. Membership was limited to Master Masons, one of whom claimed initiation from German Rosicrucian adepts.

Interest in esoteric matters and the existence of esoteric groups was much rarer in the 1930s than it is today. So Gerald determined that, when he had settled down, he would try and find out more about the theatre.

In the meantime, however, Gerald had found the house that he was looking for. He had a good idea of the sort of thing he wanted. He was not short of money and needed a reasonably big house with plenty of room for his ever-expanding library and collection of weapons. He also wanted a large and preferably secluded garden where he could carry on his nude sunbathing without interference.

So he was very pleased when he chanced upon a house in Highcliffe, about four miles east of the New Forest Club. Highcliffe takes its name from the high cliffs which characterise the coast at this point but it is actually a relatively recent name. Until the beginning of the 19th Century it was largely open farmland, with the nearest settlements being at Chewton and Walkford. There was also a group of cottages at Slop Pond on the main Christchurch to Lymington road. Further houses were built here in the 1830s and the residents decided on a change of name to Newtown. It gained its own church, St. Mark's, in 1843. Development continued and at the turn of the 20th Century the name was changed to Highcliff. (The 'e' at the end seems to have gained in popularity as the century progressed.) Highcliffe expanded greatly during the 1920s and 1930s as part of the growth of Bournemouth and other seaside locations, being particularly popular with retired people. It is on the fringe of the New Forest and on the coast with magnificent views to the Isle of Wight, so was, and still is, considered a desirable place to live.

The house Gerald had found was called 'Southridge' and was situated on the corner of Highland Avenue and Elphinstone Road. Also known as no. 3 or no. 5 Highland Avenue, it was built in 1923 on a substantial plot measuring 150 feet in length and extending to one third of an acre. The plot had several mature trees and was quite secluded, particularly in summer. The house was in red brick, with a tiled roof and tall chimneys. The ground floor consisted of a porch leading into what is described as a "Lounge Hall" (21ft x 14ft), from which the stairs led to the upper floor. Adjoining this was a large (16ft square) dining room, really a projection from the house, with windows looking out onto the garden from three sides. There was originally a verandah around the western and southern elevations of the house, which included a balcony accessible from the southern bedroom, which I think in Gerald's time was his library.

In about March or early April 1938, the owners, the Misses Caroline and Ethel Estcourt, moved out and subsequently put Southridge up for sale. This must have been around the time when Gerald was looking for property, and it seemed to suit him, for he moved in, probably in July 1938.

A Highcliffe resident remembers visiting Gerald and Donna at Southridge regularly during the war when she was a child:

> *The house struck me as being rather sombre and dark, with beautiful dark stained wood panelling, and he had the most beautiful hall. And on the stairway it had a suit of armour: I was always expecting to flap to go up and a face to appear! And up on the wall he had these beautiful daggers, spears and pistols, which I think were all in firing order. It was a very interesting house. Upstairs in his library there were three tables with books out everywhere. And he said "Any book you want to borrow, just take it!" He had a lot of history books. He was able to talk to me, as an ordinary person. I wasn't spoken to as if I was a child and not understand what he was talking about.*[7]

Donna seemed to fulfill the archetypal role of the 'little woman' in the background of Gerald's life. The same Highcliffe resident says:

7. Interview Ian Stevenson and 'MD', 8 April 2005.

She reminded me of a little sparrow. She was very, very short, almost black hair, very tiny, very petite person. ... I never, ever saw them go out together. She seemed to live a quite different life. She was a very shy person. ... I think it used to concern my mother, because she used to think that perhaps she'd be a little lonely, because she didn't seem to have any friends.[8]

Immediately to the north, on Highland Avenue in a house called 'Trapsun', lived A.V. Ridout, local builder and funeral director. Gerald gave the firm substantial business in the first year, including quite a substantial number of repairs and renovations at a total cost of over £300, which makes it clear that he had bought 'Southridge' from the Misses Estcourt and was not merely renting it.

By November 1938, Gerald already had plans for the addition of a sun lounge to the house, presumably to pursue his naturist activities. The works probably involved the glazing-in of the ground floor verandah. The fact that these were the first major works carried out on Gerald's behalf shows, to my mind, the importance of sunlight in his life. His thinking was probably that, if war came (which by that time nearly everyone thought was a near certainty) he would not be able to winter abroad for the duration and therefore it was a priority on his part to make alternative provision. He had probably initially got the idea from the sun lounge at the New Forest Club. Plans for the sun lounge were submitted by Ridout to the local authority and approved under the Building Regulations in February 1939 and it was certainly in use by the summer of 1939, as a tongue-in-cheek item in the local paper makes clear:

The instant success (with the neighbours) of the Elphinstone Road Nudist Colony has been marked. Rooms with an uninterrupted view of the Island – and other items of interest, are, they tell me, at a premium. One old gentleman who has rented a second floor back says his outlook on life generally has entirely changed in the last few weeks. He has now

---

8. Ibid.

no use for his car or fishing tackle, and wishes to exchange
them for anything useful, such as telescopes, binoculars, or
camera. Nearby householders have taken furiously to gar-
dening and hedge trimming, putting in hours with their
*heads and shoulders buried in the macracarpa.*9

The way this piece was written suggests that it was not just Gerald sunbathing in the nude but that he had some female company.

The resident referred to above also tells the story of the retired school-mistress who lived next door to Gerald on Elphinstone Road. She phoned the police and asked them to come round and see her, so Police Constable King cycled up to her house. She told him: "I've got some rather disturbing news: there's a not very desirable man that lives next door to me. I'll show you. You'll have to follow me." So she led him upstairs to the attic and said "I can see him from my window". P.C. King asked how, and she said she had to stand on a box. When he stood on the box he could see Gerald sunbathing in the nude! He told her: "Well, I really shouldn't bother. If you've got to go to all those lengths to see it, it doesn't really matter!"

Now, this is well-known as a humorous tale. I have certainly heard it myself, almost an "urban myth". Was such a tale in circulation at the time and got itself attached to the situation at 'Southridge'? Or could it possibly be the origin from which such tales all emerged? I strongly suspect the former.

Other works to 'Southridge' were in progress throughout most of 1939. These included an asbestos garage and the construction of a drive and gates, for which an application for approval was submitted in March 1939. It was thought locally that Gerald did have a car, but wartime petrol restrictions meant that it was rarely used. Gerald also had an underground air-raid shelter added. This was no Anderson shelter but something more elaborate. It was about 6ft. square, adjacent to the house in the south-east corner. Access was obtained via a stone staircase. Gerald also had another access directly from the dining room. This seems not to have been carried out by Ridouts.

---

9. *Christchurch Times*, 24 June 1939.

In January 1939, work began in converting the roof space into an extra room, which seemed to involve putting an extra floor in the roof and removing and repositioning the collar beams. Electric light and power sockets were added and water was laid on. Repairs to the roof were carried out, and a trap-door and steps were fitted. By May of that year, it is being described as a Dark Room, and that is what I suspect it was for, to develop photographs, probably particularly those taken at the naturist club which might be difficult to have processed by the normal chemists![10]

Kenneth Grant told me[11] that Gerald showed him "a lovely photo of his wife, Donna, in the nude, with a gong (?)" when Grant visited him in London in the late 1940s, which suggests that Gerald was in the habit of taking such photographs. I have seen photographs of Donna in the nude with various 'props' such as one of Gerald's serrated-edged swords. They are in colour and probably date from when they were living in Buckingham Palace Mansions in the 1936-1938 period.

Whether the Dark Room was used at any time for anything else, such as secret rituals, I do not know!

While Gerald was getting 'Southridge' how he wanted it, he did find some time to pursue his other interests, as we shall see in the next chapter. One organisation which he did join was the Folk-Lore Society. He applied for membership in early 1939. It was a group that Gerald remained associated with for twenty years. Founded in 1878, it held regular meetings in London and produced the journal *Folk-Lore*. Folklore is defined by the Society as being "the everyday culture and cultural traditions of all social groups".

By this definition, Gerald became interested in folklore as soon as he went "out East" in 1901, getting to know the local peoples in Ceylon, Borneo and Malaya and learning from them about their customs and beliefs. His folklore interests were not limited to the East, however, for when he was back in England on leave in

10. A. V. Ridout ledgers 15, 16 and 17.
11. Letter from Kenneth Grant to the author, 5 March 2007.

*Highcliffe, Walkford and Chewton Common in 1939
(based upon the 25-inch Ordnance Survey map)*

1927 we have noted that he applied for a reader's ticket at the British Museum to study Basque and Welsh folklore.[12]

Gerald first attended a meeting of the Folk-Lore Society on Wednesday 15th March 1939, when the announcement of his name as a new member was made, the decision having been taken at the previous meeting. He was proposed by Dr. W.L. Hildburgh, who had been a member since 1906. Gerald's address is given as 23A Buckingham Palace Mansions, so it is clear that he kept on his London flat for at least eight months after moving to Highcliffe in July 1938.

Although it was the first Folk-Lore Society meeting he had attended, Gerald was called upon (or offered) to exhibit and talk about his collection of witch relics. He does not say how he acquired them, merely stating that: "Within recent years a box containing what appear to be witchcraft relics has come into my possession". One clue as to their origin is provided by a label on the back of the box, written, according to Gerald, about 1890 to 1900, stating that it was "given to me by my father Joseph Carter, of Home Farm, Hill Top, near Marlborough ... Signed S. Carter".[13] It is possible that this is Sydney Carter, a member of the Society whom Gerald knew. These relics were supposed, on rather slim evidence, to have been at one time in the ownership of the so-called 'Witchfinder General', Matthew Hopkins.

In fact, this was the only meeting of the Society which Gerald attended before it ceased meetings during the war.

12. I am indebted to Roger Dearnaley for this information.
13. G.B. Gardner, *Collectanea: Witchcraft, Folk-Lore*, Vol. 50, No 2, (June 1939), 188-190.

CHAPTER FOURTEEN

The Most Interesting Element

Gerald had never forgotten the strange theatre building he had come across on his travels. So when he had settled into 'Southridge', in July 1938, he took it upon himself to enquire about the people responsible for the theatre. He talked to local people. The general opinion was: "They are a queer lot, the ones running the theatre".[1] Gerald could get no more details out of them, however. There was nothing for it: he would have to go and see for himself!

Gerald cycled up to the front door of the theatre and spoke to the woman in the box office. He had read in the local paper[2] that the theatre had had a Grand Opening not much more than a month previously, attended by the Mayor of Christchurch. The posters outside the theatre were advertising a week-long Festival at the beginning of August, and Gerald booked tickets for Donna and himself to see a performance of 'Pythagoras', a new play by Alex Mathews, a playwright of whom until that moment he had never heard. Reviews of the play the last time it had been performed the previous August were very good:

---

1. Bracelin, 162.
2. *Christchurch Times*, 18 June 1938.

*The players ... seemed to catch the spirit of the Grecian era
... The classic form in which the play is written is ... the per-
fect medium for the teachings of Pythagoras ... The ora-
tions of Pythagoras, spoken with an understanding
modulation of inflection, synchronised well with the strong
dramatic action of the play.[3]*

The author of this piece was one Edith Woodford-Grimes,
someone whom Gerald was to get to know very well indeed, but
who could well be accused of being biased, as she was taking one
of the main roles in the play herself.

As it happened, Gerald's and Donna's own conclusions were
rather different:

*All the costumes were home-made, and not very professional.
Many of the parts were rather badly acted. Pythagoras was
played by a short, sturdy, black-haired individual. He was no
actor, and the lines which he had to say were little better.
Mrs. Gardner, who was an experienced amateur actress,
hated it all, and said she would never go there again.[4]*

Gerald, however, started to attend meetings at the Ashrama
Hall, behind the theatre, partly because he had learned a little
about Rosicrucianism and wanted to find out if these people
really knew anything. His first impression of the leader of the
whole enterprise, Sullivan (the "short, sturdy black-haired individual") was confirmed:

*His ideas could be very puzzling. The first time he met
Gardner, he asked him: "Do you remember the days when
you were a noble Roman and wore a sari?" He also showed
him a genuine African witch-doctor's wand with a devil's
head knob on it – which Gardner recognised to be a Persian
or Indian mace, and not an unusual one at that. Among the
claims made by the gentleman were that he had been the
sage Pythagoras, the magician Cornelius Agrippa and Francis Bacon in past lives.[5]*

3. E. Woodford-Grimes, "An Appreciation of 'Pythagoras'", *Christchurch Times*, 28 August 1937.
4. Bracelin, 162.
5. Bracelin, 163.

Very soon, Gerald got talking to others at the meeting. The organisation was apparently called the Rosicrucian Order Crotona Fellowship. He was interested to learn that the Fellowship had originated in Liverpool, which was the birthplace of its head, George Alexander Sullivan (stage name Alex Mathews). They were rather vague about his early years, though we now know that he was born in 1890 to Catherine Sullivan and her husband, Charles Washington Sullivan, a ship's steward.

The Fellowship was established in 1920, and many slim publications, mostly written by Sullivan, who made his living as a journalist, appeared, printed on his own press. From Liverpool, Sullivan started a correspondence course. The main influences seem to have been Rosicrucian tradition, Theosophical ideas and Masonic practices, together with Sullivan's personal contribution, often by means of inspired or guided writings which he issued under the name of "Aureolis". This is the middle name of Paracelsus (though sometimes spelt 'Aureolus'), a Renaissance medic and occultist, who was thought, certainly by Sullivan, to have been a Rosicrucian.

In 1935 came the move to Christchurch. One member of the Fellowship was Catherine Chalk, who, following the death of her husband, offered her house, Meadow Way, off Somerford Road, and substantial garden, to the Fellowship and moved into a smaller house next door. A wooden building, known as the Ashrama Hall, was erected in the garden the following year, and the Fellowship started having its meetings there. These involved study, religious ritual and dramatics.

The plays performed were largely written by Sullivan and, by 1937, members had the idea of a larger purpose-built theatre. Plans were drawn up, the total cost of £4000 was raised (probably from wealthy benefactors) and the building was erected in the Spring of 1938. Sullivan was one of those who believed that the plays attributed to Shakespeare were actually written by Francis Bacon, an idea familiar to Gerald as his mother had held similar views. It is an intriguing thought to wonder whether she may have met Sullivan at some meeting for devotees of the matter in Liverpool.

As Gerald got to know members, they told him more out-landish things about Sullivan:

The chief of the Order was immortal. Because people won-dered why he did not grow old like them, he was compelled to slip away every few score years, to make another name in a fresh place. In the Ashrama ... was a great plaque with the various identities under which he had lived through the ages inscribed thereon. ... Eventually Gardner was let into a great secret. They had part of an old (Dutch or Italian) lamp, hanging by chains from a ceiling. This, it was con-fided in him, was the Holy Grail ...[6]

Despite some of the stranger ideas, Gerald continued to go to the various activities of the Crotona Fellowship. After he had been going for some time, he began to be aware of something interesting:

Now, at meetings, Gardner had noticed a group of people apart from the rest. They seemed rather brow-beaten by the others, kept themselves to themselves. They were the most interesting element, however. Unlike many of the others, they had to earn their livings, were cheerful and optimistic and had a real interest in the occult. They had carefully read many books on the subject: Unlike the general mass, who were sup-posed to have read all but seemed to know nothing.[7]

Now, this makes a good story (the down-trodden minority who keep cheerful because they possess some great secret) but in fact it is somewhat misleading, at least in the case of some of the group, who were well-respected and held responsible positions within the Fellowship, for, from certain details which are given later in the account, we can identify the group referred to. They include Ernie Mason, Susie Mason, Rosetta Fudge and the afore-mentioned Edith Woodford-Grimes. Edith, who took the part of Pythagoras' wife, Theano, in the production and played a major part in the teaching work of the Fellowship, particularly speech and drama, could never be described as "brow-beaten".

---

6. Bracelin, 163.
7. Bracelin, 164-165.

It seems as if Gerald and Edith enjoyed each other's company right from the start and they were able to converse at a certain intellectual level. It was not long before Edith invited Gerald round to her bungalow in Dennistoun Avenue, which was only five minutes' walk from the theatre. He noticed that the house was named 'Theano' – Pythagoras' wife – the part which Edith played in the recent production. He also noticed that Edith had a plaque on the house advertising her profession as a teacher of elocution and dramatic art. It also gave her qualifications, ALCM, ALAM Eloc (Associate of the London College of Music and Associate of the London Academy of Music – Elocution). Some, in later years, seeing these qualifications, have assumed, wrongly, that she had been a music teacher. Her grandson has confirmed to me that she could not play a musical instrument.

Once inside the bungalow, Gerald was introduced to Rosanne, Edith's seventeen year old daughter. She was a very attractive girl with plenty of admirers and I am sure that Gerald was immediately added to that number!

We can, perhaps, speculate on how it might have been. They sat down and, over a cup of tea, Gerald told Edith something about himself, his life, interests and beliefs. When he had finished, Edith took a moment to think and then spoke about her own background.

She had been born Edith Rose Wray on 18th December 1887 in the town of Malton in the North Riding of Yorkshire. Her mother was Caroline Wray (formerly Harrison) and her father was William Henry Wray, an implement maker at the local waterworks. Edith was the second oldest of seven children, the others being Arthur (born 1884), Ethel and Carrie (born 1890), Violet (born 1891), Albert (born 1893) and Olive (born 1898).

Gerald got the impression that Edith was reasonably well educated, particularly in languages and literature, but he didn't enquire as to how she left Malton and ended up in Christchurch. When he learned that until recently she had been living in Southampton, he assumed that it had been something to do with the war and that she may have been a V.A.D., as he had been in

Liverpool. She told him that previously she had been a ladies'
maid in Baildon in Yorkshire.

In June 1920, she married Samuel William Woodford Grimes,
who had been born in Bangalore, India in 1880. At the time they
were married, he was a clerk in the War Pensions Office in
Southampton. Their only child, Rosanne, was born in June 1921.

Edith worked as a Tutor in English and Dramatic Literature to
various student groups authorised by the Workers' Educational
Association and the Extra-Mural Department of the University
College, Southampton (now the University), also teaching Elocu-
tion and Dramatic Art at various Evening Institutes for the
Southampton Education Authority.

Edith had, moreover, a growing interest in esoteric matters,
and at some stage she made contact with the Mason family, a
contact which was to change her life. This may have been in
about 1925, when the Masons moved into a large detached early
Victorian house standing in its own grounds, which contained
many mature beech trees, which probably suggested the name
given to it – Beechwood. It was in the very street where Edith
lived – Osborne Road, Portswood, a suburb of Southampton.

When Edith mentioned the Mason family, Gerald realised
that he had already met Ernie and Susie Mason and their sister,
Rosetta Fudge, as they were all members of the Crotona Fellowship and visited the Ashrama and theatre regularly. He was to get
to know them a lot better before long. The various members of
the Mason family seem to have been involved in quite a few different esoteric movements, including anthroposophy, theosophy,
Co-Masonry and Rosicrucianism. I do not know how Edith got to
know them, perhaps through one of her classes, through a meeting of one of the organisations that they belonged to or merely
because they only lived a few hundred yards from each other. She
also met their father, George Miles Mason and his wife, Rosetta.
George had been born in Southampton in 1860 and had had a
variety of trades, including umbrella maker, photographer and
sculptor. By the time Edith got to know him, he was engaged in
the business of lantern-slide manufacture, involving him in optics
and photography, in which both his wife and Ernie played an

active part. They had a shop in Carlton Place, Southampton. George was also very much of an inventor and an astronomer, having constructed an observatory in the large garden attached to the house.

Edith was excited by the range of esoteric activities in which the family were involved. Young Rosetta, who had married William Fudge in 1903, had a limited edition of one of the first books to be translated into English by Rudolf Steiner, the founder of anthroposophy, which shows a more than passing interest in the subject. Susie Mason was the Hon. Secretary of the Southampton Lodge of the Theosophical Society. However, the latest interest of the Mason family at the time when Edith got to know them was Co-Masonry.

Co-Masonry, or, to give it its full name, International Co-Freemasonry, is a form of Freemasonry that is open to both men and women. It started in France in 1882 and, in 1900, a Supreme Council was established to administer the Order and to take in the full 33 degrees of the Ancient and Accepted Scottish Rite.

Annie Besant (1847-1933), socialist and theosophist, had long felt that Masonry should be open to both men and women, and on hearing about the French lodge, she applied to be initiated, and subsequently obtained permission to form the first lodge in Britain open to both men and women. On 26th September 1902, a Co-Masonic Lodge was consecrated in London by officers of the Supreme Council in Paris, and it was given the title Lodge Human Duty No. 6, of which Annie Besant was the first ruler. The fact that she was involved meant that there was a tendency towards an interest in esoteric and occult ideas amongst English members.

Anyway, the Mason family were attracted to Co-Masonry and, certainly by 1928, Harmony Lodge No. 25 was established at 32 Carlton Crescent, Southampton. In 1934, George Miles Mason had plans drawn up to erect a meeting hall within the grounds of Beechwood. This was a substantial building, 30 feet by 20 feet in area. It had full height windows on two sides and had its own kitchen and lavatory. It is described on the 1948 Ordnance Survey map as a Church Mission Hall. Whilst one does not lightly criticise the Ordnance Survey, particularly in matters concerning its home town of Southampton, it was actually nothing of the sort! It was known as Beechwood Hall and seems to have been used for meetings of the various esoteric groups in which the family were involved, primarily Harmony Lodge No. 25. On Sunday 13th January 1935, what is described as the new Temple (i.e. Beechwood Hall) was consecrated "with the assistance of a large and distinguished gathering of Brethren from many parts of the country". Present, as well as the Grand Secretary of the Order, was the Most Puissant Grand Commander of the British Federation, Mabel Besant-Scott, Annie Besant's daughter.

As Edith mentioned that name, Gerald remembered meeting Mabel at the Ashrama. She was: "... a rather pleasant, sometimes uncertain old lady. She spent quite a lot of her time trying to remember a former incarnation as Queen Elizabeth. She had no occult powers, she told him, and neither, she admitted, had her mother."[8] Edith told Gerald something of Mabel and how she came to be living in Christchurch. Born in 1870, she married the newspaper reporter, Ernest Scott, in 1892, emigrating to Australia the same year. He eventually became Professor of History at the University of Melbourne, but she became estranged from him and returned to England in 1909. She became interested in Co-Masonry and, in 1934, following the death of her mother, she was made Most Puissant Grand Commander of the British Federation, the top post.

However, only a year later, in July 1935, Mabel resigned very suddenly from the Co-Masons, apparently for "personal reasons" and seems to have cut off all contact with them. At the same time, the whole of the Mason family and Edith Woodford-Grimes also resigned.

"What had gone wrong?" Gerald enquired. The story that Edith told him was an interesting one.

There was disquiet within the British Federation of the Co-Masons and it all seemed to come to a head in the first two weeks of July 1935. It centred around the relationship between the British Federation and the Supreme Council in France. One major issue was that the Supreme Council had established 'fraternal relations' with the Grand Orient. The Grand Orient de France

---

8. Bracelin, 163.

was founded in 1733, but in 1877, in the strong anti-religious climate that was present following the defeat of Napoleon III, it abolished one of the basic Masonic principles, that of the necessity for Masons to profess a belief in a Supreme Being, and admitted atheists and free-thinkers into its lodges. It also went against another fundamental principle when it involved itself directly in politics. The rest of the Masonic world reacted by casting the Grand Orient out of the fold. As well as being in 'fraternal relations' with this exiled body, the Supreme Council was also accused of 'writing the Masonic secrets' and having no belief in a Supreme Being. These criticisms came right from the top of the British Federation – from Mabel Besant-Scott herself.

A petition had been circulated and Mabel wrote that there were those "who are truly torn between their loyalty to the Supreme Council and their loyalty to King and Country, which might become suspect, (they believe) on account of our relations with the Grand Orient ..." Some argued that the British Federation should break away from the Supreme Council. Mabel continued:

> ... members recognise with gratitude the great debt they owe to the Supreme Council for the great tolerance and liberty given to them since the beginning of our Masonic work. The Supreme Council is our masonic mother; but the children have arrived at the age of thirty-three years, the full masonic age, and should now leave their mother's house and build a house for themselves.[9]

Several members of Harmony Lodge No. 25 in Southampton felt the same way. Ernie and Susie Mason and Gavin Harris circulated a letter drumming up support for secession from the jurisdiction of the Supreme Council. They continued:

> ... the political situation in Europe is at present strained to breaking point, and trouble may be expected of so serious a nature that it behoves every British subject to free himself from any foreign entanglement – such as obedience to the Supreme Council of International Co-Freemasonry. ...

9. Letter from Mabel Besant-Scott to the M. P. Sov. Gr. Master, 1 July 1935.

the attitude of the present Consistory Council is such as
would associate the Brethren with suspicion of political
intrigue.[10]

As a result, the Supreme Council for the British Federation
suspended these three "from all Masonic rights and privileges" for
what was described as "gross disloyalty".

Apart from Mabel Besant-Scott herself, there did not appear
to be any desire amongst the leaders of the British Federation to
secede from the Supreme Council. So, in the end, virtually the
whole of Harmony Lodge, certainly the most active members,
including Ernie and Susie Mason and Edith Woodford-Grimes
took the lead from Mabel Besant-Scott and resigned from the
British Federation. Edith, for example, wrote: "I wish to tender
my resignation from the Order of International Co-Freemasonry
... I feel I can no longer owe allegiance to the Supreme Council ...
I am not insensible to the many privileges I have received from
Co-Freemasonry and shall always acknowledge that debt."[11]

Mabel had become close to the members of the Harmony
Lodge for the support which they gave her leading up to her resignation. So when she mentioned a new Rosicrucian community
which had just been established in Christchurch, only some
twenty or so miles away, to which she was going to move, they
were all very interested and decided to investigate. Bracelin
records it thus: "They explained that they had been co-masons,
and had followed Mabs (Mrs. Scott) when she had moved to this
place".[12] They were all very much taken with Sullivan's teaching
and the activities of the Ashrama. We don't know how Mabel first
contacted Sullivan and the Crotona Fellowship. I suspect that it
was via Catherine Chalk, who had also been a Co-Mason. Mabel
bought a bungalow very close to the ashrama, calling it 'Locris'
after the town in Sullivan's play 'Pythagoras'. There was a lot of
interchange between esoteric groups in those days anyway.

Now that Edith had given Gerald some background to the
various individuals in the Fellowship, he could understand better

10. Circular letter from Susie M. Mason, Ernest W Mason, and Gavin Harris, 10 July 1935.
11. In the Toronto collection.
12. Bracelin 165.

the various relationships involved. He was beginning to understand that their shared background explained to some extent the closeness that existed between Edith and the Mason family. He began to rely on them more and more, particularly Edith, and he became a regular visitor to her house.

Although she was always known in the family as 'Daff', Gerald began to refer to her as 'Dafo'. I don't think this was intended to be a magical name in any way, probably just a nickname. During his trip to China in 1934 he had probably heard of and possibly even seen the giant statues of the Buddha carved out of solid rock, such as the one at Leshan, Szechuan province, which is over 230 feet tall, and which is known as 'Dafo'. Gerald probably started to call her that as a term of endearment.

At some stage he confided in her that he was writing, indeed had substantially written, a novel about a life which he remembered having lived in ancient Cyprus. Edith was, for some reason, particularly interested in the fact that Gerald could remember a previous lifetime in such great detail, and told him that she, too, could remember a previous lifetime as a witch, where she was burned at the stake. She even gave him a poem which he understood that she had written. It was entitled "Hymn to Fire" and was, in fact, written by the Russian poet, Konstantin Balmont (1867-1942). She had obviously been attracted by the subject matter and had copied it into what was probably a commonplace book.

This was the first indication to Gerald that Edith believed that she had had an earlier lifetime as a witch. It is perhaps significant that Gerald publishes a slightly amended version in *Witchcraft Today*, where he entitles it "The Witch Remembers her Last Incarnation". Whenever he referred to Edith latterly, he usually called her "the witch". He is, however, vague about its origin, writing that the poem was "in a witch's book I possess", adding that there was "no indication of who wrote them"[13] and this is probably correct.

Gerald gave the manuscript of what was to become *A Goddess Arrives* to Edith to look through, admitting that he was well aware that the spelling and grammar left a lot to be desired. Edith

---

13. Gardner (1954), 123..

read through the manuscript and then tackled Gerald. She was quite blunt: it would need far more than just tinkering around with the grammar and spelling. Indeed, it really needed a complete re-write. However, if Gerald agreed, she would be willing to tackle it with him, for she thought it was worth it.[14]

One can imagine that Edith was in a rather difficult position. She was well aware that he was writing about the witch cult. She was a very secretive person and it is clear that she did not reveal herself as being a member of the witch cult herself until half way through his initiation in September 1939, so any influence she had on what Gerald wrote would have to be done in a very subtle way. She obviously kept quiet when Gerald introduced ideas which were alien to the Craft as she knew it, including animal and even human sacrifice. Of course, we don't know what Gerald's first draft was like and how much she may have influenced the final version.

---

14. I am informed by Edith's grandson that she was "directly involved in at least one of Gerald's books, as an editor, hacking it around". This, because of the timing, is highly likely to have been *A Goddess Arrives*. He told me "she was literate and could do this easily".

CHAPTER FIFTEEN

Into The Witch Cult

We now come to the one event in Gerald's life for which he is known. The whole of his life was leading up to probably the most significant thing that ever happened to him: his initiation into witchcraft. His life had so far been exciting but nothing special. It is this moment of initiation that distinguishes Gerald Gardner from other retired ex-Colonials.

In this chapter I try to unravel the threads of what was going on. I cannot, however, give the complete picture: there are too many things of which I claim complete ignorance. And yet, I hope that this account will be more complete and considered than any written so far. I have tried to be honest about when I am not sure about something and where I am speculating. And I could be completely wrong. I am sure there is much more to be discovered. I try to write from Gerald's perspective – what *he* thought was going on, for that is what ultimately became important, even if it turns out that he was mistaken. And it is important to realise that he didn't know everything that was going on, at least not immediately.

We only have Gerald's account that any of it ever took place: small sections in *Witchcraft Today* and *The Meaning of Witchcraft*, the account in *Gerald Gardner Witch* plus one or two letters. There are, however, internal hints in his writings plus some circumstantial evidence which enable us to take things a little further. Bracelin gives the fullest account:

> *He felt sure that they had some secret, there must be something which allowed them to take the slights at the theatre without really caring. He still thought that they might be mooting Yoga, or something of that nature. ...*
>
> *Gardner felt delighted that he was to be let into their secret. Thus it was that, a few days after the war had started, he was taken to a big house in the neighbourhood. This belonged to "Old Dorothy" – a lady of note in the district, "county" and very well-to-do. She invariably wore a pearl necklace, worth some £5,000 at the time.*
>
> *It was in this house that he was initiated into witchcraft. He was very amused at first, when he was stripped naked and brought into a place "properly prepared" to undergo his initiation.*
>
> *It was halfway through when the word Wica was first mentioned: "and I knew that that which I had thought burnt out hundreds of years ago still survived."*[1]

Let us look at this in some detail. First, as is the nature with secrets, he knew they had a secret, but didn't know what it was. As we have seen, he had already got to know them very well and knew something of their interests. We know from what he says that they were interested in Yoga, "had a real interest in the occult" and "had all sorts of magical beliefs".

Then there is the question of when Gerald was initiated. Bracelin is clear: it happened "a few days after the war had started", which was 3rd September 1939. In other words, it was presumably some time in September 1939. However, it is important to face the problem with chronology during this period, which is not just the matter of a few dates being wrong but the

---

1. Bracelin, 165.

order in which things happened, which is crucial for our under-standing of how Gerald became aware that his friends were witches. We have seen that *A Goddess Arrives* includes many of the elements which are later to be found in his description of the practices of the witches. I have always assumed that Gerald had written the book before he had met any witches, but that he added witchcraft elements (which are not essential to the story) after he had come into contact with the witches. However, Bracelin recounts the following:

> *Gardner always felt at home with them, was invited to their houses, and had many talks with them. The day came when one said:*

> *"I have seen you before". Gardner, interested, asked where. "In a former life". Then all gathered around and agreed that this was so. What made it all remarkable to Gardner was that one of the number proceeded to describe a scene "exactly like one which I had written in A Goddess Arrives, which was due to be published any day then, and which in fact came out the following week".*

> *Then someone said, "You belonged to us in the past – why don't you come back to us?"*[2]

The implication of this is that it happened before Gerald's ini-tiation in September 1939 yet *A Goddess Arrives* was not pub-lished until December 1939. Gerald was, as many of us are, particularly as we get older, somewhat uncertain about dates and particularly the order in which things happened and whether they were contemporaneous with each other. The comments about a previous lifetime could well have happened before his initiation and the incident that was similar to the scene in *A God-dess Arrives* could well be three months later. At least, that seems to me to be the most likely explanation.

This could tie in with an incident that is supposed to have happened that same month:

---

2. Bracelin, 165.

Christmas, 1939 was the occasion of a prank which Gardner played upon the master. He gave a girl a bracelet to wear. A psychometrist was at once called, who said that the bracelet and its engraved characters were very old, had certainly belonged to an ancient Egyptian priest. Then Aurelius [sic] insisted that the characters were ancient Celtic. He pompously ended the discussion with the pronouncement: "It is ancient Celtic – older than anything you know".

Then it was revealed that Gardner had had the trinket made, and that the signs upon it came from Cornelius Agrippa's private code. Since he had once assumed this personality in his deathless existence, Gardner felt that Aurelius should have known this. In any case, this was the last time that he went to their meetings.[3]

We know that later in his life, Gerald made quite a few bracelets, particularly for the women he had initiated, with their magical name in the Theban alphabet. It would appear that the item referred to was similar, since Theban was also known as Cornelius Agrippa's private code. Doreen Valiente[4] has indicated that the "girl" concerned was Edith, who was hardly a girl, being 52 years old at the time. It is at least possible that Gerald had given it to Edith as a present to celebrate his initiation as well as the more usual birthday and Christmas present.

It is significant that Bracelin states that "this was the last time that he went to their meetings". Perhaps Gerald no longer felt that he needed what the Crotona Fellowship had to offer and that he could therefore make a fool of Sullivan without fear of reprisal. Whether Edith and the Masons left at the same time I do not know but they are never mentioned subsequently in any press reports of Crotona Fellowship activity. Gerald's initiation and the publication of *A Goddess Arrives* would contribute to this feeling that he no longer needed the Crotona Fellowship.

There was, however, an existing commitment to the Fellowship that Gerald needed to fulfill before he severed ties completely. In

3. Bracelin, 164.
4. Annotation in her copy of *Gerald Gardner Witch*.

January 1940, Sullivan's play, "The Demon Monk" was put on for three performances in St Peter's Hall, Bournemouth:

He acted the drunken monk in Liveda ("a devil" spelt back-wards) when the play was produced in Bournemouth ... one monk corrupts others, and causes three of them to die. Their hearts are flung upon the stage. He prays to the devil, only for the ghosts of the monks to appear. Eventually he is sentenced to death by the abbot of their monastery.[5]

The *Christchurch Times*[6] states that Gerald played an ordinary monk, not the drunken one, so either the paper got it wrong, Gerald's memory was at fault, or Gerald was exaggerating his role in the production. It should also be noted that Liveda is the name of one of the characters, not that of the play itself.

⚜

But what of the location of Gerald's initiation? It was in a "big house in the neighbourhood" which "belonged to "Old Dorothy"". The clues are sufficient to identify "Old Dorothy" as Dorothy St. Quintin Fordham (née Clutterbuck), who was indeed a prominent resident of Highcliffe. She had been born in India in 1880, the daughter of Thomas St. Quintin Clutterbuck, a Lieutenant Colonel in the Indian Army, and his wife, Ellen Anne, née Morgan. Thomas retired in about 1887 and returned to England, ending up in 1908 by purchasing Chewton Mill House, in Highcliffe.

The Mill House is situated in the steep-sided and wooded Chewton Glen, which carries the Walkford Brook, which rises at the southern edge of the New Forest, down to the sea near Highcliffe. It is the first building you come across in the glen itself on walking up the footpath alongside Walkford Brook from the sea shore. It is on a traditional smuggling route. There are records of a mill in Chewton Glen as early as the 13th Century. The present building dates from the early to mid 18th Century. There is a depression in the ground to the north of the present house, which is all that remains of the mill pond. The mill continued

5. Bracelin, 164.
6. *Christchurch Times*, 27 January 1940.

working until 1908, when Thomas and Ellen moved in. They carried out considerable alterations to the house, including a two-storey extension, a porch and complete re-roofing, including a dormer window.

Thomas died in 1910 and Ellen in 1920. From then on, Dorothy was the sole occupant, together with her companion, Elizabeth Slatter, and various servants. In 1930, Dorothy met Rupert Fordham, heir to a brewing fortune, and had a further extension to Mill House built for him in 1931. Although spacious by most standards, Mill House was not really big enough for Rupert and, in 1933, he bought a larger house, Latimers, the other side of Highcliffe. He and Dorothy moved in there, leaving Mill House unoccupied.

In *The Witches' Way* by Janet and Stewart Farrar,[7] is a photograph of The Mill House, Highcliffe, with the caption "The house on the edge of the New Forest where Dorothy Clutterbuck initiated Gerald Gardner". Now, whilst, as I hope to demonstrate, Dorothy was not Gerald's initiator and it is somewhat stretching the point to refer to the house as being "on the edge of the New Forest", it is clear that it is Mill House that is being illustrated. The information that this was the venue of Gerald's initiation came from Doreen Valiente, who had discussions with Gerald on this very point.

It is evident to me from Bracelin's words that Dorothy was not present at Gerald's initiation. Note what he says. The house "belonged to" Old Dorothy. If she were actually there, living in the house, I submit that one would not use such a phrase. One would be more likely to say something like: "He was taken to a big house, where he met the owner, Dorothy Clutterbuck". However, the phrase "belonged to" is just the sort of thing one would say if she were not actually present. Also, the phrase "she invariably wore ..." suggests to me hearsay – what Gerald had been told – rather than what he would have seen for himself if she had been there. Moreover, Gerald says nothing about his initial impression of Dorothy, a further indication that she was not actually present at that time. And certainly Dorothy had "a big house in the neighbourhood" that was not currently occupied, probably the only person in Highcliffe to which such a statement would apply.

---

7. Janet and Stewart Farrar, *The Witches' Way*, (Robert Hale 1984).

But, if Gerald was initiated at Mill House, surely the witches weren't "breaking and entering"? No, it seems clear to me that Dorothy gave permission for Mill House to be used. I'm not saying that she knew exactly what was going on. She was sufficiently separate from it not to attend personally but also sufficiently sympathetic to allow her "spare house" to be used in this way. I suspect strongly that there was an intermediary and we shall investigate who this might have been in due course.

⚜

Gerald says little of the initiation ritual itself:

He was very amused at first, when he was stripped naked and brought into a place "properly prepared" to undergo his initiation.[8]

... I was half-initiated before the word "Wica" which they used hit me like a thunderbolt, and I knew where I was, and that the Old Religion still existed.[9]

It was half way though when the word Wica was first mentioned: "and I then knew that that which I had thought burnt out hundreds of years ago still survived".[10]

One can imagine Gerald, blindfolded, being taken through the ritual, hearing the word 'Wica' repeated several times and turning it over in his mind. What did the word "Wica" mean? They talked about "the Wica" as people: who could they be? What did the word "Wica" sound like? And then, as he says, the answer "hit him like a thunderbolt". One can imagine how Gerald felt, and it is clear to me that this is not a made-up story on his part; this actually happened.

Candidates for initiation today are in a very different position. They know perfectly well what they are asking to be initiated into, and, indeed, they would not be admitted if they did not know! Gerald, on the contrary, if we are to believe him, did not

---

8. Bracelin, 165.
9. Gardner, (1959), p 19.
10. Bracelin, 165.

know until half way through the ritual. I think we must try to see this from his point of view and from those of his initiators. Gerald trusted Edith and the others. If he was to be let into their secret then he was content. He was in their hands and perfectly prepared for what it might be. From their point of view, they probably felt that it would have more impact on Gerald if he did not know in advance.

Let us imagine the scene. At some stage, his blindfold was taken off, and he gradually made out the figures which were surrounding him in the dim candlelight and in the smoky atmosphere of the burning incense. There was Edith, of course, his initiator. And the other members of his small circle of friends – Susie Mason, Rosetta Fudge and Ernie Mason. And there in the background was Rosanne, smiling at him. They all embraced him and welcomed him into formal membership of their group: he was now a witch.

There were so many questions springing up in his mind, but the warm feelings that he had for them, and they for him, made any serious questioning impossible. It was a time for feasting and dancing. In 1954, in *Witchcraft Today*, he writes "Fifteen years ago, I heard many of the old tunes. Unfortunately I know nothing about music and I did not write them down."[11]

Gerald says very little else about the form of the ritual:

> ... *I soon found myself in the circle and took the usual oaths of secrecy which bound me not to reveal any secrets of the cult.*[12]

Gerald gives what are likely to be more details about his initiation in a letter which he wrote to Gerald Yorke of Riders in the period before the publication of his book, *Witchcraft Today*. It is interesting that this is all about actions. Few words are mentioned, which makes me think that the description is based on Gerald's own initiation. He would remember actions far more than the words that may have been used:

11. Gardner, (1954), 141-142.
12. Op. cit., 19.

... there are two, things they do, As soon as the Circle is cast &
purified, they go round, what I call, evoking the Mighty Ones.
To attend, to guard the Circle & witness the rites, These are
meny. they are supposed to stand outside, & watch, seeing all
is correct. Candidates for initiation are peraded round, intro-
duced to them, & they are supposed to be satisfied all is in
order, Also at certain rites, The, God, or Goddess Is invoked to
descend & come into the Body of the Priestess or Priest, but
first these are purified, & perade round so the mighty ones
outside see all is in order, this we speak of as invoking. At ordi-
nary meetings, the God & Goddess are not so invoked, the
Priestess & Priest are simply their representitives, & are not
the Gods themselves, I think I did not refer to this rite, if I did,
I dont think theyll pass it.[13]

I think that Gerald revealed further details of the initiation
ritual in his novel, *High Magic's Aid*, which was published in 1949
and which we shall look at in Chapter 22.

⁂

Gerald's mind would have been buzzing with possibilities: he
couldn't have slept that night even if he didn't get to bed until
dawn. However, I am sure that later the following day he would
have visited Edith and asked her all sorts of questions, but she
would probably have appeared strangely different and more circumspect. Gerald would have asked her how she got into the
witch cult:

He found that his friends, after following Mabs to her set-
tlement, had discovered an old Coven, and remained here
because of that. "I found that Old Dorothy and some like
her, plus a number of New Forest people, had kept the light
shining".[14]

Whilst this passage needs a lot of interpretation, it is clear
that there are two distinct groups of people here. One group was

---

13. Letter, Gerald Gardner to Gerald Yorke, 24 October 1952 (in Yorke Collection, Warburg
Institute).
14. Bracelin, 166.

Gerald's friends (Edith and the Mason family) who "followed Mabs to her settlement". The other group, what Bracelin calls "an old coven" consisted of "Old Dorothy, some like her, plus a number of New Forest people".

Let us go back to Southampton in 1935. Edith and the Mason family had resigned en masse from the Co-Masons and, in effect, taken Beechwood Hall with them. They were following the lead of Mabel Besant-Scott (Mabs) and it was probably natural for them to be interested when she told them that she had moved down to Christchurch, probably at the invitation of Catherine Chalk, who had also been a Co-Mason, to join her Rosicrucian group. This was just after the time when Sullivan had been invited by Catherine Chalk to move the headquarters of the Crotona Fellowship from Liverpool to Christchurch. Edith and the Mason family subsequently started to attend meetings of the Crotona Fellowship in Christchurch, becoming heavily involved in their plays and other activities.

It is interesting that it is only the second group which Bracelin describes as a "coven". Whether it was actually what would nowadays be recognised as a coven I very much doubt. But who was in the group and what did they do and believe?

It is clear from Bracelin's statement that 'Old Dorothy' was a member of this group. It is most fortunate that we do have an insight into Dorothy's inner thoughts and feelings, particularly about nature, as some of her 'commonplace books' have survived, where she wrote, usually in verse, about matters which interested her. In my book *Wiccan Roots* I give details of how those for 1942 and 1943 survived.[15] They are illustrated by her friend, Christine Wells, and are currently in private ownership.

In that book, I concluded that the deepest emotions present in Dorothy's commonplace books, apart from those which are concerned with relationships, are engendered by Nature rather than orthodox religion. Let us look at a few examples. Her entries for the Christian festivals relate Easter Day with New Birth, Christmas with a feminine entity, and Whit Sunday with contact with those who have died. Just where one would most expect a

---

15. Philip Heselton, *Wiccan Roots*, (Capall Bann 2000), 156-158.

reference to Jesus and to the Christian significance of the festival, we get instead a divinity which is expressed through and found in the local landscape, and the legends and spirits associated with it. And of what day did Dorothy write:

> *Of all the days of the wonderful year*
> *This is the day of all days most dear.?*

Not Easter, nor Christmas, nor any of the Christian festivals: she was writing about Midsummer Day.

It is abundantly clear that Dorothy's main inspiration is Nature. She was acutely aware of the cycle of the seasons and of the birds, animals and flowers that marked it. And, whether to be interpreted literally or not, the pages of her books are liberally scattered with accounts of fairies and a nameless being whom we can only identify with a Goddess. Indeed, it is no exaggeration to say that much of Dorothy's verse would not look out of place in any of today's Pagan journals.

I have been criticised for my opinion that Dorothy's writings were Pagan. I shall try and be clearer about what I mean. First of all, I do not mean that she would have called herself Pagan or that she was a member of a Pagan organisation. She was, in fact, a member of the Church of England. All I meant was that her approach to Nature was one that would be compatible with that of present-day Pagans. She was aware of the cycle of the year, the natural markers of that cycle, particularly the "old" festivals, and the entities that embody such seasons, whether they be goddesses, fairies or woodland spirits generally. At present, my conclusions are that the almost complete absence of Christian imagery and observance, and the presence of a strong and deeply felt expression of an awareness of the divinity of and in Nature, seem to me so clear as to demonstrate that Dorothy was pagan in all but name.

Dorothy Fordham's commonplace books and her life in general are worthy of more detailed consideration, which I intend to give in a future book. Dorothy had a somewhat unusual private life. She was probably strongly bi-sexual, living with her companion, Elizabeth Slatter, known as 'John', until her death in 1933.

There are also strong hints of her bisexuality in her commonplace books. In 1935, she went through a marriage ceremony with Rupert Fordham, which was invalid because Rupert's previous wife was still alive. It was widely believed locally that Dorothy married Rupert for his money, and it is certainly true that there are hints of this in her commonplace books. Because of her invalid marriage, she was refused communion and, as a result, went off to confront the Bishop of Winchester, but to no avail. When I write about Dorothy at greater length, I shall tell the story of the 'fake funeral'! Dorothy was a complex personality. I hope that I have written enough about her to make clear her approach to Nature.

Another member of the group I believe to have been Rosamund Sabine. I got the clue when looking at Doreen Valiente's copy of *Gerald Gardner Witch*. After the phrase "a number of New Forest people" she had put an asterisk and written the name "Mother Sabine". Rosamund Sabine was living in Highcliffe at the time. She had also been a member of an Order associated with the Golden Dawn.

Contrary to the embarrasingly wrong information I gave in my previous book, *Gerald Gardner and the Cauldron of Inspiration*,[16] she was born Rosamund Isabella Charlotte Carnsew on 5th February 1865, the daughter of Henry Carnsew, solicitor, and his wife, Henrietta Maria (née Donnithorne) at the family home of Somers Place, a fine Victorian Gothic mansion near Billingshurst in Sussex.

In 1905, at the age of 40, she applied for membership of the Order of the M[orgen] R[othe], also known as the Independent and Rectified Order R.R. et A.C. (Rosae Rubae et Aureae Crucis – the Red Rose and the Cross of Gold) or the Independent and Rectified Rite of the Golden Dawn, an offshoot of what was probably the most famous and influential magical orders of all time – the Hermetic Order of the Golden Dawn. On the application form, she gave her Sacramental Name, the name by which she desired to be known if admitted to the Order, as 'Vacuna'.

Vacuna was a Roman Sabine Goddess, and I think it is no coincidence that six years later, in May 1911, she married Thomas George Alford Broadfield Sabine in the Catholic Church of Saints

---

16. Philip Heselton, *Gerald Gardner and the Cauldron of Inspiration*, (Capall Bann, 2003), 65.

Anthony and George at Burton Park, in Sussex. Most of those applying for membership of the Order chose a Latin motto for their Sacramental Name: she was the only one of the 80 or so applicants to give the name of a goddess.[17]

In August 1930 she wrote an article entitled 'Rose of the World' about the Golden Dawn lamen in the well-respected journal, *The Occult Review*.[18] Gareth Medway, who drew my attention to the article, tells me that such an article at that date "must be by an initiate, so she must have gained admission to some branch of the Golden Dawn". The Golden Dawn scholar, R.A. Gilbert, states "...she clearly was familiar with the Golden Dawn form which suggests that she had entered one branch of the original Order; probably Waite's, but possibly one of the others".[19] 'Rosamund', of course, means 'Rose of the World', and one could well speculate on this coincidence.

In 1923 or 1924, the Sabines moved into a house near Chewton Glen Farm, Walkford, not far from Highcliffe. They named the house 'Whinchat'. It seems to have been one of the first houses in what was to become Avenue Road, Walkford, the very road which would later be home to Edith Woodford-Grimes. The house was referred to as No. 1 Avenue Road. It has now been demolished and a bungalow, which retains the name, built in its place.

The whinchat is a small, short-tailed bird, common on open farmland. However, the name also has the property that if you take alternate letters, thus – W̲h̲i̲n̲c̲h̲a̲t̲ – you get 'Wica'. I offer no comment except that it shows the same sort of mind as that which chose 'Vacuna' as Rosamund's Sacramental Name – a subtle joke for those 'in the know'.

Gerald refers to 'Mother Sabine' in a letter to Cecil Williamson, written in December 1953: "Old Mother Sabine died recently & Ive got her very nice little cabinet of little draws & lots of little Boxes & things etc. but the Herbs have mostly mouldered away. It smells wonderful though, & theres an Old Culpepper with 1684 Original binding."[20]

17. R A Gilbert, *The Golden Dawn Companion*, (The Aquarian Press, 1986), 170.
18. R. Sabine, "The Rose of the World", *Occult Review*, Vol. 52, No 2, (August 1930), 107-110.
19. Letter, R. A. Gilbert to the author, 6 March 2003.
20. Letter, Gerald Gardner to Cecil Williamson, 23 December 1953 (Document 89, Boscastle Museum of Witchcraft).

Rosamund died in May 1948, over five years before Gerald is writing that "Old Mother Sabine died recently". I think the explanation for this is that Gerald never had very much, if any, direct contact with Rosamund: it was all done via Edith, who was, as it is sometimes put, "economical with the truth".

The third member of the group is merely my deduction, but I think it highly likely. She was Katherine Oldmeadow, author of children's stories and good friend of 'Old Dorothy'. From circumstantial evidence, I think it highly likely that she knew Rosamund Sabine. Katherine Louise Oldmeadow (1878-1963) lived with her married sister, Edith, Edith's husband, Arthur Lawrie, and her other sister, Annie, in The Glen House, on the corner of Lymington Road and Mill Lane, Highcliffe. The Lawries had lived in India and had moved to Highcliffe some time before 1913.

Katherine was a writer of girls' school stories and had over 23 books published. Their pages show their author had a rich appreciation of Nature and of its experience evoking deep feelings in her characters, particularly of the New Forest, which she loved and knew well:

> *The quiet, open glades were rather different from the thick Forest of her fancy, but the scampering Forest ponies enchanted her, and far away in the distance were great belts of fairy blue pine-trees.*[21]

Katherine was well aware of fairies and nature spirits and considered them to be real. She brought them into many of her stories and there is much vivid description about fairies in the landscape. Ian Stevenson says: "Chewton Glen was a magical place to her. Whenever she brought it into her stories it seemed fairy folk lurked behind every tree."[22]

Orthodox Christian religion is rarely given a mention in Katherine's books, where divinity is represented almost exclusively by reference to Pagan gods and goddesses:

> *"It's lucky we had classical dancing this term," said Nancy, "it will be jolly to have the nymphs barefoot, and those*

21. K. L. Oldmeadow, *Madcap Judy*, (Collins, 1919), 41.
22. Letter, Ian Stevenson to the author, 5 December 2000.

green Greek dresses will just do". ... "We must have twelve nymphs," said Barbara ...[23]

... in the middle of the door there swung an old copper knocker – the head of Pan, the woodland god, holding a round copper ring between his grinning lips.[24]

Similarly, Easter and Christmas are hardly mentioned, but there is one festival which dominates the books – May Day. The descriptions certainly have a pagan resonance about them:

A great, spreading, pink thorn-tree grew there, which would make a flowery and fragrant canopy for a May Queen. ...The evening before the birthday was spent in the woods, and the girls returned laden with wild flowers, and great branches of pink and white May ...[25]

Bettine, dressed as a wood-nymph, all in green, danced in with a crown of golden flowers, which she placed on the May Queen's head. Then very soft music sounded, and twelve nymphs in silver and green came running from the pine-wood in the distance, garlanded with flowers, six of them bearing great branches of white May, and six carrying Spring flowers of blue and gold.[26]

By "pagan resonance" I should perhaps explain that I do not mean that Katherine thought of herself as or called herself pagan, but the way she wrote about the things which interested her would accord with the approach of present-day pagans.

Divination, through crystal balls and numerology, secret societies and rituals also feature prominently.

The one non-fiction book which Katherine wrote was entitled *The Folklore of Herbs.*[27]

She also brought witchcraft into her stories. In her earlier books, most of the mentions are negative, describing witchcraft as something to be feared:

23. Oldmeadow, (1919), 273.
24. K.L. Oldmeadow, *Princess Charming*, (Collins, 1923), 101.
25. Oldmeadow, (1919), 276 and 278.
26. Oldmeadow, (1919), 284.
27. K. L. Oldmeadow, *The Folklore of Herbs*, (Cornish Brothers Limited, 1946).

... she hated going to bed alone with a witch living under the staircase![28]

"She's a witch, you know. If you poked your nose through that door which leads into her part of the house, she'll cast an awful spell on you."[29]

Whenever witches are mentioned in the earlier books, they are referred to in such terms. However, a change seems to occur in about 1925 or 1926. After that time, witchcraft is shown in a more positive light. Katherine was certainly sufficiently aware by 1926 to know that there were witches who healed. She calls them "white witches", and there are extended passages in *The Folklore of Herbs* where she makes a clear distinction between "white" and "black" witches, after which she makes a very interesting statement: "The white witch of today still holds queer beliefs about ..."[30] This is a very clear statement which implies that witches existed when she was writing and that she knew at least one of them sufficiently well to know what they believed. She states that "witches always had herb gardens", a very definite statement, perhaps implying that she knew some who did.

Her continuing distinction between "white" and "black" witches clearly demonstrates that she was aware that there are witches who do not do harm (presumably because she had personal knowledge of them) and wanted to distinguish them from the "other kind". This distinction is totally absent from her pre-1926 books, which refer to witchcraft in purely negative terms.

This down-to-earth attitude to witchcraft appears to be firmly established by the time *When George III was King* was published in 1934. When one of the heroines of the story, which is set at the time of the threatened Napoleonic invasion, was asked what she would like to be, she replied that she wanted to be a travel writer, but that because she was a girl, she couldn't, and she would have to stay at home:

28. K L Oldmeadow, *Ragged Robin*, (Collins, 1920), 93.
29. K. L. Oldmeadow, *Princess Anne*, (Collins, 1925), 156.
30. Oldmeadow, (1946), 15.

"But I shan't be only a housewife," continued Charlotte. "I shall be a witch too."

"A witch! Oh, Charlotte, but witches are wicked!" cried Susan in distress.

"Not a white witch ... They are wise old women and know all about herbs that heal. I shall learn Latin, and study plants and herbs, and grow them in the garden and make them into medicines and ointments for Father's patients. I shall be a wise young woman ... You can't be a white witch and a wise woman unless you understand all about herbs ..."[31]

What caused Katherine's sudden change of approach to witch-craft? She can't just have read *The Witch Cult in Western Europe*, because of the emphasis on herbs. Could it be that she met some-one in about 1925 who caused her to change her opinions? Some-one who healed people through the use of herbs? Someone who revealed to Katherine that she was a witch? I am of the opinion that it was meeting Rosamund that changed how Katherine wrote about witches, and this was because at some stage Rosamund iden-tified herself to Katherine as a witch. The timing is right and so is Katherine's association of witches with herb-growing. I have not yet established any definite connection between them, but I would be most surprised if Katherine Oldmeadow and Rosamund Sabine did not know each other. Highcliffe was not a large village in the 1920s and 1930s. It is not unlikely that long-term residents would get to know each other. Katherine and Rosamund lived only half a mile apart on the edge of Chewton Common for 24 years. They both had a great interest in herbs; in Rosamund's case possessing a 1684 edition of Culpeper and a cabinet with drawers for keeping herbs; in Katherine's case, having written about herbs and having a book on them published. Is it not highly likely that they would have met whilst walking on the Common or in Chewton Glen and the conversation getting around to their common interest in herbs? They would then have found that they had other interests as well – pagan gods and goddesses, fairies and divination.

---

31. K. L. Oldmeadow, *When George The Third Was King,* (Hutchinson, 1934), 61.

Dorothy and Katherine were near neighbours, living at each end of Mill Lane. We know from Dorothy's commonplace books that she knew and respected Katherine greatly. Indeed, she gave the completed books to Katherine, who, probably more than anyone, would qualify to be Dorothy's "best friend".

So we have this triangle of older women (in 1939, Dorothy was 59, Katherine 61 and Rosamund 74), all past retirement age and certainly "ladies of leisure". They had probably known each other since the mid 1920s. Katherine and Dorothy had in common a love of nature such that their expressions would be totally compatible with what could appear today in pagan publications. Rosamund had a background in occult and magical traditions and was also a practitioner of herbalism. Katherine was also very much aware of the occult side of nature and was interested in herbs. Yet there was something intimate linking them and I think it was something to do with roses. I intend to explore this in my next book.

I also suspect that Catherine Chalk may have been a member of that group, partly because she had been a Co-Mason[32] and also because she had lived in the area for longer than most of the Crotona Fellowship members. Indeed, her offer of land was the reason for the Fellowship moving its headquarters to Somerford in the first place. Catherine Chalk was also the same generation as Rosamund, Katherine and Dorothy. Being interested in esoteric matters and living within four miles of the others, it would not be surprising if some contact had been established in the years from the early 1920s to the late 1930s.

I don't think Gerald really ever got to know these people at all well, even after his initiation. For example, he gets the dates when Dorothy and Rosamund died significantly wrong, which suggests that he did not keep in regular or indeed any contact with them, which in any case would have been via Edith. Ronald Hutton[33] states that the social worlds of Dorothy Fordham and Gerald Gardner never overlapped. Yet in one respect at least, they certainly did. As suggested by his taking of the *Daily Telegraph*, Gerald was conservative in his political opinions. He was also a member of the Highcliffe Branch of the New Forest and

32. Christchurch Times, 11 December 1931 and letter from Phyllis G. Croft to the author, 9 November 2001.
33. Hutton, 211.

Christchurch Conservative and Unionist Association. He did not seem to take a very active part, but he did attend the Annual General Meeting on 20th November 1940. Dorothy Fordham had been President of the branch for three years and was being proposed for re-election. Gerald seconded the proposal, which was adopted.[34]

I think that whatever it was that bound these women together, it was not a coven as we would know it today. These were mature ladies: they were not cavorting around naked in the middle of the Forest! It probably all started with Margaret Murray's *The Witch Cult in Western Europe* which was published in 1921. Gerald's use of the term "the witch cult" to describe what he was initiated into suggests that that is what they themselves called it. I suspect that the determining factor may have been an article which appeared in the leading monthly journal, *The Occult Review*, in March 1922. This was by J.W. Brodie-Innes and was entitled "The Cult of the Witch", which appears to have included a review of *The Witch Cult in Western Europe*.[35] We know that Rosamund had been interested in the occult since at least 1905 and that she had an article published in *The Occult Review* in 1930, so it is at least likely that she read the Brodie-Innes article in 1922. This is actually more likely than that she had read the book since its sales had actually been very slow.

Rosamund was knowledgeable about esoteric topics and would certainly have been familiar with the doctrine of reincarnation. At some stage, I think she came to a realisation, whether by dream recognition, more formal regression or just an inner knowing, that she had been a witch in a previous lifetime. I suspect that she was the first to claim to have memories of a previous lifetime as a witch. She was somewhat older than the others (hence, perhaps, the appellation "Mother Sabine") and, after moving to Walkford, she called her house 'Whinchat', which suggests that by at least 1924 the concept of "the Wica" to mean members of "the witch cult" had already been formed in her mind.

I think that Ralph Merrifield (1913-1995), Curator of the Guildhall Museum, London, has hit on the essence of the matter:

34. *Christchurch Times*, 23 November 1940.
35. J. W. Brodie-Innes, "The Cult of the Witch", *The Occult Review*, Vol. 35, No 3, (March 1922).

> *Margaret Murray in The Witch Cult in Western Europe in*
> *1921 and subsequently in The God of the Witches had*
> *removed the whiff of sulphur from witchcraft and repre-*
> *sented it as a respectable pagan religion, driven underground*
> *by persecution. Alan Smith has demonstrated that folklorists*
> *can be suspected of practising what they study, and this is*
> *likely to have been the case with Dr. Murray herself. That*
> *diminutive and kindly scholar, who radiated intelligence and*
> *strength of character into extreme old age, may well have*
> *seemed to some a role-model for the beneficent witch, oblit-*
> *erating the traditional image of the squalid hag, with whom*
> *they cannot have wished to identify. For such people Mar-*
> *garet Murray may have seemed the ideal fairy godmother,*
> *and her theory became the pumpkin coach that could trans-*
> *port them into the realm of fantasy for which they longed.*
> *Were there any 'Sunday newspaper' covens before 1921?*[36]

If we assume that these two groups (the traditional group from Southampton consisting of the Mason family and Edith; and what we might call the 'Rose' group from Highcliffe, consisting of Rosamund Sabine, Katherine Oldmeadow and Dorothy Fordham) made some sort of contact with each other in the autumn of 1935, some of the individual members may have drawn close to each other in the three years before Gerald Gardner came to Highcliffe in 1938 and started attending the Crotona Fellowship meetings. During that time there could well have been a cross-fertilisation of ideas centred on witchcraft, both on what seems to have been a surviving tradition and on individual memories of a previous lifetime as a witch. They had four years together, from 1935 to 1939, before Gerald's initiation. I suspect that these core elements plus a wealth of experience in many esoteric and practical fields were mixed together in the cauldron of inspiration to create a potent brew in the course of those four years, whereby an ethos of being witches developed strongly into a firm belief.

I think that the contact between the two groups was a fertile one, with ideas passing around both groups. I suspect that, as

---

36. Ralph Merrifield, "G. B. Gardner and the 20th Century 'Witches'", *Folklore Society News*, no. 17, (June 1993), 10.

well as Rosamund, Edith also had memories of a previous lifetime as a witch. The coincidence of two individuals both remembering such previous lifetimes was enough to spark creative thoughts and feelings. During that time, there grew within them a very vivid feeling of being witches. The idea of being a witch and of being a group of witches reincarnated together was a very powerful image and I think it was enough to excite each member of the group and draw them together.

The vivid feeling that at least two of them had of having been witches in a previous lifetime, the consequent firm belief in reincarnation, an awareness of esoteric matters strengthened by membership of a variety of bodies, a strong feeling of finding divinity in nature, and the importance of the mind in working magic all came together in the melting-pot which produced what they saw as a living representation of 'the witch cult'.

Perhaps they didn't *do* much, but they were very strongly aware of what they were. Each contributed something to the whole, not in an organised way, but in an organic fashion. It was more an awareness and a recognition than something for which one trained and joined. That, I think, is the reason why they were so interested in Gerald's supposed ancestor, Grissell Gairdner and his memories of a previous lifetime in Cyprus. They felt he was one of them.

There are still far too many unanswered questions in this whole business. For example, did the Mason family come from a hereditary line of witches? In Gerald's manuscript, "New Light on Witchcraft", there is the following statement:

Grandfathers and great-grandmothers have told folk still living of meetings they attended about a hundred and thirty years ago ...[37]

This is subtly different from what finally appeared in *Witchcraft Today* and very much more specific: "grandfathers and great-grandmothers". If, as I strongly suspect, this is the Mason family, then we can probably track down who of their ancestors were around in the early 1820s.

37. Gerald Gardner, "New Light on Witchcraft", (manuscript in Toronto collection), 76.

One important unanswered question is how the former Co-Masons, Edith Woodford-Grimes, Susie Mason, Ernie Mason and Rosetta Fudge, after "following Mabs to her settlement" could have "discovered an old Coven". We can imagine that they initially came over to Christchurch from Southampton for the day or the evening by train, a distance of some 30 miles. And back again the same day. Eventually, in 1938, Edith bought a house in Somerford, adjacent to the Theatre, and Susie moved to Barrack Road, Christchurch. The others remained living in Southampton.

How were they to have "discovered an old Coven" which was centred on Highcliffe? There is only one realistic place that they could have come across a member of that group, and that is within the ranks of the Crotona Fellowship itself.

So far, we have not established the identity of this "missing link". Of the group in Highcliffe, Rosamund is by far the most likely. By 1935, she had been interested in the occult for well over 30 years and would have been highly likely to have heard about and been interested in the Crotona Fellowship when there began to be mentions of it in the local paper. The fact that her name never appears in connection with the theatrical productions staged at the Ashrama, Garden Theatre or elsewhere does not necessarily mean that she was not a member of the Fellowship. At present, she is the most likely candidate for the "missing link". Catherine Chalk, who provided the land for the Ashrama and Theatre, is another possibility, as I have already suggested.

A lot more research is clearly needed. Our one consolation is that almost certainly Gerald didn't know the answers to these questions either. The only witches that he was in regular contact with were Edith and Rosanne. I am firmly of the opinion that it was Edith who taught him what he subsequently reproduced about the witches' beliefs and practices in *High Magic's Aid, Witchcraft Today* and *The Meaning of Witchcraft*.

CHAPTER SIXTEEN

Guarding His Native Land

When Gerald had settled in Highcliffe in July 1938, he offered himself as an Air Raid Precautions (ARP) warden to the local headquarters and was accepted enthusiastically. He was quickly promoted to Sector Warden, and wore a white helmet. He was in charge of Sector E (the Walkford area) and had ten wardens, as well as himself, including Edith after she had moved to Highcliffe in August 1940. As well as the normal warden's job of patrolling to make sure the blackout was being strictly observed, he would also be responsible for handing out gas masks and making sure that everyone could use them properly. The ARP post was his own house, although by 1941 it had moved to the junction of Glenville and Ringwood Roads.

On the evening of Tuesday 14th May 1940, the Secretary of State for War, Anthony Eden, made a broadcast in which he referred to the numerous ordinary citizens who, whilst not being able to enlist in the regular armed forces, wanted to do their part in helping to defend their country in its hour of need. He asked for men aged between 17 and 65 to put their names down at their local police station to join what was to be called the Local Defence Volunteers. They would not be paid but would have uniforms and would be armed.

The response was overwhelming: long queues formed outside police stations and during that day over a quarter of a million men put their names down. By the end of June there were almost one and a half million volunteers. Organisation was haphazard, however, and arms were in very short supply, as were uniforms.

This was where Gerald felt that he could make a real contribution. He had knowledge of weapons and, in fact, many weapons themselves in his collection which could be put to good use. He knew how to use them, he was fit after a lifetime of physical work and he was still of an age where he could be actively employed. If the country's coastline needed defending, then he was just the one to do it. I have no reason to doubt that Gerald performed his ARP duties conscientiously, but when the formation of the Local Defence Volunteers was announced on the radio he immediately offered himself for service: he applied to join the LDV – and was turned down! Apparently they were not taking Civil Defence personnel because those in charge of Civil Defence were rather afraid that many of their best people would be siphoned off by the new force.

Gerald was not one to take this lying down. He armed his wardens with some of the weapons from his collection, including pikes and coshes. Gerald himself had a Luger with a "snail" magazine, which acted as a miniature machine-gun. This did not make ARP Headquarters enamoured of Gerald.[1]

It was probably this reaction to his attempt to arm his wardens that caused Gerald to respond in two ways. The first was typically English: he wrote to the papers.

Gerald was a Conservative politically. As we have seen, he attended and voted in the 1940 Highcliffe Conservative Association A.G.M. However, as we have also seen, he was not the typical retired colonial type. He did, however, read the *Daily Telegraph*, which was then, and remains today, the archetypal reading matter for Conservatives. Using his writing skills, he sent a letter, for publication, to the editor. It was headed "Resisting the Invader" and was sub-titled "Delaying Actions by Civilians". It read:

1. Bracelin, 161.

Belgium and France were lost because the civil population bolted instead of staying and delaying the invaders. It has been proved in many wars that if the civil population will fight delaying actions they can be most troublesome to invaders and may even beat them.

It is part of German tactics to make it believed that civilians cannot, and may not, resist invaders, because the Germans well know how difficult they are to fight. In the last war the Germans encouraged civilians in East Prussia and Poland to snipe when the army had retreated.

The made-in-Germany rules of war mean that Germany does not obey the rules of war as they have hitherto been understood. Why should we? Everyone willing should be given arms when they are available and taught how to use them.

If the French villages had resisted the German motor-cycle troops could not have come on as they did. If each village and town had defended itself, France would never have fallen as she did, and Germany might well have been on the way to defeat now.

Why should people who wish to defend themselves be prevented just to make it easy for Germany? By Magna Carta every free-born Englishman is entitled to have arms to defend himself and his household. Let us now claim our right.[2]

This letter did not emerge unbidden. There had been correspondence over the previous week or two and Gerald's letter continued the theme. It was, however, his letter that drew attention, both in England and in Germany. Further letters in the *Daily Telegraph* generally supported Gerald's point of view.

Not everyone approved, however. The *Daily Telegraph* in its issue of Thursday 22nd August carried a report by its correspondent in Zurich from the previous day. Entitled "Daily Telegraph Annoys Nazis" and subtitled "Magna Carta Letter", the report reads:

---

2. *Daily Telegraph*, 13 August 1940.

The letter in The Daily Telegraph last week on civilian resistance to invaders has galvanised the Wilhelmstrasse in Berlin into fervent protestations. ... Today's Frankfurter Zeitung, in a prominent front-page cable from Berlin, rants against the writer of the letter and the conditions in which it obtained publicity. The writer must know, says the cable, that human ethics have advanced in the last 700 years. His suggestion is condemned as mediaeval and as an infringement of international law.

The following Saturday, 24th August, the *Christchurch Times* reported on the local angle in a front page piece entitled "Highcliffe Resident Annoys Nazis: Berlin Resents Civil Resistance". It concluded:

Dr. Gardner, commenting to our representative this week on the annoyance expressed in Berlin, emphasised that the country should organise to defend our homes, particularly in delaying action by the enemy, it is a factor that has played a definite part in previous wars. He points out with regard to the Berlin objection that this is contrary to international law, Germany has so ruthlessly discarded international law that she can no longer plead what is right or not right.

As to annoying the Nazis, Dr. Gardner says he does not like annoying anybody, but in this case it affords him very much pleasure.

There was a postscript to this episode in that on Thursday 22nd August 1940, two days after the *Frankfurter Zeitung* article, it is rumoured that a German aircraft flew very low over the Highcliffe area. The following day, New Milton, a small town just two miles east of Highcliffe, was the subject of an air raid. A lone Heinkel 111 flew very low and dropped a stick of bombs over the town causing much damage, 23 deaths and 20 injuries. Cable damaged in the raid meant that the air-raid siren did not sound. As a result, and because the raider flew so low, many did not realise that it was an enemy aircraft until too late, so did not take cover, which probably contributed to the casualty figures. The fact that it was a single aircraft so near to Highcliffe led some to speculate that the raid may have been in retaliation for Gerald's letter and some blamed him, saying: "If you hadn't written that letter that annoyed Hitler, this would never have happened."[3]

Bracelin suggested that Gerald's letter: "... might have had some effect upon Whitehall – for it was soon announced that the L.D.V. (Local Defence Volunteers) was to be formed, civilian formations with rifles and uniform arm-bands."[4] In fact, the timing is rather different: as we have seen, the formation of the Local Defence Volunteers was announced by Anthony Eden on 14th May 1940, whereas Gerald's letter was not published until three months later, on 13th August.

Apart from the letter, Gerald had other plans for joining the LDV, or what had then become known as the Home Guard. He began to be aware that not all those in authority were quite as "stuffy" as others. He had already made contact with Major Frederick Merriott Fish, the Company Commander of the local Home Guard unit in Highcliffe. This was the "A" (Avon Mouth) Company of the Hampshire Home Guard, which had been quickly established and which consisted of platoons from Highcliffe, Walkford, Mudeford, Friars Cliff and the Airspeed aircraft factory at Somerford. It had its HQ at Hengistbury House, on the cliff top at Highcliffe. There was also a platoon from the top secret Air Defence Experimental Establishment (ADEE) at Steamer Point, Highcliffe, which was known locally as "The Hush-Hush Factory" and which was devoted to the development of radar.

Fish had been born at Croydon in Surrey in 1896 and was brought up at Bransgore near Highcliffe before emigrating to Canada some time after 1911. He had served in the Canadian Army in World War I and stood as a candidate for the Co-operative Commonwealth Party in the Canadian Federal Election of 1935. He returned to England in 1938 and was subsequently invalided out of the Army. He was working as a researcher at ADEE when the call to form the Local Defence Volunteers was made and, as Major Fish, he was appointed commanding officer of "A" Company in 1940. In an interview he said that in his battalion there were:

---

3. Bracelin, 161.
4. Ibid.

*... two titled men ... one, a viscount who was junior to a Trade Union chairman. There was an Australian foreman ... ex-schoolmasters, engineers, a novelist [this was probably Gerald], an ex-sergeant major in the Coldstream Guards, several holding university degrees, and an ex-group captain of the R.A.F. – A grand mixture of men ... all of whom are now trained.*5

One of his company remembers Fish as a "likeable, cheerful, humorous chap". He went on to say:

*Politically, he was very radical, keen on anything left-wing. He spoke strongly of his support for the Republicans in the Spanish Civil War. Fish was a maverick and rebelled against traditional authority. ...He was the right chap for the job because of the nature of the Home Guard. He ran things with a loose rein.*6

Although one suspects that he and Gerald would not have had much in common politically, Gerald was certainly also a maverick who rebelled against authority, particularly where he thought it was being short-sighted and bureaucratic. So it seems as if Fish and Gerald would have got on well together and enjoyed trying to circumvent the regulations! He could see that it would obviously be advantageous to have Gerald in the Home Guard, so they looked up the regulations and found that a Home Guard commander could take on technical staff without permission, so Fish enrolled Gerald as an armourer.

Gerald had a lot of support from the other ARP Wardens, who were annoyed that, according to the regulations, they were forbidden from taking up arms in the event of invasion. At a meeting, it was confirmed that Wardens could not be taken into the Home Guard. Until then, Gerald had been hidden in the audience. At that moment he stepped forward, quite clearly in Home Guard uniform, with a lance-corporal's chevron and the armourer's crossed-pincers badge on his arm. He explained how he had been working hard fitting Sten guns for the Home Guard and was

5. *Christchurch Times*, 1 February 1941.
6. Interview Ian Stevenson and 'GB', 19 November 2004.

not worried in the slightest by threats from the Wardens' commanding officers:

> *"They could sack me from the Wardens; but my house was the A.R.P. Post. They could stop the Home Guard from recruiting a Warden. Once taken on, however, there was no rule about giving him back, and a man could be a warden during raids and a Home Guard during the All Clears".*[7]

After Gerald had joined the Home Guard as Armourer, he realised how desperate the situation was:

> *"We expected Hitler on the seashore any day. We had no weapons worth the name. In my three-mile beach sector there were six shotguns, my Luger and Donna's revolver, and a few other pistols, with about six rounds apiece for them. Then there were my pikes and swords. By the end of that week, six soldiers and a sergeant were sent to defend the three miles. In another seven days these had been augmented by fifty men under an officer. Later, dribs and drabs came; but, barring rifles and not much ammunition, they had nothing. No artillery, no automatic weapons. I tried to get an old Malay cannon going, with some blasting power [sic] for explosives, but nothing came of this."* [8]

The Highcliffe Home Guard had their own training area on the cliff-top, which had slit trenches and hanging dummies used for bayonet practice. A fellow member of the Home Guard remarked: "... at the outset, when we were trying to get any weapons together that we could, ... he [Gerald] manufactured some Molotov cocktails to his own recipe. These things were very dangerous indeed! I don't know whether they frightened the enemy, but they frightened everyone over this side!"[9]

Gerald enjoyed talking to people and getting them to talk to him, and his technique was the same whether they were the natives of Borneo or Highcliffe. In 1946, in his notes for a talk on Amulets, he wrote: "4 years ago, a Commando Regiment was

7. Bracelin, 161-162.
8. Bracelin, 166-167.
9. Interview Ian Stevenson and 'GB', 19 November 2004.

guarding the beach at Highcliffe where I was + the sergeant Major showed me the Amulet that kept him safe, + I asked if many men wore them, + he said I think every man in the Regiment has one except some Irish men. They have whole necklaces of them."

Local historian, Ian Stevenson, gives a vivid account of life during this period, when he was a boy in Highcliffe:

The dreaded wailing of a siren sent Highcliffe families scurrying to air-raid shelters or specially-reinforced parts of their homes. Searchlights based at Walkford swept the night sky, looking for German bombers that could be targeted by local anti-aircraft guns.

Usually the bombers would pass overhead on their way to blitz targets inland. But many bombs did fall on and around Highcliffe, so no one relaxed until the all-clear siren sounded.

The threat that villagers faced was not just from the air. Highcliffe's position on the South Coast meant that it was a possible landing place if the Germans launched an invasion across the Channel.

Public access to the beach was shut off and elaborate coastal defences were set up. These included mile upon mile of barbed wire. "We felt like chickens in a hen-run," recalled the village's leading figure, Mrs Violet Stuart Wortley of Highcliffe Castle. ...

The main road buzzed with military vehicles and men in uniform. Walls of sandbags protected important posts and many windows were criss-crossed with tape to reduce the risk of flying glass in a bomb blast.

At night, the village was blacked out so that it could not be seen from the air. No street lights were lit and any home showing a chink of light through its black-out curtains would get a visit from an air-raid warden and, in some cases, a £5 fine.[10]

---

10. Ian Stevenson, Highcliffe at War Exhibition Souvenir 2005.

It was considered by those who had access to information that the threat to the Christchurch area would come from the German 6th Army which was stationed on the Cherbourg peninsula. Gerald was keen to do everything he could to help stop the threatened invasion. In an important sense it was a real-life acting out of the situation portrayed in *A Goddess Arrives* and, just as in that book, he turned to magic in an hour of need. He mentioned on several occasions in his writings and to other people a momentous series of rituals which he said had taken place in the New Forest to try to stop the threatened invasion. Some have questioned whether these ever took place. I think it would actually be more surprising if they had not occurred.

The group into which Gerald was initiated were mostly not in the first flush of youth and could therefore not enlist in the regular forces. Gerald, as we have seen, was a Sector Warden in the ARP, of which Edith, Rosanne and her husband, Tommy, were also members, and Gerald was also in the Home Guard. However, they knew, or believed, that they had certain skills – magical ones – which they were willing to employ to protect their native land from threat of invasion.

I don't know who first suggested a magical working: it was probably something of a joint decision amongst the group. The crucial moment was probably when some of them (presumably the Masons) revealed that their families had lived in the area for many years and that they had a tradition that when there had been invasion threats in the past, from the Spanish Armada in 1588 and from Napoleon in 1805, they had successfully carried out magical workings to stop them.

This resonated very strongly with Gerald. After all, it had been a theme of his novel, *A Goddess Arrives*, and he was all for taking such action as was necessary. Indeed, I think it was likely to have been Gerald who first suggested that what had been done once could be done again! If so, then he obviously convinced them, as it was decided to perform a ritual or rituals to help stop the threatened invasion.

I suspect that there was much discussion about the form and objective of the magical working. The working of magic, which can be called the witch's stock-in-trade is, in my experience and that of many others, undoubtedly a reality. It can move physical objects, but it is a lot easier to affect things that are more fluid, such as an individual's state of mind and, significantly in the present context, the weather.

The Mason family would have told Gerald about the traditions of magical working to achieve such objectives, and reminded him that threatened invasions of England had been affected by a combination of adverse weather conditions and bad decisions on the part of those in charge, just the sort of thing that magical working might be expected to influence. One of the earliest was during the Hundred Years War, in 1386-87: "The French readied themselves to invade England, assembling a fleet of ships in the Scheldt estuary. On standby were 100,000 men and nearly 1,000 barrels of wine. But a combination of bad weather and dithering scuppered their plans and the French went home."[11] They knew more about the Spanish Armada in 1588 and told Gerald what had been passed down to them:

> At the time of the Spanish Armada the invading force was off the coast before the cult really heard about it. They knew it was useless trying to get at King Philip; he was out of touch with and could not change the Armada's course, and they had not the slightest idea who was in command. The only thing they could do was to send out a general idea: "Go on," "Go on," "Go on," "You cannot land," "You cannot land," and hope it would take effect. If they could have raised a storm, they would have done so, but they did not know how, though naturally they would pray to their gods to bring disaster to the fleet and this would probably include storms.[12]

Perhaps tales of the witches' ancestors had come down over almost 400 years but, if so, I don't understand why Gerald seems to be implying that they did not know how to raise a storm. Elsewhere he says that: "The witch generally does not believe it is possible to alter nature – to cause storms, for instance ...".[13] This

---

11. *The Guardian*, 2 March 1999.
12. Gardner (1954), 104.
13. Op. cit. p 183.

is one of the traditional skills that a witch possessed and one of the main reasons for the defeat of the Armada is traditionally said to have been a sudden storm which blew them off course. Perhaps there was a psychological element to it as well, making the Spaniards think the weather was worse than it was:

> ... *it is worth recording that the Spaniards on the whole were less experienced than the English in encountering gales at sea, and it is noticeable that they seem to have recorded worse storms and sea conditions than did their adversaries. This storm, for example, ... has been described in a Spanish log as having "the sea so high that all the mariners said they had never seen the like in July". Yet it rates no mention at all in the English reports except for the casual remark by John Hawkins that "a little flaw took them".*[14]

Invasion was threatened again in 1803-4, when Napoleon Bonaparte had organised the construction of some 2000 invasion craft and military camps in the coastal area of northern France, accommodating upwards of 150,000 soldiers. He is quoted as having said of the Channel that "it is a ditch which will be leaped whenever one has the boldness to try". Older members of the coven, those who came from a generation when magic enjoyed a matter-of-fact acceptance in some households, could remember family talk of a similar rite against "Boney" at the time of the threatened Napoleonic invasion.[15] Gerald writes: "The witches told me that their great-grandfathers had tried to project the same idea [that he could not cross the Channel] into Boney's mind."[16]

Napoleon's grand plan was to group the French and Spanish fleets in the West Indies and then sail for Boulogne. Unfortunately for Bonaparte, things didn't work out that way. A combination of a lack of communications and poor weather resulted in the non-appearance of the fleet. Having arrived at Boulogne on 3rd August 1805, Bonaparte had by 25th August turned his attention to the east, and by 28th August the army was in full march

---

14. David A. Thomas, *The Illustrated Armada Handbook*, (Harrap, 1988), 69.
15. Allen Andrews, "Witchcraft in Britain" in *Illustrated*, 27 September 1952, 41.
16. Gardner (1954), 104.

towards Germany and would then attract the military attention of Russia and Austria.

This seems to accord with Gerald's account of the oral tradition which the witches claimed to have about the threatened Napoleonic invasion, and it is most interesting to note that the same thing happened as took place following the 1940 threat – that the potential invasion was recognised to be too difficult and attention was refocused on the east.

It is quite likely that if those who had performed the magical workings at the time had carried out some ritual to deter the invasion they would have told their grandchildren about it some time in the middle of the 19th Century. And it is quite possible that the oldest members of the group which Gerald joined could be those same grandchildren. In any case, the events were sufficiently recent to have been handed down orally through not more than three generations. The ancestors of the Mason family, for example, lived in Southampton and Portsmouth in the early 19th Century, just the area where 'invasion fever' was likely to be the strongest.

War had been declared on 3rd September 1939, but it was only on 10th May 1940 when German troops invaded Holland and Belgium and Winston Churchill became Prime Minister, that a sense of urgency started to come into focus. Very quickly the German troops over-ran those two smaller countries and they surrendered on 28th May. British troops were forced back on the small French coastal town of Dunquerque (Dunkirk), but, with the help of a flotilla of assorted vessels, over 300,000 British and French troops were safely evacuated. By 14th June, German troops had reached Paris and, on 22nd June, the French government surrendered.

In 1954, Gerald told Ithell Colquhoun that Hitler's first big mistake, ordering the tanks to stop on 24th May (thus allowing the Dunkirk evacuation) might have been the result of the coven working on his unconscious mind. For this information I am indebted to Gareth Medway, who comments:

Since no-one really expected an invasion before the start of the German advance on 10 May, one may presume that the rite was done between these two dates, probably on the full moon of 21 May.[17]

As Churchill said: "After Dunkirk, and still more when three weeks later the French Government capitulated, the questions whether Hitler would, or secondly, could invade and conquer our Island rose, as we have seen, in all British minds."[18] "As the month of June ground itself out, the sense of potential invasion at any moment grew upon us all."[19]

And those living on the coast were more likely to be taking such possibilities seriously than the rest of the population. Highcliffe and the New Forest were potentially very vulnerable to invasion, being right on the south coast, close to the undoubted military targets of Southampton and Portsmouth. The Highcliffe historian, Ian Stevenson, told me that his family always had their bags packed ready for retreat at a moment's notice.

Time was pressing and history was in the making. Every day brought changing circumstances, from the evacuation of Dunkirk, completed on 4th June, to the fall of France on 22nd June. It was clear by Midsummer at the latest that something would have to be done! Churchill's speech on the 18th June was probably the determining factor:

> *What General Weygand called the "Battle of France" is over. I expect that the battle of Britain is about to begin. Upon this battle depends the survival of Christian civilisation. Upon it depends our own British life and the long continuity of our institutions and our Empire. The whole fury and might of the enemy must very soon be turned on us. Hitler knows that he will have to break us in this island or lose the war.*
>
> *If we can stand up to him, all Europe may be free, and the life of the world may move forward into broad, sunlit uplands; but if we fail, then the whole world, including the United States, and all that we have known and cared for, will sink into the abyss of a new dark age made more sinister, and perhaps more protracted, by the lights of a perverted science.*

17. Gareth Medway, personal communication with the author, October 2009.
18. Winston S. Churchill, *The Second World War Volume II: Their Finest Hour,* (Cassell, 1949), 247.
19. Op. cit., 152.

*Let us therefore brace ourselves to our duty and so bear
ourselves that if the British Empire and its Commonwealth
lasts for a thousand years men will still say, "This was their
finest hour".*[20]

The effect of this speech cannot be overestimated. It set the
atmosphere for determined action, and it is my guess that it was
this moment, more than any other, which decided the witches to
do what they could: to work magic to prevent invasion occurring.
With the sense of urgency felt by all at the time, it need only have
taken a day or two to organise and it is my guess that they would
have attempted some sort of magical working within a few days
of Churchill's speech.

Those who have written about the workings, however, seem
clear that Lammas (1st August) was the date. Patricia Crowther[21]
says "Lammas Eve"; Doreen Valiente[22] says "Lammas", and Allen
Andrews[23] says unambiguously "the night of 1st August". In fact,
Gerald says: "We repeated the ritual four times."[24] Whether this was
four (or strictly speaking five) separate occasions, or four times during one ritual, I do not know. It is not clear from Gerald's account. I
am inclined to think there was a build-up, from individual magical
workings at the end of May – a sort of stop-gap measure – building
up to a more organised ritual with more people involved for the
night of either Wednesday 31st July or Thursday 1st August 1940.

I suspect that there was much discussion about the form and
objective of the magical working. As Bill Wakefield has said, the
Masons were all "mind control people" and I think that it gradually emerged that the thing that would be most effective would be
to get at the minds of Hitler and the German High Command to
get them to change their minds about invading Britain. Further
discussion would have come up with the idea of reinforcing that
thought, which was almost certainly in their minds anyway, that
it was too difficult to attempt a cross-channel invasion, indeed
that it was impossible, as was supposedly done with Napoleon.

---

20. Martin Gilbert, *Finest Hour: Winston S. Churchill 1939-1941*, (Heniemann, 1983), 570-571.
21. Patricia Crowther, *One Witch's World*, (Robert Hale, 1998), 21.
22. Doreen Valiente, *The Rebirth of Witchcraft*, (Robert Hale, 1989), 45.
23. Andrews, (1952), 41.
24. Bracelin, 167.

The ritual was to be both special and serious. Gerald sets the tone when he writes: "...that was done which may not be done except in great emergency."25 By this, he suggests something which was known about, and which had been done before (perhaps in the oral tradition dating back to Napoleonic and Spanish Armada times) but could only be used in an emergency of that magnitude. It was clearly felt that the present state of imminent invasion met that criterion amply.

So, who performed the ritual? Gerald, being interviewed by Allen Andrews in 1952, told him that "... an extraordinary summons was sent out to members of the Southern coven of British Witches. It brought seventeen men and women to a clearing in the New Forest."26

This seems the right number of people that could reasonably be brought together for such an activity. I suspect that they consisted of the members of the little group into which Gerald was initiated, but also of their friends who would be likely to be sympathetic to the whole enterprise. However, if there had been any more then the rituals would be likely to attract the attention of the Home Guard or ARP wardens. Indeed, I suspect that Gerald may have used his influence in both organisations to draw attention away from such activities.

I have no way of knowing who was actually present, but I can set out a provisional list of "possibles", arranged in order of certainty, which would go something like this: Gerald Gardner; Edith Woodford-Grimes; Ernie Mason; Susie Mason; Rosetta Fudge; William Fudge; Rosetta Mason; Amy Morgan; Edith Ethel Morgan ("Queen") (both close relatives of the Masons); Katherine Oldmeadow; Rosamund Sabine; George Sabine; Rosanne Woodford-Grimes; 'Tommy' Thompson; Walter Forder; Dorothy Fordham; Donna Gardner. I don't claim this in any way as a definitive list: I could be almost completely wrong, but it is a first attempt!

The location of the ritual was clearly something to be determined. There were rumours of traditional witch meeting-places in the New Forest and it was decided to go out there to perform the ritual. The edge of the Forest was only some four miles from

25. Bracelin, 167.
26. Andrews, (1952), 41.

Highcliffe and it is highly likely that Gerald would have included the Forest in his "long cycle rambles". So he probably got to know the Forest quite well during his time in Highcliffe.

However, Gerald says: "We were taken at night to a place in the Forest ...",[27] which suggests that there was someone who knew the Forest even better than Gerald. There was one person in the little group into which Gerald was initiated who knew the Forest better than the others, and that was Katherine Old-meadow. Although not native to the Forest, having been born in Chester, Katherine had lived in Highcliffe for almost thirty years and had got to know and love the Forest well. It featured in many of her stories and what she wrote showed a natural understanding, as the following extract shows:

> *Great deep glades, where the beech-leaves lay like a fairy carpet of magic colours, and scarlet and orange and yellow toadstools grew all ready to be spread for some elfin feast. The bracken was a baby forest of golden trees, and across the purple-brown, autumn-scented heather big spiders were spinning shining silver webs in the sunshine.*[28]

She has one marvellous description of what would be a wonderful ritual site. It may be pure imagination, but it has the essence of a real location:

> *To see the Forest in all its fairy loveliness you must leave the king's highway and plunge boldly into the greenwood, or make friends with some tiny stream and let it lead you onward like a gay, singing comrade. It will show you the Forest's noblest trees, its most magical colours, and its rarest wild-flowers. Pandora and Rory knew this, and before they had gone many miles they left the forest road and plunged into a rough track through pine-woods. "We'll show you the King's Council Chamber," promised Rory. "Pan and I call this wood that – the old King is the dar-lingest pine-tree, and he's got twenty-four courtiers." They emerged suddenly into a wide clearing, where a ring of fine*

27. Bracelin, 167.
28. K. L. Oldmeadow, *Madcap Judy*, (Collins, 1919), 223.

old pines surrounded an immense tree, covered with cones as
big as babies' heads. They lay fallen among the scented pine-
needles, too, and Rory called them the king's treasures and
began to pick them up to burn with the Christmas log.[29]

There are clues, which I am currently investigating, as to
exactly where the ritual site may have been. It was probably in the
vicinity of the Naked Man. This is now just a tree stump, but in the
18th Century it was known as Wilverley Oak and was reputedly
used for hanging highwaymen and smugglers. It has been dead
with the bark stripped for many years, gradually decaying. It is still
a visitor attraction and has protective fences around it. It is an area
that is really quite remote from human habitation and would, I
think, in 1940, be quite safe from prying eyes. They seem to have
assembled there and then probably walked to the ritual site. In the
height of summer, it did not begin to get dark until late in the
evening. They would, however, have been equipped with lanterns
and electric torches, quietly assembling at the Naked Man, having
parked cars or bikes in the bushes some distance away so as not to
alert suspicion. Katherine would have led them, seventeen in total,
in single file, along the footpath that led away from the Naked
Man and the road, along a ridge and then down into a valley,
across a stream, which would not be very deep at that time of year,
over another ridge, across another stream and up to the place
where they were to hold the ritual. Of course, we can't be sure that
this was where the anti-invasion rituals took place, but the clues
we have point to this area. Perhaps unorthodox methods such as
dowsing or scrying might locate the site more precisely.

Anyway, Gerald says: "We were taken at night to a place in the
Forest, where the Great Circle was erected ..."[30]

A very large circle was marked out on the ground in brushwood in a clear space between the trees. This was presumably
done beforehand and would obviously be in an area where brushwood, i.e. twigs and small branches, was easy enough to find. One
can perhaps imagine the gathering of brushwood into several
piles a day or two before, and then on the evening of the ritual
laying it out immediately outside the circle which would be cast

29. K. L.Oldmeadow, *Princess Charming*, (Collins, 1923), 256-257.
30. Bracelin, 167.

in the normal fashion. The brushwood could then be returned to its piles before dawn to be ready for the repeat of the ritual in the near future.

Writing about the usual (9 foot diameter) witches' circle, Gerald refers back to the special circle they cast in the Forest: "The only time I have seen a larger circle used was when we tried to work on Hitler's mind, and that was a totally different operation, 'Sending Forth', performed in an entirely different way, needing as many people as we could get together and plenty of room to work in."[31] If there were seventeen people holding hands and rushing across a circle, then it would have to be pretty big, probably fifty feet across at a minimum and preferably quite a bit more.

Doreen Valiente gives the following details about the illumination:

> *A fire or candle was within* [the circle], *in the direction where the object of the rite was supposed to be ... The candle referred to would have been in a lantern ... and the fire, not too large because of wartime blackout restrictions, was lit in what was roughly the direction the invasion was thought likely to come from, presumably the south-east."*[32]

Andrews adds that: "Their ceremonial firebrands were expertly kept dim, yet alive, by such of the company as were air-raid wardens..."[33] These, as we have seen, included Gerald himself, Edith, Rosanne and Tommy. It was a recognition that, in wartime, any light could draw unwanted attention. This statement is, however, interesting in that no other candle or light is mentioned, certainly not at the four quarters, plus two altar candles as would be usual today. It seems as if they only had what was absolutely necessary, but the statement is ambiguous as to whether the candle and the fire were alternatives or if both had to be present. The latter seems likely, as details about both are given. It is also clear that the candle and fire are directly related to the object of the rite and not mere decorations.

---

31. Gardner, (1954), 115.
32. Doreen Valiente, *The Rebirth of Witchcraft*, (Robert Hale, 1989), 45-46.
33. Andrews, (1952), 41.

The "ceremonial firebrands" were presumably some sort of stick held by each of the participants, which were lit at one end but perhaps impregnated with something which kept them from going out but which didn't give too much flame, much like a large joss-stick. The implication of this statement is that this was a substance with which the air-raid wardens were familiar, though it certainly sounds the sort of thing that Ernie Mason would have known about.

Gerald was told by the witches that power resides in their bodies and that this can be released by various techniques including chanting and dancing. By working together within the magic circle, they can raise what they call a "cone of power", which can then be directed towards a particular objective. "The Cone of Power. This was the old way."[34] It is this that they were intending to raise through the ritual. Andrews says that: "... the coven proceeded to conduct rites intended to raise the first colossal "cone of power" they had ever produced – and direct it against Hitler.[35] And the great Cone of Power was raised and slowly directed in the general direction of Hitler." This seems to indicate that they (i.e. those particular individuals) had raised a cone of power before, but never anything on this scale, although they knew, from tradition, that it could be done.

There were at least three aspects to this – the dancing itself and the energy generated; the chanting; and the state of mind of the participants. Valiente writes, from notes made as Gerald was talking: "Then all danced round until they felt they had raised enough power. If the rite was to banish, they started deosil and finished widdershins, so many rounds of each."[36] Valiente also records that people were "stationed to whip up the dancers". This reminded her of a reference to: "... a Scottish witch meeting which took place in August 1678, when a leading male witch, one Gideon Penman, '...was in the rear in all their dances, and beat up all those that were slow'. This is mentioned in *The Geography of Witchcraft* by Montague Summers."[37] This was obviously during

---

34. Valiente, (1989), 45.
35. Andrews, (1952), 41.
36. Valiente, (1989), 45.
37. Op. cit., 46.

the part of the rite when everyone (presumably excluding the 'whips') danced round in a circle to raise the cone of power.

The raising of the cone of power was only the first stage in the proceedings, however,. The next stage was actually to send it with its message to its destination. So what was the message and what was the destination? Valiente gives the following details of what they were trying to achieve:

> *... when the witches raised the Cone of Power against Hitler's invasion, they sought to reach the minds of the German High Command and persuade them that the invasion could not succeed, or alternatively to muddle and stultify their thinking so that the plans for the invasion fell through. Generally, old Gerald said, there was someone somewhere whose actions would vitally affect whatever it was that the witch ceremony was trying to bring about. This person's mind would be acted upon, without their knowledge, so that they would behave in one way rather than another, and thus the desired result would happen.*[38]

It is clear that this was mind magic – trying to get to those who were in a position to make decisions, and ultimately Hitler himself, to put into their minds that they could not succeed with the invasion. The way in which they did this was quite distinctive. Valiente, quoting Gerald, says: "Then they formed a line with linked hands and rushed towards the fire shouting the thing they wanted."[39] This is a variation of holding hands in a circle, dancing in toward the centre and then out as far as one can without letting go of the hand of the person next to you, which is an old witch dance and is still a feature of many country dances.

We can now see the real purpose of the fire being on the edge of the circle in the direction in which the Cone of Power was to be sent. As it was on the edge, people wouldn't be able to dance round it. So, as Gerald describes, they formed a line, then rushing towards the fire shouting, and then back again, so that the efforts were focused in the right direction. As Andrews says: "The climax

38. Doreen Valiente, *Witchcraft for Tomorrow*, (Robert Hale, 1978),73.
39. Valiente, (1989), 45.

of a long ritual came with the members, in a state of tense excitement, projecting their defiance in shouts of rhythmic unison ..."[40]

So, what were they shouting? Gerald records two concise commands: "You cannot cross the sea. You cannot cross the sea. YOU CANNOT COME. YOU CANNOT COME."[41] Valiente gives a slightly different version, and one that would probably be easier to chant: "Can't cross the sea! Can't cross the sea! Not able to come! Not able to come!" As she says: "The words had to be simple and capable of falling into a chanted rhythm that expressed the purpose of the rite."[42] Gerald told Patricia Crowther that the two phrases were "You cannot cross the sea" and "Not able to come".[43] It is said that they directed the thought at Hitler's brain. Valiente, quoting Gerald, says that: "They kept it up till they were exhausted or until someone fell in a faint, when they were said to have taken the spell to its destination."[44]

It probably does not need to be said that this was not just an evening party in the Forest. The country was in peril and it was a willing duty on the part of each individual to do what they could to help stop the threatened invasion. Gerald, Edith, Rosanne and Tommy were ARP wardens and, as we have seen, Gerald was also in the Home Guard. Yet, members of the group were well aware that they had psychic and magical abilities which they could, and indeed should, employ. They knew that there was a genuine and very real threat of invasion. It is perhaps an obvious point but one that can be subtly overlooked, and that is that they didn't know how things were going to work out. For all they knew, Britain would be invaded, and in the very near future indeed – perhaps a matter of days. In other words, there was a crisis, and if their working involved sacrifice, then that was no more than what thousands of their compatriots were facing every day.

It is also important to recognise that what the group was doing was to raise a very large cone of power and to direct it towards its objectives. Gerald says: "... mighty forces were used, of which I may not speak. Now to do this means using one's life-

40. Andrews, (1952), 41.
41. Bracelin, 167.
42. Valiente, (1989), 46.
43. Patricia Crowther, Personal communication with the author.
44. Valiente, (1989), 45.

force; and many of us died a few days after we did this. My asthma, which I had never had since I first went out East, came back badly."[45] Gerald is obviously not intending to go into detail, but we have a possible clue in what he wrote about magicians in the Far East and how they operated. He says: "How do they do it? By starving themselves or weakening the bodily functions in some way ... They do it by taking away a part of their life – dying in part, if you like – in order to obtain this power."[46] Whatever it was, it was certainly something which, by his own account, used mighty forces, used the life-force of the individual and resulted in the deaths of several individuals a few days later. The more energy that could be put into it the better, and I think this is why Gerald spoke about "using one's life-force". I take this to mean the energy which sustains one's life and that if too much is taken one may die or be severely affected. Doreen Valiente writes: "I was told that a number of the older and frailer people who took part died shortly afterwards, and it was believed that the cold and the exertion had contributed to their deaths. They were regarded as having died for the cult and for the success of the ritual and were honoured accordingly."[47] And Gerald said: "We repeated the ritual four times; and the Elders said: 'We feel we have stopped him. We must not kill too many of our people. Keep them until we need them'."[48]

This was not deliberate sacrifice. It was carrying out an operation that was known to be risky. Sacrifice is thus merely a possible by-product of this course of action, certainly not the intention. It is similar to the RAF airmen who knowingly put themselves in danger in order to fulfil their objectives. They did not want to die or be injured and it was certainly not a requirement for the success of their mission. But they were prepared to die, and if they did so, 'sacrifice' would be an appropriate word to use. So, I think, it was with the group that met to perform the ritual.

It is possible that "we repeated the ritual four times..." means that the Cone of Power was raised several times on the same night, but this is highly unlikely as it would be too exhausting physically and mentally for those involved. Indeed, the Cone of

45. Bracelin, 167.
46. Bracelin, 113-114.
47. Valiente, (1989), 46.
48. Bracelin, 167.

Power would only be successful if those raising it 'gave their all', which they would be unlikely to do if they knew they would have to repeat it immediately.

We don't know the identity of those who died following the rituals, or, indeed, how many. I suspect that Gerald was exaggerating but in my earlier book, *Wiccan Roots*,[49] I speculated on the identity of one of those as being the editor of the local paper, Walter Forder, who died on 11th August 1940 at the relatively young age of 58. I think I put up a reasonable case for suggesting that he was one of those involved, but there is no way in which we can be sure. It all happened almost 70 years ago, and it undoubtedly took place in secret, so there is bound to be a great deal of uncertainty surrounding the whole event.

And did it achieve anything? We know, of course, that no invasion took place nor was even started, but did the New Forest ritual actually have the desired effect on the minds of Hitler and the German High Command?

The timing certainly looks interesting. On 2nd July, following the fall of France on 22nd June, a directive was issued for planning the invasion: "The Fuehrer has decided that under certain conditions – the most important of which is achieving air superiority – a landing in England may take place."[50] Another directive was issued on 16th July: "Since England in spite of her militarily hopeless position shows no sign of coming to terms, I have decided to prepare a landing operation against England, and if necessary to carry it out. ... The preparations for the entire operation must be completed by mid-August."[51] On 21st July, Hitler stated that: "The execution of 'Sea Lion' ... must be regarded as the most effective means of bringing about a rapid conclusion of the war."[52] And yet, towards the end of July, Hitler is reported to have said to one of his Field Marshals: "I do not intend to carry out Sealion. There is no bridge across the sea. On land I'm a hero: on water I'm a coward."[53] And at a meeting on 31st July: "... Hitler told the

---

49. Heselton, (2000), 243-248.
50. Churchill, (1949), 267.
51. Ibid.
52. Churchill, (1949), 268.
53. BBC Television programme "Timewatch: Hitler and the Invasion of Britain", 7 April 1998.

leaders of the army that he was sceptical about the practicalities of an invasion, given the strength of the British Navy."[54]

Recent research has shown that: "... between July and the middle of September 1940 ... the Germans had removed at least half of their divisions in the west to the east of the Reich to become part of the preparations for an attack on the Soviet Union in the following year."[55] The Luftwaffe failed to gain the necessary air superiority and on 17th September 1940, Hitler decided to postpone the invasion indefinitely.

So, did the rituals in the New Forest influence things? The timing was certainly right, but we must not forget that there were other magical groups and individuals doing things in their own way. Dion Fortune writes about a prolonged magical working in *The Magical Battle of Britain*;[56] Doug Pickford tells of a working that took place at Alderley Edge in Cheshire;[57] and Paddy Slade tells of a working that involved sprinkling "go away powder" into the sea off the North Foreland in Kent. And doubtless there were many others that have not come to public attention.

Perhaps Gerald's own conclusion is the best:

I am not saying that they stopped Hitler. All I say is that I saw a very interesting ceremony performed with the intention of putting a certain idea into his mind ... and this was repeated several times afterwards; and though all the invasion barges were ready, the fact was that Hitler never even tried to come.[58]

54. Ibid.
55. Ibid.
56. Dion Fortune, *The Magical Battle of Britain*, (Golden Gates, 1993).
57. Doug Pickford, *Cheshire: Its Magic and Mystery*, (Sigma Leisure, 1994), 107.
58. Gardner, (1954), 104.

CHAPTER SEVENTEEN

The Wica

A As a result of the activities at the theatre, their collaboration over *A Goddess Arrives*, his initiation and the momentous rituals in the Forest, Gerald grew particularly close to Edith, as might be expected between those experiencing the depths of an initiation, particularly between the two directly involved. That this proximity turned to love is indicated by a comment made by Ralph Merrifield, of the Museum of London: *... in 1954, I received a visit at the Guildhall from [Gerald Gardner], and took the opportunity of asking where he had learnt his witchcraft. His reply was "I fell in love with a witch when we were fire-watching together during the war."*[1]

The journalist, Marjorie Proops, following an interview with Gerald[2] in 1957, wrote: *I asked the doctor how he started. He said that twenty years ago he met a girl witch named Dafo and that was it. Dafo brought out the occult in Gerald.* I think he genuinely saw Edith as a "girl". Even though she was 50 years of age and only three years younger than Gerald he definitely saw her in that way.

---

1. Ralph Merrifield, G. B. Gardner and the 20th Century 'Witches'", *Folklore Society News*, no. 17, (June 1993), 10.
2. Marjorie Proops, "I Got the Low-down on this Witch Lark!", *Daily Mirror*, 10 April 1957.

I think a clue to Gerald's relationship with Edith is provided by a passage which appears in *A Goddess Arrives*:

> *Dayonis and he were constantly together and her quick observation and essentially practical mind saw deficiencies and made suggestions which were of real value to him. Their friendship and understanding of each other grew rapidly and he found her a charming, intelligent companion, one who would enter into his schemes and his moods in a way which he had never experienced with a woman before.*[3]

I do not know whether the relationship was a sexual one: it probably was. I hinted at this in my book *Wiccan Roots*[4] but it was Adrian Bott[5] who first stated this unambiguously. No correspondence between Gerald and Edith appears to have survived.

An indication of the closeness between Gerald and, not just Edith but Rosanne as well, is that he was the one who gave Rosanne away at her wedding. It is clear from this that Edith's marriage must have broken down completely, since it would normally be her husband's role to do this. Gerald is described as 'a close friend'.[6] Rosanne, aged 19, married Cecil Albert Thompson, known as Tommy, on Saturday 17th August 1940 at Christchurch Priory. The reception, which was attended by between 50 and 60 guests, was held at the Nelson Hotel, Mudeford which, perhaps significantly, was only 100 yards from the New Forest naturist club at Rushford Warren.

Indeed, the list of those giving wedding presents to the couple includes several people with naturist links, including a dispensing chemist from Southbourne, Mr. O. Saul and his wife, who used to advertise a discreet photographic developing service in naturist magazines. There was also Miss Mary Dowding, from London, who was a friend of Gerald's and was a member of various naturist clubs. This certainly suggests that there was a link between Edith, Rosanne and the New Forest Club. Whether this pre-dated their friendship with Gerald, I do not know, but it is at least a possibility.

3. Gardner, (1939), 174-175.
4. Heselton, (2000), 264-268.
5. Adrian Bott, "The Great Wicca Hoax?", *White Dragon*, (Lughnasa 2001), 13-15.
6. *Christchurch Times*, 24 August 1940.

The couple had a few days' honeymoon in Somerset and returned to live in 'Theano'.

Edith had taken the opportunity to move into her new house, Avenue Cottage, in Avenue Road, Highcliffe. Sometimes the address is given as Walkford, as it is between the two places. It was only just over half a mile's walk from 'Southridge'. Avenue Cottage was rather larger than its name might suggest and was, in fact, a substantial house with a long garden, the bottom part of which extended behind neighbouring gardens on both sides. I understand that Edith also owned the neighbouring house, letting it to tenants.

How could a modest teacher of elocution afford such a property? Edith's mother, Caroline, died in March 1939, but the likelihood of any financially significant legacy from that direction is very low. Firstly, Edith's father was an agricultural engineer and, whilst he was a J.P. (Justice of the Peace), his income could not have been great. Secondly, any financial legacy would very likely be shared amongst the surviving six children. Edith's grandson believes that Gerald financed the whole enterprise, a conclusion which I had already reached independently. If so, it is another indication of how close Gerald and Edith had become by that time.

And what did Donna make of all this? She is always represented as being a really nice person, but someone who didn't particularly want to get involved in his witchcraft activities. Indeed, there is a hint of this in *Witchcraft Today*. After writing about married or other couples, Gerald says:

> There are ... some unattached people, or some whose resepctive spouses are for some reason or another not members of the cult. I have heard fierce purists declare that no married man or woman should belong to, or attend, any club or society to which their respective partners did not also belong; but such strict views are not part of witchcraft.[7]

Donna, who seems to have been liked by everybody, was, I am sure, aware of Gerald's relationship with Edith. Whilst one might have expected that, being the daughter, grand-daughter, niece

7. Gardner, (1954), 29.

and sister of clergymen, she would have a conventional attitude to Gerald's relationship with Edith, this does not seem to have been the case. Fred Lamond says of her that she:

> ... did not belong to witchcraft but was very tolerant of his activities. According to Cecil Williamson (not the most reliable of sources) she said on one occasion: "I don't mind how many young women Gerald can get to whip him, as long as I don't have to be involved!" [8]

It is quite possible, and indeed even probable, that Rosanne had also been initiated. She would have been well known to the Mason family, having lived in the same street in Southampton during her childhood. Certainly in many hereditary traditions, children are initiated at quite a young age. It is quite possible that Edith's grandson is referred to in the following passage from *Witchcraft Today*, suitably altered: "I have heard it said 'I'd simply love to bring Diana in, she would adore it and she has the powers, I know; but suppose in some unguarded moment she let it out at school that I was a witch...'"[9]

⁂

Gerald writes in *Witchcraft Today* and *The Meaning of Witchcraft* something of the beliefs and practices of the people who initiated him into 'the witch cult'. By looking at these passages, we get a vivid impression of what it must have been like to know these people.

We are probably talking primarily about Rosetta Mason, Susie Mason, Ernie Mason and Rosetta Fudge, plus Edith and Rosanne. They are the ones that Gerald would have seen on a fairly regular basis. In contrast, Dorothy Fordham, Katherine Oldmeadow and Rosamund Sabine were rather distant figures, talked about rather than met on most occasions.

I can imagine that Gerald wanted to spend quite a lot of time with Edith, first in Dennistoun Avenue and later at Avenue Cottage, both because he enjoyed her company, but also because he

---

8. Lamond, (2003), 11.
9. Gardner, (1954), 129.

desperately wanted to know more about 'the witch cult'. Gerald referred to her as "the witch", which suggests to me that she was, if not the only one, at least the main, member of 'the witch cult' with whom Gerald retained contact.

I think it likely that together they devised and performed rituals both there and out in the woods and heaths of the nearby New Forest. There was a multitude of suitable isolated woodland glades to choose from, as there is for groups of witches and pagans today. We shall probably never know, although I have seen reference to an "Autumn leaf-fall" ritual which was performed under a beech tree.

Gerald would undoubtedly have been asking a lot of questions which Edith would have had to deal with. There would not be any 'course of instruction' and Gerald would probably have been frustrated at the number of topics where Edith was being deliberately vague or evasive. Things were rarely imparted in a straightforward way. They might be ambiguous - a piece of information might be taken in different ways, and Gerald might only learn which was right some time later. It is probably only on looking back on it that he could see that he was being taught, but in a very subtle way.

There was, I believe, certain written material that Gerald copied, nothing that would today be given the title 'Book of Shadows', but I shall refer to something of what this material contained later. Most of the information was probably given in informal chats with the various individuals I mention above, or imparted directly during any rituals which they performed together.

We get quite a vivid impression of the group as a whole. Gerald was not, usually, an emotional person: he was very much more someone who had ideas about things. And I don't think he often had what might be called a "religious experience": he just wasn't that sort of person. Yet, towards the group of people into which he was initiated he certainly expressed an unusual degree of emotion. I have already mentioned that, even before his initiation, they had become close enough for him to say: "... I was really very fond of them ... I would have gone through hell and high water even then for any of them".[10]

---

10. Bracelin, 165.

Following his initiation and experiencing their rites for himself, Gerald had an even greater emotional response when he wrote: "I found, too, what it was that made so many of our ancestors dare imprisonment, torture and death rather than give up the worship of the Old Gods and the love of the old ways."[11]

It is clear from this that it was Gerald's relationship with the individuals in the group and his emotional response to the rites in which he participated with them that were most important: everything else stemmed from that. Beliefs and written material, where they existed at all, were secondary. Theirs was a 'cult' where what they did was based on their experience, not on book-learning. It is clear that feelings and emotions were an important part of their experience of life and this was reflected in their magical and ritual practice.

They referred to themselves as 'the Wica' and what comes over in Gerald's writings is that they were strong in their belief that their magic worked and that it was important to keep their methods secret. Yet in other ways they were surprisingly modest and humble, freely admitting when they didn't know something. They seemed to be quite happy not to be noticed at all, just getting on with their everyday lives. As Edith said: "... I am the sort of person who likes to go about affairs of interest in as unobtrusive a way as possible so that many people who meet me do not really notice me, which is the way I prefer."[12] This is, of course, one of the magical techniques of invisibility. She also commented: "I was taught to be cautious".

As late as 1952, Gerald was still very protective of them: "Now, I simply cant and wont let my friends, the people who trusted me, be bothered & badgered about ..."[13] Consistent through all Gerald's statements about the Wica is the obvious respect and indeed love which he had for them. The above statement is, for me, so obviously genuine and from the heart, and it sums up his attitude to them.

---

11. Gardner (1959), 11.
12. Letter from Edith Woodford-Grimes to Cecil Williamson, 4 January 1955 (in the Boscastle Museum of Witchcraft archives).
13. Letter, Gerald Gardner to Gerald Yorke, 24 October 1952 (in the Yorke Collection, Warburg Institute).

The character of these individuals made a deep impression on Gerald. Indeed, he began to realise that one had to be a certain type of person to be a witch:

> *Witches have for hundreds of years held their meetings in private; they are people who want release from this world into the world of fantasy. To certain kinds of person the relief gained has been of enormous benefit and these occasional nights of release are something to live for.*[14]

> *Witchcraft was, and is, not a cult for everybody. Unless you have an attraction towards the occult, a sense of wonder, a feeling that you can slip for a few minutes out of this world into the other world of faery, it is of no use to you. By it you can obtain peace, the soothing of jangled nerves and many other benefits, just from the companionship, but to obtain the more fundamental effects you must attempt to develop any occult power you may have.*[15]

In what might be called 'theology', they were very weak. Essentially, the Wica seemed to focus on practice rather than beliefs. Gerald put down in writing what he had been told:

> *My great trouble in discovering what their beliefs were is that they have forgotten practically all about their god; all I can get is from the rites and prayers addressed to him. ... The witches do not know the origin of their cult.*[16]

> *To them the cult has existed unchanged from the beginning of time, though there is also a vague notion that the old people came from the East ...*[17]

> *Exactly what the present-day witch believes I find it hard to say ...*[18]

---

14. Gardner (1954), 111.
15. Op.cit., 29-30.
16. Op. cit., 43.
17. Op. cit., 24.
18. Op. cit., 40.

One can imagine Gerald querying Edith with innumerable requests for information which were never answered directly. This must have been frustrating for him, even though he was a master of that technique himself!

I have commented that if Gerald was, as some people have claimed, making it all up, he would surely have done better than this!

What there was in the way of theology was related to their firm belief in reincarnation:

> *The cult god is thought of as the god of the next world, or of death and resurrection, or of reincarnation, the comforter, the consoler. After life, you go gladly to his realms for rest and refreshment, becoming young and strong, waiting for the time to be reborn on earth again, and you pray to him to send back the spirits of your beloved dead to rejoice with you at your festivals.*[19]

Gerald states this very strongly when he relates it to the continuity of the tradition:

> *The witches are firm believers in reincarnation, and they say that "Once a witch, always a witch." They believe that people who have been initiated into the cult, and have really accepted the Old Religion and the Old Gods in their hearts, will return to it or have an urge towards it in life after life, even though they may have no conscious knowledge of their previous associations with it. There may be something in this; because I know personally of three people in one coven who discovered that, subsequent to their coming into the cult in this life, their ancestors had had links with it, and I have already mentioned the witches who "recommended" me.*[20]

They also talked of:

> *... a sort of happy hunting ground, where ordinary folk go and forgather with like-minded people; it may be pleasant or unpleasant according to your nature. According to your*

19. Gardner, (1954), 40.
20.Gardner, (1959), 14.

merits you may be reincarnated in time, and take your chance where and among whom this takes place; but the god has a special paradise for his worshippers, who have conditioned their bodies and natures on earth, who enjoy special advantages and are prepared more swiftly for reincarnation which is done by the power of the goddess in such circumstances as to ensure that you will be reborn into your own tribe again. This is taken nowadays to mean into witch circles. It would seem to involve an unending series of reincarnations; but I am told that in time you may become one of the mighty ones, who are also called the mighty dead. I can learn nothing about them, but they seem to be like demigods – or one might call them saints.[21]

I think Gerald genuinely believed that what he had been initiated into had ancient roots, regardless of the somewhat ambivalent attitude which they presented to him.

The working of magic was a major theme for the Wica. And this was primarily a matter of directing the mind and of various techniques to help such a process. Underlying any magical working, however, was an understanding and use of what might be called popular psychology: giving people misleading impressions by their actions or words. This was something that Gerald was very good at anyway, so it was natural to him to use their psychological techniques.

As Thur says in Gerald's novel, *High Magic's Aid*: "... witchcraft ... is very much a thing of the mind ... the dominance of the witch's mind over her surroundings."[22] And someone who had known the Mason family told me that the whole family were "mind control people". Indeed, it is generally recognised in many different traditions that the main essential in working any form of magic is concentration of the mind.

Gerald hints at certain magical techniques which they used, some of which have at least a component, often a major one, of what might be called 'psychology'. An example is where he seems to be quoting from some earlier text:

---

21. Gardner, (1954), 32-33.
22. Scire (G. B. Gardner), *High Magic's Aid*, (Michael Houghton, 1949), 140.

... a charm to make a young couple love each other ends with: "Try to ensure that the pair are thrown together alone, in exciting and if possible dangerous circumstances (or let them think they are dangerous). Soon they will begin to rely on each other; then let them know that a love charm has been made. If they be of the cult, make them perform the rites together and the charm will soon act." [23]

Gerald adds: "If I were only a quarter of my age, I wish that someone would try that charm on me." [24]

Other magical techniques are barely hinted at, but this is probably deliberate:

... the witches have formulae for producing [a] form of intoxication, of escape into the world of faery. It cannot be induced, however, if people are unsympathetic ... [25]

... the witches have a rite which involves kissing and then beating an object, with the intention of charging it with power. [26]

... some curious things can be done with the right sort of wand ... [27]

Another skill which seems to have been lost is referred to when Gerald writes: "Witches have many formulae for making all sorts of charms, though few use them nowadays ..." [28]

Gerald wrote that "witches are good leg-pullers". I think one example of this is when he writes:

They ... tell me that in most villages the witches arranged that the first and last house was occupied by a member of the cult, and any strange witch, travelling or 'on the run', could go where she would be sure of help and protection. [29]

---

23. Gardner, (1954), 148.
24. Ibid.
25. Gardner, (1954), 65.
26. Op. cit., 79.
27. Gardner, (1959), 99.
28. Gardner, (1954), 147.
29. Op. cit. p 54.

Realistically, even in a period with little new housing development on the outskirts of villages, this would have been very difficult to arrange, and certainly not something to rely on in a time of persecution.

So, where did this most implausible idea originate? I think someone was looking at the map of Highcliffe one day and noticed that Mill House, the Glen House and 'Whinchat' (homes of the Fordhams, the Oldmeadows and the Sabines) were all right on the edge of the village and therefore all could be considered the first (or last) house. At some point, someone noticed this and made a joke of it, perhaps fooling Gerald into taking it seriously, or perhaps he was in on it or even originated the joke himself. It certainly confirms his comment (that witches are good leg-pullers), which is on the same page of *Witchcraft Today*.

The point here is that something is observed but that a totally spurious reason for it is then given. I remember that the main meeting room in the Quaker Meeting House in Pickering in Yorkshire had the seating arranged in a square around an old-fashioned stove with a stove-pipe going up to the ceiling. It was a well-known quip by certain individuals that "Quakers worship a stove"!

There is also the technique of saying something literally true but which is designed to mislead. Gerald himself was particularly good at this, an attitude summed up by what he wrote about Joan of Arc: "It is evident from her trial that Joan did not like telling a direct lie, but that she was an adept at evasion; she could dodge about like a lawyer."[30]

Gerald included their techniques of invisibility in *High Magic's Aid*, the main principle being that "invisibility is not a lack of sight in all beholders, *but lack of observation*".[31]

He referred to their use of mind power:

They showed me one queer trick with music which I described in my novel High Magic's Aid, in the chapter called 'Music Magic'. They told me they could make me fighting mad; I did not believe it, so they got me to sit, fixed in a chair so that I could not get out. Then one sat in front of me playing a little drum; not a tune, just a steady

---

30. Gardner, (1959), 123-124.
31. Gardner, (1949), 140.

tom-tom-tom. We were laughing and talking at first ... it seemed a long time, although I could see the clock and knew it was not. The tom-tom-tom went on and I felt silly; they were watching me and grinning and those grins made me angry. I did not realise that the tom-tomming seemed to be a little quicker and my heart seemed to be beating very hard. I felt flushes of heat, I was angry at their silly grins. Suddenly I felt furiously angry and wanted to pull loose out of the chair; I tugged out and would have gone for them, but as soon as I started moving they changed their beat and I was not angry any longer.

I said: 'It is just suggestion,' but they insisted it was something more – that it was an old secret and could be used to make men fighting mad before a charge.[32]

It is clear that they were proficient at using music, sound in general and the other senses in magical workings. Psychic ability (which we all possess, however buried beneath the trappings of society) and the ability to work magic are like two sides of the same coin, and the Wica seemed to be proficient at both. Gerald definitely had this psychic ability. It seemed to be centred around his solar plexus and Donna often used to ask: "Gerald, what does your tummy feel about so-and-so?" And he admitted in a 1958 'Panorama' interview that he could see auras. He wrote:

Being initiated into the witch cult does not give a witch supernatural powers as I reckon them, but instructions are given, in rather veiled terms, in processes which develop various clairvoyant and other powers, in those who naturally possess them slightly. If they have none they can create none. Some of these powers are akin to magnetism, mesmerism and suggestion, and depend on the possibility of forming a sort of human battery, as it were, of combined human wills working together to influence persons or events at a distance. They have instructions in how to learn to do this by practice. It would take many people a long

32. Gardner, (1954), 142.

time, if I understand the directions aright. ... to a witch it is
all MAGIC, and magic is the art of getting results. To do
this certain processes are necessary and the rites are such
that these processes may be used. In other words, they con-
dition you. This is the secret of the cult.[33]

Magic happens when the concentrated mind and power are
brought together. Gerald is, however, very definite when he says:
"... they do not wish it to be known how they raise power."[34]
However, he also writes:

Witches are taught and believe that the power resides
within their bodies which they can release in various ways,
the simplest being dancing round in a circle, singing or
shouting, to induce a frenzy; this power they believe exudes
from their bodies, clothes impending its release.[35]

There are several other ways in which present-day witches
raise power, but I suspect that the way that they often did it but
which they didn't want known was by the use of the scourge. Fred
Lamond has confirmed[36] that this was the method which was
used when he first joined Gerald's coven, and in the Doreen
Valiente collection there is a scourge which Gerald told her was
originally owned by the 'New Forest Coven', one of the few ritual
tools which date from that period. This is probably the background to Gerald's statement that:

... it is no use trying to develop these powers unless you
have time and a suitable partner, and it is no place to take
your maiden aunt, even if she is romantic; for witches,
being realists, have few inhibitions and if they want to pro-
duce certain effects they do so in the most simple way.[37]

That this power could be used for various purposes is made
clear by Gerald as follows:

33. Gardner, (1954), 28-29.
34. Op. cit., 26.
35. Op. cit., 20.
36. Frederic Lamond, "Fifty Years of Wicca", (*Green Magic*, 2004), 20.
37. Gardner, (1954), 30.

They say that witches by constant practice can train their wills to blend this nerve force, or whatever it is, and that their united wills can project this as a beam of force, or that they can use it in other ways to gain clairvoyance, or even to release the astral body. These practises include increasing and quickening the blood supply, or in other cases slowing it down, as well as the use of will-power ...[38]

With regard to the morality of magical working, Gerald writes:

... they believe a certain law to be important, 'You must not use magic for anything which will cause harm to anyone, and if, to prevent a greater wrong being done, you must discommode someone, you must do it only in a way which will abate the harm. This involves every magical action being discussed first, to see that it can do no damage ...[39]

He adds: "They are inclined to the morality of the legendary Good King Pausol, "Do what you like so long as you harm no one"."[40] Gerald is referring here to *The Adventures of King Pausole* by Pierre Louÿs, where the actual wording is given as the Code of Tryphemia:

I. Thou shalt not harm thy neighbour.
II. This being understood, do as thou wouldst.[41]

This has echoes both in Aleister Crowley's maxim: "Do what thou wilt shall be the whole of the Law. Love is the law, love under will." and in the subsequent 'Wiccan Rede': "Eight words the Wiccan Rede fulfill – An it harm none do what you will."

It is clear from Gerald's statements that the Wica used to cast a magic circle in which to perform their rites. He says:

I am ... permitted to tell for the first time in print the true reason why the important thing in all their ceremonies is 'Casting the Circle'. They are taught that the circle is

---

38. Op.cit., 20-21.
39. Gardner, (1959), 127.
40. Ibid.
41. Pierre Louÿs, *The Adventures of King Pausole*, (Privately Printed for William Godwin, Inc. in New York in 1933), 16.

'between the worlds', that is between this world and the next, the dominion of the gods. … When drawn, this circle is carefully purified, as also are all who celebrate the rites. Witches attach great importance to this, for within the circle is the gods' domain.[42]

One of the main functions of the circle is to keep the power that is raised contained within a small area so that it can be focused into what they call a Cone of Power, such as we saw in the previous chapter when they raised one in an attempt to stop the threatened invasion. They told Gerald that they worked naked because only in that way could they obtain power:

They believe the power is within themselves and exudes from their bodies. It would be dissipated were it not for the circle cast … to keep the power in …[43]

It is a tradition that fire in some form, generally a candle, must be present on the altar, which is placed in the middle of the circle, and candles are also placed about the circle itself.[44]

It seems as if the rites which they performed were not fully scripted with ritual words that had to be learned – they were far more spontaneous, as Gerald describes:

Rites are performed for certain purposes. These take time, but when they are finished the assembly have a little meal, then dance and enjoy themselves.[45]

I have attended many of these cult rites … There may be a fertility dance, but the other rites are simple, and with a purpose … sometimes there is a short ceremony when cakes and wine are blessed and eaten. (They tell me that in the old days mead or ale was often used.) … The ceremony is simply intended as a short repast, though it is definitely religious.[46]

---

42. Gardner, (1954), 26.
43. Op. cit., 47.
44. Gardner, (1959), 17.
45. Gardner, (1954), 27.
46. Gardner, (1954), 22-23.

The dances that follow are more like children's games than modern dances – they might be called boisterous and noisy, with much laughter. In fact, they are more or less children's games performed by grown-ups, and like children's games they have a story, or are done for a certain definite purpose other than mere enjoyment.[47]

Among primitive people dancing was the usual religious expression. In witch tradition it was the necessary preliminary to the climax of the sabbat, the producing of power; it may have had other objects, to bring joy and to express beauty.[48]

... These dances are intoxicating, and this intoxication is the condition for producing what they call magic.[49]

We don't know what seasonal rites they carried out. Cecil Williamson refers to an 'Autumn leaf-fall' ritual and Gerald mentions attending a May Eve rite. I suspect that they kept the cross-quarter days (February, May, August and November eves) and probably Yule, but we don't know!

One of the things which witches have historically been knowledgeable about are herbs, herbal remedies and potions generally. Yet the people who initiated Gerald seemed strangely ignorant of this area. Writing about poisons, he says:

... the present-day ones have no real knowledge of them. They know vaguely that hellebore is deadly, as they know weed-killer is, but they do not know the correct dose of either, and do not know where to get hellebore.[50]

When he writes about herbs to aid clairvoyance, he implies that there was lost knowledge:

I am told that in the olden days witches had knowledge of a herb called Kat which, when mixed with incense, would release the inner eye, the subconscious, but unless another

---

47. Op. cit., 26.
48. Op. cit., 111.
49. Op. cit., 115.
50. Op. cit., 103.

herb, Sumach, was mixed with it, it could not be used for long as it would produce hallucinations. If you used both correctly, it was possible to leave the body. Unfortunately they do not know what these herbs were; but both are said to grow in England. It is said that if a man breathes incense with Kat in it, then woman becomes more beautiful, so it is possible that it contained wild hemp.[51]

This seems to be similar to a substance which Gerald said they called 'Soma' or 'Sume'. In answer to a query by Gerald Yorke, he wrote:

This was not a drink. They had somthing which mixed with the Incense. Burning this they said it opened the inner eye, but you could only use very little, & for a short time only, or it produced Halucanations, but if you mixed some other herb with it it kept off the bad effects, you could use the first stronger, & keep on using it, & could obtain wonderful results, & both of these were things that grew in England, but they dont know what they were, anyhow Ive left the name out.[52]

They were not totally ignorant, however, of ingredients, for he writes about aromatic oils:

They have a very powerful scented oil, which nowadays they speak of as anointing oil. This is only used by the ladies, who dab it on their shoulders, behind their ears, etc., much as ordinary perfume. When they are heated with dancing, this gives off very strong fumes, and most certainly produces a very curious effect. What it is made of is kept a great secret; they had to do without it during the war and for some time afterwards but supplies are coming forward again.[53]

Since Gerald was really only in contact with Edith and Rosanne after the war, they were probably the ones who told him that they were able to obtain the ingredient again. It was probably

51. Gardner ,(1954), 111.

52. Letter, Gerald Gardner to Gerald Yorke 24 October 1952 (in Yorke Collection, Warburg Institute).

53. Gardner, (1954), 53.

patchouli. Gerald does describe another oil, the ingredients for which would have been readily available:

> *I have never known witches anoint themselves all over, but I have been shown a recipe for an anointing oil. This consisted of vervain, or mint crushed and steeped in olive oil or lard, left overnight, then squeezed through a cloth to remove the leaves. Fresh leaves were then added and the squeezing repeated three or four times until it was strongly scented and ready for use.*[54]

I think I have demonstrated that both Rosamund Sabine and Katherine Oldmeadow were deeply interested in herbs. Yet the group into which Gerald was initiated were aware of certain potions but largely ignorant of the ingredients. And the implication of this, to my mind, is that, certainly by the time Gerald was asking his questions, Rosamund and Katherine were no longer closely involved in their activities. I will present further evidence that the Wica (in practice probably just Edith by that time) were not very heavily involved in herbalism when I examine the loan in 1952 to the Museum of quite a few items to do with the preparation of herbs because they were no longer used by the coven.

And that, in essence, is what Gerald wrote, in *Witchcraft Today, The Meaning of Witchcraft* and elsewhere, about the beliefs and practices of the group into which he was initiated – the people that called themselves 'The Wica'. Everything else grew from that.

---

54. Gardner, (1954), 53.

Index

A selection of other titles from Thoth Publications

THE TREASURE OF THE SILVER WEB
By Marian Green

Magic is a subject which fascinates many people, both young and old. Popular books may have drawn it to the attention of a new generation, yet magical tales of quest and mysteries, of symbols and discoveries seem to go back through human history.

The Treasure of the Silver Web is the story of friendship, discovery and magic set in the simpler times of the pre-computer age. It reveals secrets of the countryside the gifts of nature as well as describing magical arts and methods still used today. Readers will have to decide for themselves where the facts stop and fiction begins.

Marian Green is well known for her many books on folklore, occult philosophy, modern magic and witchcraft so her approach to these matters, even in a story book setting, are based on many years of practical experience and study.

ISBN 978-1-870450-77-5 eBook
ISBN 978-1-870450-78-2 paperback

A MODERN MAGICIANS HANDBOOK
By Marian Green

This book presents the ancient arts of magic, ritual and practical occult arts as used by modern ceremonial magicians and witches in a way that everyone can master, bringing them into the Age of Aquarius. Drawing on over three decades of practical experience, Marian Green offers a simple approach to the various skills and techniques that are needed to turn an interest into a working knowledge of magic.

Each section offers explanation, guidance and practical exercises in meditation, inner journeying, preparation for ritual, the arts of divination and many more of today's esoteric practices. No student is too young or too old to benefit from the material set out for them in this book, and its simple language may help even experienced magicians and witches understand their arts in greater depth.

ISBN 978-1-870450-43-0

THE GRAIL SEEKER'S COMPANION
By John Matthews & Marian Green

There have been many books about the Grail, written from many differing standpoints. Some have been practical, some purely historical, others literary, but this is the first Grail book which sets out to help the esoterically inclined seeker through the maze of symbolism, character and myth which surrounds the central point of the Grail.

In today's frantic world when many people have their material needs met some still seek spiritual fulfilment. They are drawn to explore the old philosophers and traditions, particularly that of our Western Celtic Heritage. It is here they encounter the quest for the Holy Grail, that mysterious object which will bring hope and healing to all. Some have come to recognise that they dwell in a spiritual wasteland and now search that symbol of the grail which may be the only remedy. Here is the guide book for the modern seeker, explaining the history and pointing clearly towards the Aquarian grail of the future.

John Matthews and Marian Green have each been involved in the study of the mysteries of Britain and the Grail myth for over thirty- five years. In the Grail Seeker's Companion they have provided a guidebook not just to places, but to people, stories and theories surrounding the Grail. A reference book of Grailology, including history, ritual, meditation, advice and instruction. In short, everything you are likely to need before you set out on the most important adventure of your life.

This is the only book that points the way to the Holy Grail Quest in the 21st. century.

ISBN 978-1-870450-49-2

THE HIDDEN VALUES OF THE GOLDEN DAWN
Volume One: **We call thee to the Gentle Light**
By Rick Falconer
Forward by Charles Chic Cicero and Sandra Tabatha Cicero

These volumes are indispensible for any with a genuine interest in the Golden Dawn. They are no beginner's guides, for you are no beginner. *The Hidden Values of the Golden Dawn* is a series of Psycho/Spiritual Magical treatise aiding transformation to a Higher Magical Awareness. The Adept, student, and all with an interest in the Golden Dawn will find aspects of themselves within these volumes. They each form experiential and insightful importance, revealing an alchemical infusion and a depth shaping magical undercurrents to ever take you deeper into your spiritual journey with a gradual potential of Divine perfection.

Rick Falconer is an Adept of the Golden Dawn System and a member of various Rosicrucian and Esoteric bodies. Living in England he is a lifelong student of more than thirty years involvement in Hermeticism, including Golden Dawn, Esoteric, Pagan, Theosophical, Psychical Research and Spiritualist Organisations. He began his magical and spiritual vocation at the age of 11 with three Middle England Spiritualist Mediums in the mid 1970's.

ISBN 978-1-870450-88-1 paperback
ISBN 978-1-870450-89-8 eBook

PRACTICAL MAGIC AND THE WESTERN MYSTERY TRADITION
Unpublished Essays and Articles by W. E. Butler.

W. E. Butler, a devoted friend and colleague of the celebrated occultist Dion Fortune, was among those who helped build the Society of the Inner Light into the foremost Mystery School of its day. He then went on to found his own school, the Servants of the Light, which still continues under the guidance of Dolores Ashcroft- Nowicki, herself an occultist and author of note and the editor and compiler of this volume.

Practical Magic and the Western Tradition is a collection of previously unpublished articles, training papers, and lectures covering many aspects of practical magic in the context of western occultism that show W. E. Butler not only as a leading figure in the magical tradition of the West, but also as one of its greatest teachers.

Subjects covered include: What makes an Occultist
Ritual Training
Inner Plane Contacts and Rays
The Witch Cult
Keys in Practical Magic Telesmatic Images Words of Power
An Explanation of Some Psychic Phenomena

ISBN 978-1-870450-32-4

PRACTICAL OCCULTISM
By Dion Fortune supplemented by Gareth Knight

This book contains the complete text of Dion Fortune's Practical Occultism in Daily Life which she wrote to explain, simply and practically, enough of the occult doctrines and methods to enable any reasonably intelligent and well balanced person to make practical use of them in the circumstances of daily life. She gives sound advice on remembering past incarnations, working out karma, divination, the use and abuse of mind power and much more.

Gareth Knight has delved into the Dion Fortune archive to provide additional material not available before outside Dion Fortune's immediate circle. It includes instruction on astral magic, the discipline of the mysteries, inner plane communicators, black magic and mental trespassing, nature contracts and elemental shrines.

In addition, Dion Fortune's review of The Literature of Illuminism describes the books she found most useful in her own quest, ranging from books for beginners to those on initiation, Qabalah, occult fiction, the old gods of England, Atlantis, witchcraft and yoga. In conclusion there is an interpretation by Dion Fortune's close friend Netta Fornario of The Immortal Hour, that haunting work of faery magic by Fiona Macleod, first performed at Glastonbury.

ISBN 978-1-870450-47-8

SPIRITUALISM AND OCCULTISM
By Dion Fortune with commentary edited by Gareth Knight

As well as being an occultist of the first rank, Dion Fortune was an accomplished medium. Thus she is able to explain the methods, technicalities and practical problems of trance mediumship from firsthand experience. She describes exactly what it feels like to go into trance and the different types of being one may meet with beyond the usual spirit guides.

For most of her life her mediumistic abilities were known only to her immediate circle until, in the war years, she responded to the call to try to make a united front of occultists and spiritualists against the forces of materialism in the post-war world. At this point she wrote various articles for the spiritualist press and appeared as a speaker on several spiritualist platforms

This book contains her original work Spiritualism in the Light of Occult Science with commentaries by Gareth Knight that quote extensively from now largely unobtainable material that she wrote on the subject during her life, including transcripts from her own trance work and rare articles from old magazines and journals.

This book represents the fourth collaborative work between the two. An Introduction to Ritual Magic, The Circuit of Force, and Principles of Hermetic Philosophy being already published in this series.

ISBN 978-1-870450-38-6

DION FORTUNE AND THE INNER LIGHT
By Gareth Knight

At last – a comprehensive biography of Dion Fortune based upon the archives of the Society of the Inner Light. As a result much comes to light that has never before been revealed. This includes:

Her early experiments in trance mediumship with her Golden Dawn teacher Maiya Curtis-Webb and in Glastonbury with Frederick Bligh Bond, famous for his psychic investigations of Glastonbury Abbey.

The circumstances of her first contact with the Masters and reception of "The Cosmic Doctrine" The ambitious plans of the Master of Medicine and the projected esoteric clinic with her husband in the role of Dr.Taverner.

The inside story of the confrontation between the Christian Mystic Lodge of the Theosophical Society of which she was president, and Bishop Piggot of the Liberal Catholic church, over the Star in the East movement and Krishnamurti. Also her group's experience of the magical conflict with Moina MacGregor Mathers.

How she and her husband befriended the young Israel Regardie, were present at his initiation into the Hermes Temple of the Stella Matutina, and suffered a second ejection from the Golden Dawn on his subsequent falling out with it.

Her renewed and highly secret contact with her old Golden Dawn teacher Maiya Tranchell-Hayes and their development of the esoteric side of the Arthurian legends.

Her peculiar and hitherto unknown work in policing the occult jurisdiction of the Master for whom she worked which brought her into unlikely contact with occultists such as Aleister Crowley.

Nor does the remarkable story end with her physical death for, through the mediumship of Margaret Lumley Brown and others, continued contacts with Dion Fortune have been reported over subsequent years.

ISBN 978-1-870450-45-4

AN INTRODUCTION TO RITUAL MAGIC
By Dion Fortune & Gareth Knight

At the time this was something of a unique event in esoteric publishing - a new book by the legendary Dion Fortune. Especially with its teachings on the theory and practice of ritual or ceremonial magic, by one who, like the heroine of two of her other novels, was undoubtedly "a mistress of that art".

In this work Dion Fortune deals in successive chapters with Types of Mind Working; Mind Training; The Use of Ritual; Psychic Perception; Ritual Initiation; The Reality of the Subtle Planes; Focusing the Magic Mirror; Channelling the Forces; The Form of the Ceremony; and The Purpose of Magic - with appendices on Talisman Magic and Astral Forms.

Each chapter is supplemented and expanded by a companion chapter on the same subject by Gareth Knight. In Dion Fortune's day the conventions of occult secrecy prevented her from being too explicit on the practical details of magic, except in works of fiction. These veils of secrecy having now been drawn back, Gareth Knight has taken the opportunity to fill in much practical information that Dion Fortune might well have included had she been writing today. In short, in this unique collaboration of two magical practitioners and teachers, we are presented with a valuable and up-to-date text on the practice of ritual or ceremonial magic "as it is". That is to say, as a practical, spiritual, and psychic discipline, far removed from the lurid superstition and speculation that are the hall mark of its treatment in sensational journalism and channels of popular entertainment.

ISBN 978-1-870450-26-3 Soft cover edition

PRINCIPLES OF HERMETIC PHILOSOPHY
By Dion Fortune & Gareth Knight

Principles of Hermetic Philosophy was the last known work written by Dion Fortune. It appeared in her Monthly letters to members and associates of the Society of the Inner Light between November 1942 and March 1944.

Her intention in this work is summed up in her own words: "The observations in these pages are an attempt to gather together the fragments of a forgotten wisdom and explain and expand them in the light of personal observation."

She was uniquely equipped to make highly significant personal observations in these matters as one of the leading practical occultists of her time. What is more, in these later works she feels less constrained by traditions of occult secrecy and takes an altogether more practical approach than in her earlier, well known textbooks.

Gareth Knight takes the opportunity to amplify her explanations and practical exercises with a series of full page illustrations, and provides a commentary on her work

ISBN 978-1-870450-34-8

THE STORY OF DION FORTUNE
As told to Charles Fielding and Carr Collins.

Dion Fortune and Aleister Crowley stand as the twentieth century's most influential leaders of the Western Esoteric Tradition. They were very different in their backgrounds, scholarship and style.

But, for many, Dion Fortune is the chosen exemplar of the Tradition - with no drugs, no homosexuality and no kinks. This book tells of her formative years and of her development.

At the end, she remains a complex and enigmatic figure, who can only be understood in the light of the system she evolved and worked to great effect.

There can be no definitive "Story of Dion Fortune". This book must remain incomplete and full of errors. However, readers may find themselves led into an experience of initiation as envisaged by this fearless and dedicated woman.

ISBN 978-1-870450-33-1

THE FORGOTTEN MAGE
The Magical Lectures of Colonel C.R.F. Seymour.
Edited by Dolores Ashcroft-Nowicki

Charles Seymour was a man of many talents and considerable occult skills. The friend and confidant of Dion Fortune, he worked with her and his magical partner, Christine Hartley, for many productive years.

As one of the Inner Circle of Dion Fortune's Society of the Inner Light, Seymour was a High Priest in every sense of the word, but he was also one of the finest teachers of the occult art to emerge this century.

In the past, little of Seymour's work has been widely available, but in this volume Dolores Ashcroft-Nowicki, Director of Studies of the Servants of the Light School of Occult Science, has gathered together a selection of the best of Seymour's work. His complex scholarship and broad background knowledge of the Pagan traditions shine through in articles which include: The Meaning of Initiation; Magic in the Ancient Mystery Religions; The Esoteric Aspect of Religion; Meditations for Temple Novices; The Old Gods; The Ancient Nature Worship and The Children of the Great Mother.

ISBN 978-1870450-39-3

THE WESTERN MYSTERY TRADITION
By Christine Hartley

A reissue of a classic work, by a pupil of Dion Fortune, on the mythical and historical roots of Western occultism.

Christine Hartley's aim was to demonstrate that we in the West, far from being dependent upon Eastern esoteric teachings, possess a rich and potent mystery tradition of our own, evoked and defined in myth, legend, folklore and song, and embodied in the legacy of Druidic culture.

More importantly, she provides practical guidelines for modern students of the ancient mysteries, 'The Western Mystery Tradition,' in Christine Hartley's view, 'is the basis of the Western religious feeling, the foundation of our spiritual life, the matrix of our religious formulae, whither we are aware of it or not. To it we owe the life and force of our spiritual life.'

ISBN 9781913660161